DATE DUE

*Twayne's United States Authors Series*

Sylvia E. Bowman, *Editor*

INDIANA UNIVERSITY

*John William De Forest*

# JOHN WILLIAM DE FOREST

By JAMES F. LIGHT

Indiana State University

 82

Twayne Publishers, Inc.   ::   New York

For
SHELDON, MATTHEW, AND JAMA ROWENA

MANUFACTURED IN THE UNITED STATES OF AMERICA BY
UNITED PRINTING SERVICES, INC.
NEW HAVEN, CONN.

# Preface

DURING THE EARLY PART of his authorial career John William De Forest had an independent income and a grandiose concept of the writer; and during these years De Forest wrote a number of witty, graceful, scholarly, and psychological works—all of them indicating a remarkable, though youthful, talent. In his middle years De Forest served as a professional soldier during the Civil War and the Reconstruction. During this period his writing was an avocation, and he strove to tell of things that came from his own experience and about which he felt deeply; these works are the most realistic and most penetrating of his career. Later on in his life, De Forest came to depend upon his pen for the livelihood of his family, and the consequence of this was a desperate effort to find a subject and a style that would bring him a popular audience. When that search, after a number of extremely varied novels, proved a failure, De Forest gradually ceased writing.

To his writing De Forest brought a mentality that could see numerous sides to any argument and that consistently strove to reconcile extremes in order to achieve some golden mean. This mentality often drove him to satirize political and social excesses and to counsel moderation, but at the same time this mode of thought made him unable to choose permanently between Realism and Romanticism as modes of expression. Because he could see so clearly the virtues and weaknesses of each kind of writing, he tended to sway back and forth between them, often in the same work; and he only wrote well when he wrote satirically and realistically. He would have been a far greater writer if he had seen his strength clearly from the beginning and never strayed from it, but his fate as a transitional writer was to see only occasionally where his genius lay.

Because his perception was not constant, De Forest wrote a vast amount of trash; because his vision was at times dim, he wrote a considerable amount that is a mixture of trash and merit; and because at times De Forest saw with great clarity, he occasionally wrote well enough and consistently enough to approach greatness.

During his lifetime De Forest gained only a small audience, and he was almost forgotten by the time of his death in 1906. Since 1921, however, De Forest, on the strength of his best work, has slowly been gaining critical recognition. In 1921 Carl Van Doren indicated his approval of De Forest's art in *The American Novel*. In the mid-1930's Mrs. Anne Jenovese was at work on the first doctoral dissertation on De Forest, and, though her work was never completed, at least seven doctoral theses have since been devoted to De Forest. In 1936 Arthur Hobson Quinn included a lengthy discussion of De Forest in his *American Fiction;* in 1948 Alexander Cowie in *The Rise of the American Novel* devoted a long, perceptive chapter to the major work of De Forest; in 1952 Edward Wagenknecht proclaimed in *The Cavalcade of the American Novel* that De Forest's work "might well be tagged Exhibit A in the museum of American literature to refute the comfortable claim that all good books somehow find the readers they deserve automatically." As if to give official sanction to this rising chorus of recognition, *The Literary History of the United States* in 1953 asserted that De Forest was "The first American writer to deserve the name of realist," and in 1962 Edmund Wilson, probably America's foremost literary critic, devoted some seventy-two pages of *Patriotic Gore,* his study of American Civil War literature, to the writing of De Forest.

In addition to the praise of De Forest, some of his works seem at last to be finding an audience. In 1939 *Miss Ravenel's Conversion,* probably De Forest's best novel, was reprinted by Harper; and in 1955 *Miss Ravenel,* with an introduction by Professor Gordon S. Haight, was published as a paperback in "Rinehart Editions." In 1946 De Forest's journalistic writings upon the Civil War were published by Yale University Press under the title *A Volunteer's Adventures;* in 1948 the same press published De Forest's accounts of his experiences in the South after the war under the title *A Union Officer in the Reconstruction;* and in 1964 Archon Books published the fifth edition of De Forest's pioneering scholarly work *History of the Indians of Connecticut*. At the present time the Bald Eagle Press is publishing, under the editorial direction of Professor Joseph Jay Rubin, a handsome "Monument Edition" of De Forest's works; of this edition three novels—*Honest John Vane, Playing the Mischief,* and *Kate Beaumont*—have already been published. Finally, Twayne Publishers is scheduled to include, in Twayne's United

States Classics Series, De Forest's initial novel *Witching Times*, a work that has never been published in book form.

The name of De Forest is becoming more than a footnote in American letters, and it is just that this should be so. De Forest's best work has both historic and artistic importance. His best novels are probably the earliest examples of American Realism, and typically this Realism covers three broad areas. Around each of these interests De Forest produced a pioneering novel of mature art: *Miss Ravenel's Conversion from Secession to Loyalty* (the Civil War); *Kate Beaumont* (the folly and decadence of Southern aristocracy); and *Playing the Mischief* (political corruption in Washington). In addition De Forest wrote numerous other novels, as well as dozens of short stories and journalistic essays, and these indicate his concern for contemporary events—among them such diverse matters as Reconstruction and American feminism. These lesser novels, as well as his major ones, reveal De Forest's dramatization, sometimes done humorously, sometimes tragically, of the eternal weaknesses and strengths of human-kind.

Perhaps it is at last time for the publication of a relatively comprehensive study of De Forest's life, mind, and art. That is the purpose of this study—to reveal the relationship between the life and the work and by doing so to exhibit each a little more clearly. In fulfilling this aim, I have attempted to analyze De Forest's major works at some length, and in a number of these works I have found justification for my belief that De Forest was consistently a rational and moderate human being, a man who from his youth took his direction from the Greeks and who through his life worshiped the Golden Mean.

JAMES F. LIGHT

*Indiana State University*
*Terre Haute, Indiana*

# Acknowledgments

In a work of this sort it is customary to acknowledge the assistance the writer has received, and I do this with deep gratitude. To no source am I more indebted than to the libraries that have been so generous and have so kindly granted me permission to quote from manuscripts in their possession. Foremost among my debts of this kind is that to the Collection of American Literature of Yale University Library and the Curator of that Collection, Mr. Donald C. Gallup; and only slightly less am I indebted to the Yale University Library for the use of the David Curtis DeForest materials held in the Historical Manuscripts Room of the Library. Other libraries that have generously granted me aid are the Houghton Library of Harvard University; the New York Public Library; the Columbia University Library; the Rutherford B. Hayes Library of Fremont, Ohio; the Johns Hopkins University Library; the Riggs Memorial Library of George Washington University; the Library of the University of Illinois; the Indiana University Library; the Library of the Chicago Historical Society; and the Library of the Historical Society of Pennsylvania. To the staff of the Library of Indiana State University I am grateful for unfailing courtesies, and my especial thanks must be extended to Miss Dorothy Shinoske for her assistance through the Inter-Library Borrowing Service.

To Mrs. William Durrie Waldron, the granddaughter of John W. De Forest, I am indebted for the conversations through which she shared her memories of her grandfather and father with me and for the kindness with which she allowed me to use letters and other De Forest material in her possession.

I am grateful to Indiana State University for a travel grant that enabled me to visit and work at a number of the libraries that hold De Forest materials. To the Corporation of Yaddo, and most especially to Mrs. Elizabeth Ames, the gracious director of the Yaddo Artists' Colony, I am grateful for a summer's stay during which the work began to assume tangible form.

To Miss Mary Day, the Secretary of the English Department of Indiana State University, I am appreciative of aid that went well beyond the call of duty; to Professor Sylvia Bowman of Indiana University I am indebted for advice upon the style and content of the manuscript—though I alone am responsible for any inaccuracies of content or clumsiness of expression. I am grateful to my most gentle critic, my wife, for her unfailing wisdom, charity, and love.

# Contents

# Chronology

1826    John William De Forest born March 31, 1826, at Seymour, Connecticut, the youngest of four sons born to John Hancock De Forest and Dotha Woodward De Forest.

1838    Attack of typhoid fever leaves De Forest with chronic bronchial condition that impedes his formal education and eventually leads to travel in the Orient and in Europe in search of health.

1839    Death on February 12 of John Hancock De Forest.

*circa* 1845    Invests as a silent partner in the lumber business of his brother Andrew De Forest.

1846-1847    Travels abroad in Greece, Turkey, and the Holy Land; begins residence with his brother, Dr. Henry De Forest, in Syria. On October 15, 1847, Mrs. Dotha W. De Forest dies.

1850-1854    Travels for health in Europe; dreams of writing fame.

1851    Publishes *History of the Indians of Connecticut from the Earliest Known Period to 1850.*

1856    On June 5 marries Harriet S. Shepard in New Haven, Connecticut. Publishes *Oriental Acquaintance.* In December his novel *Witching Times* begins serial publication in *Putnam's Monthly Magazine.*

1857    Son Louis Shepard De Forest born February 23 in Charleston, South Carolina.

1858    Publishes *European Acquaintance.*

1859    Publishes *Seacliff.*

1861    With his wife and son in Charleston, South Carolina, during the period of tension preceding the firing on Fort Sumter. Leaves shortly before the beginning of the Civil War.

1862    January 1, mustered into United States Army as Captain of Company I, 12th Connecticut Volunteers. Before his discharge, serves in the Louisiana campaign under generals Butler and Banks, and in the Virginia campaign under General Sheridan. All told, forty-six days under fire.

1864    Publishes "The First Time Under Fire," *Harper's New Monthly Magazine,* XXIX (September, 1864), the first of a series of articles upon his war experiences. Discharged from army, by reason of termination of service, on December 2.

1865    Commissioned on February 10 as captain in Veteran Reserve Corps and serves as acting assistant adjutant general in Washington, D. C.

1866    Receives commission as brevet major signed May 15, to date from March 13, 1865. Ordered to report for duty in the Freedmen's Bureau, July 18. Serves as bureau major in Greenville, South Carolina.

1867    Publishes *Miss Ravenel's Conversion from Secession to Loyalty.*

1868    Mustered out of service, January 1, as Captain, Veteran Reserve Corps. Publishes "Drawing Bureau Rations," *Harper's New Monthly Magazine,* XXXVI (May, 1868), the first of a series of articles on his bureau major experiences in South Carolina.

1868-   Publishes numerous short stories, poems, and essays in
1878    such places as *Harper's New Monthly Magazine, The Atlantic Monthly, The Galaxy, The Nation, Putnam's Magazine, Hearth and Home, Lippincott's Magazine,* and the Sunday New York *Times.*

1869    Returns to New Haven to live.

1870    *Overland* is serialized in *The Galaxy* (August, 1870, to July, 1871), and then published as book in 1871.

1871    *Kate Beaumont* is serialized in *The Atlantic Monthly* (January to December); appears as book in 1872.

1872    *The Wetherel Affair* is serialized in *The Galaxy* (December, 1872, to January, 1874); appears as book in 1873.

1873    *Honest John Vane* is serialized in *The Atlantic Monthly* (July to November, 1873); published in book form in 1875.

1874    *Playing The Mischief* is serialized in *Frank Leslie's Chimney Corner* (November 21, 1874, to May 22, 1875); published in volume form in 1875.

1876   Travels abroad with intent to work on a history of the Huguenots.

1878   Publishes anonymously *Justine's Lovers*. Death of Harriet Shepard De Forest.

1879   *Irene the Missionary* serialized anonymously in *The Atlantic Monthly* (April to November) and then anonymously published in book form.

1881   Publishes *The Bloody Chasm*.

1884   Begins first negotiations with publishers in hopes of a collected edition of his novels.

1885   Travels abroad and works on De Forest genealogy.

1888   Left a substantial sum, probably around $20,000, by his first cousin Erastus L. De Forest.

1890-  Considerable wandering in the American East but keeps
1904   his headquarters at the Garde Hotel, New Haven. Relatively impoverished during these years, he applies for a Civil War veteran's pension in 1890. The pension, some twelve dollars a month, does not begin until 1904.

1898   Publishes *A Lover's Revolt*.

1900   Publishes a genealogical study *The De Forests of Avesnes (and New Netherland) a Huguenot Thread in American Colonial History, 1494 to the Present Time*.

1901   Publishes *The Downing Legends: Stories in Rhyme*.

1902   Publishes *Poems: Medley and Palestina*.

1903   Hospitalized and bedridden. Dies in New Haven of heart disease on July 17, 1906.

### CHAPTER 1

# Background and Beginnings

## I *Lineage and Childhood*

JOHN WILLIAM DE FOREST was born on March 31, 1826, the son of John Hancock De Forest and Dotha Woodward De Forest. Both of De Forest's parents were of old American stock, and the De Forest lineage in America traced itself back some six generations to Jesse De Forest. That recalcitrant Huguenot forebear of the future novelist had been born at Avesnes between 1570 and 1580 and had served as a leader of some fifty-six Walloon families who wished to emigrate to America. Obsessed with the desire to find a homeland free of religious tyranny for his Protestant countrymen, Jesse De Forest recruited in Holland the group of Walloons and French which sailed from Dutch shores in March, 1623, and later founded New York (or New Amsterdam) and Albany.

Though Jesse himself probably never reached New Amsterdam,[1] his sons Isaac and Henry De Forest settled there and made the name De Forest prominent in the early history of New Amsterdam. By the time of John William's birth in 1826, the De Forest line was distinguished for its civic conscience, its piety, and its courage (some twenty-five De Forests fought in the Revolutionary War). Not the least eminent of old Jesse's descendants were the brothers John Hancock De Forest and David Curtis DeForest (the slight difference in the last name seems traditional). In 1796 the brothers were partners in business in Bridgeport, Connecticut. When their store was robbed and a clerk murdered in 1797, the business was forced into bankruptcy. With that impetus, David began an adventurous military and mercantile career that led him to South America and brought him a fortune. The aura of his past, the splendor of his hospitality, and the beauty of his South American wife made him, on his return to New Haven, a legend in his own lifetime.

His name is still remembered at Yale by his endowment of four DeForest scholarships and by the annual gift of the DeForest Gold Medal to be given yearly to that "student who writes and delivers the best oration in English."[2]

The career of John Hancock De Forest was less romantic than that of his brother David. After the Bridgeport bankruptcy, John started anew in New Haven around 1797. For six years he worked as a clerk, and he saved enough money ($2700) to join his brother Benjamin in a mercantile venture that thrived so well that the brothers were soon shipping some articles as far away as Europe. On December 5, 1811, John Hancock married Dotha Woodward. A daughter of Elijah Woodward, a veteran of the Revolutionary War, Dotha was not a well-educated woman, but her family was responsible and well connected, and she was a woman of deep religious convictions.

In 1818, primarily because of the restlessness of John Hancock, the De Forest brothers decided to dissolve their partnership. After an unfortunate experience as a broker in New York, John Hancock moved to Humphreysville, Connecticut, where he directed the formation of the Humphreysville Manufacturing Company, which was organized with a capital of $50,000 and was established with De Forest as president. In this factory town, which had been founded by General Humphreys and praised for its moral climate by President Dwight of Yale College, Mr. De Forest built in 1822 an imposing three-story mansion, where he lived with his family until his death. A model of architecture and comfort, the mansion had fourteen rooms, and everything about the house was cheerful, substantial, and aristocratic. The grounds were pleasant and filled with numerous pine and spruce trees.

An active and sociable man, Mr. De Forest soon joined the Masons of Humphreysville, and, when that organization came under attack in 1832 for godlessness and immorality, Mr. De Forest signed a declaration refuting such charges and proclaiming that the institution required its members to give strict obedience to the laws of God and man. A scholarly man who loved to read when he could spare the time, Mr. De Forest had a substantial library, and prominent among the works and authors therein were Shakespeare, Milton, Cowper, Young's *Night Thoughts*, Bunyan, Hume's *England*, Gibbon's *Decline and Fall*, Franklin's *Works*, Hamilton's *Works*, Trumbull's *M'Fingal*, Plutarch, Xenophon, Pope's *Iliad*, Dryden's Virgil, *Don Quixote*, and Sale's *Koran*. A historian of the town remembers Mr. De Forest thus:

The eyes were gray, the spectacles silver, the nose aquiline, the complexion swarthy. The coat was swallow-tailed and dark blue in color, with gilt buttons. The silk vest opened to show a ruffled shirt bosom. The cane, when he walked out, was never missing. The gig, when he drove, was weighty, durable, and of a canary yellow. A gentleman of other days. The squire![3]

Mr. De Forest's substantial position in the town is apparent in the fact that he was elected repeatedly to the state legislature and for many years was also the principal trying judge of the district.

It was in Humphreysville (later Seymour) that John William De Forest was born. He was the youngest of his parents' four living sons, his elder brothers being George (born in 1812), Henry (born in 1814), and Andrew (born in 1817); and John was given the same first name as another brother who had died in infancy in January, 1826. On April 6, 1826, John Hancock wrote George and Henry, who were attending school in Goshen, Connecticut, of the birth of a son on "the 31st of March at three o'clock in the morning. . . . We call him Tom Thumb at present."[4]

Dotha Woodward De Forest was not a strong woman, and her weakness made it necessary that John spend the first years of his life with relatives in Woodbridge, Connecticut. To his "Dear Boys" at school in Goshen, John Hancock wrote of occasional visits to see the baby. On September 30, 1826, he noted: "Little John goes to meetings every Sunday when the weather is good.— He laughed out loud in meeting time a little while ago. I suppose he didn't like the preaching." In April of 1827, John was brought home to Humphreysville, a pastoral community famed for its temperance, its morality, and its religion. John Hancock De Forest and his wife were true citizens of the village. In his letters to George and Henry in Goshen, Mr. De Forest gave the typical fatherly advice of the time and the community: Don't lie; don't cheat; brush your teeth at least twice a week; get to bed by ten o'clock; don't spend so much time at your books that you neglect to exercise; and, above all, beware of worldly vanities. Often Mr. or Mrs. De Forest warned their sons against liquor. When the elder sons, George and Henry, enlisted in the temperance army, they had little difficulty in persuading young John William, then eleven, to take the vow of total abstinence; but high-spirited Andrew needed greater persuasion. George wrote him (March 3, 1838) that it was "high time" he took the pledge, for "John is young and it will require his brothers [*sic*] example to keep him in the right track."

In addition to his advice on health and morals, John Hancock often lectured his sons upon their studies. The poor writing and spelling of Andrew, the bohemian of the family, bothered the father; and the way in which John Hancock constantly spurred on his sons in their classical studies implies the father's devotion to ancient Greece and Rome. Something of a rationalist, John Hancock showed his literary common sense when he wrote to George in 1825: "A composition is nothing else but putting down our thoughts and ideas in writing;—pretty much as you would talk it." Four years later (July 4, 1829) John Hancock commended one of Andrew's letters: "You have written down exactly what you would have wanted to tell us, if you had been here to talk with us;—and that is precisely what is wanted of in a letter."

Permeating the letters of John Hancock and his wife was religious certitude. On the death of the first John De Forest, the father wrote his "Dear Boys," on January 10, 1826, to assure them that "Both your Mother and I are perfectly reconciled to this dispensation of Providence." The tone is even more pronounced in the letters of Dotha to her boys; she longed, labored, and prayed to "see all our dear friends brought into the Kingdom of Christ,"[5] and hardly a letter she wrote to her children failed to emphasize her hope of their salvation. About Andrew especially she worried, and the news that Andrew had visited the filth and obscenity of the New York theatres upset her dreadfully. When Andrew started working in New York, she wrote to her "dear naughty good son," in September, 1839, to warn him anew of the perils there: "One thing I do know about, and that is that vice and immorality stalk abroad in your most public streets . . . beware my very dear son beware." Undoubtedly it was memories of his mother that the mature John W. De Forest drew upon many years later when he wrote the essay "Two Girls." In it he contrasted the modern girl with the old-fashioned one. The "Puritan Maiden" of that earlier time, De Forest remembered, seldom left the home; dressed simply and cheaply in calico; exercised little and as a consequence was plagued with indigestion (a constant complaint of Mrs. De Forest); read hardly at all beyond such devotional literature as the *Bible, Pilgrim's Progress, The Life of James Brainard,* and the *Missionary Herald;* and talked of few things beyond town gossip and the opinions of her mother and pastor. Such an old-fashioned girl not only attended church thrice on Sunday and prayer meetings every Wednesday but also "held that it would be wicked to marry an 'unbeliever'...; she attended a serious sewing society, taught a Bible class, and sometimes distributed tracts.... She would not have a lottery at a fair, nor would she dance at a party. If there crept into her circle a 'worldly man,' wearing whiskers, she felt no hankering after his society...."[6]

The De Forests were a family of steady habits, sturdy morality, and Congregational faith, but they were more than that. In their letters home, Henry and Andrew showed considerable wit and *joie de vivre*. Though Mr. De Forest worried that George's fondness for reading might do harm to his health, the family was generally fond of art (with conspicuous exceptions in the theater and the novel) and especially loved music. While he was working for a while in Bristol, Connecticut, Henry De Forest, by then a fledgling physician, noted that the men he met in Bristol were fortunately "of strict integrity and good moral and religious principles"; but in the same letter he complained to sympathetic ears that the businessmen of the town "have *learned* but little except what bears directly upon the making of clocks. There is no poetry at all in their composition."[7] In another letter to George, Henry chided his father for returning to the tobacco habit; enclosed a temperance paper for the perusal of young John; and then added a fervent recommendation of a singer whom he thought Dotha and George, an amateur singer himself, would especially enjoy.[8]

Into this pious, comfortably affluent, somewhat cultured environment there occasionally crept intimations of another face of reality. Sometimes members of the Woodbridge Indian tribe brought to town parti-colored baskets which they wished to sell in order to purchase provisions—most of which turned out to be rum. Among these pathetic creatures were two poignant reminders of a corrupted and decaying civilization: "Ruby was short and thick, and her face was coarse and stupid. Jim's huge form was bloated with liquor; his face was coarse and hollow; and his steps, even when he was not intoxicated, were unsteady from the evil effects of ardent spirits."[9] Another familiar figure of the town was David Sanford, a former blacksmith who had killed a man with a pitchfork and so become "Pitchfork" Sanford. Tried and branded for his crime, he was forced to wear a cord around his neck for the rest of his life. As a symbol of human crime, he became a curiosity for small boys to watch and ponder.[10]

There were other assertions that reality was multiple and complex. On January 31, 1835, the peaceful river that ran through the town went berserk and left the populace fearful and shaken. On another occasion, during the financial Depression of 1837, the Humphreysville Manufacturing Company was forced to close from May to October, and the elder De Forest complained: "We have never before had so hard and unprofitable a time as in the past six months."[11]

Yet another fact implied the uncertainties of life. Almost from infancy young John's health was delicate, and in his youth he was frequently bedfast. Most seriously he was afflicted with a bronchial ailment which often left him hoarse and out of breath and which he never completely conquered. This condition was exacerbated by an attack of typhoid fever in 1838.

Because of his health John William attended, somewhat irregularly, the nearby schools of Miss Platt and Miss Stoddard, and later he spent considerable time preparing under the tutelage of the Reverend Smith for the Yale entrance examinations. From the latter he probably gained the familiarity with Bunyan and the *Bible* that remained with him through life, but he also must have studied philosophy, Cicero, Virgil, Sallust, Xenophon, Latin and Greek grammar, Latin prosody, and English grammar and geography. When he was eleven, John wrote to his brother Henry:

> I began to study latin about three years ago. The books are Gooriches latin lessons and Andrews and Stoddards latin grammar. Father began smoking about a month ago he says he means to leave off the first April I don't think he will be an April fool but rather the reverse. we have a great deal of snow but no slaying of any consequence. we have a grate also but can't keep warm. . . . I can think of nothing more so I will lay down my pen sprinkle on some sand fold up the letter and send it off.[12]

With better grammar and punctuation and more consistency in his capitalization, John wrote Andrew on October 20, 1837: "About a week before Miss Stoddards [*sic*] school let out she had an exhibition; all the scholars that were old enough wrote compositions, each choosing their own subjects; mine was on the manners, customs and habits of the American Indians; some of the young ladies thought it rather hard to have to read their own compositions before the company; but for my part I got along very well and was much amused."

On February 12, 1839, John Hancock De Forest died. Though recent business convulsions had considerably depleted his fortune, he left his family half of the outstanding shares of the Humphreysville Manufacturing Company. These were valued at

around $25,000, and Mr. De Forest left explicit instructions,
for purposes of control, that none of the shares should be sold
unless all were. The business was indeed shaky, and for a time
after his father's death, George De Forest, who became John's
legal guardian, was so absorbed in financial affairs that injury
to his health was feared.

In 1841 Dr. Henry De Forest met and married Catherine
Sedgwick Sergeant, a lineal descendant of the first missionary to
the Indians in western Massachusetts. The piety of his wife, as
well as his own inclinations, inspired Dr. De Forest to a new
career, and late in 1841, sponsored by the Humphreysville Congregational Church, Dr. and Mrs. De Forest left for a missionary
post in Syria. In the meantime the physical fragility of young
John continued; and, as the years passed, it became evident that
it would be unwise for him to attempt the rigors of a Yale
education. The sale of the Humphreysville Manufacturing Company to Raymond French and Company on July 1, 1845, brought
a total of $17,000 to Mrs. De Forest and her sons. Since the
family now thought that it was both wise and practicable for
John to travel for his health, he set out to join his brother
in Syria.

## II   *Travels in the Orient*

When De Forest embarked for the Orient, he was a young
man of almost five feet ten inches, with a high forehead, brown
hair, deep hazel eyes, a medium aquiline nose, and a rather
dark complexion. In letters to his family and in the volume
*Oriental Acquaintance,* De Forest told of his early response to
his new environment. Early in February, he reached the Turkish
city of Smyrna, a place of "oriental strangeness...shabby
wharves...fragile minarets, and rough, red-tiled roofs."[13] Step-
ping ashore, he felt that the rotten wood of a ruinous quay
was symbolic of the decadence of the Turkish people and their
government, and he never lost a feeling of the contrast between
the decadent present and the glorious past of the Orient.
Despite the comfortable nationalism implicit in his feeling
that "the age of gold has run its sands in the East" (6), he
found from the first that his vision of man was enlarged. His
first sight of a Turkish Negro was one of a man of dignity, independence, ease, intelligence and gravity; this vision gave De
Forest new ideas of the possibilities of the African race, and
"made me look forward to a supposable time when negroes shall
have a chance with the rest of us" (5).

While De Forest waited for a boat to Beirut, he stayed with
various members of the missionary colony of Smyrna. Though he
saw no houris or odalisques, he did enjoy exchanging stares with
some of the prettier Greek girls, but he felt his callowness when
the girls unabashedly stared him down. Occasionally De Forest
traveled beyond the city limits of Smyrna, and so he was able
to see a Genoese castle, the American missionary schools, and
the country seats of some of the wealthy Turks. On one afternoon De Forest visited the country seat of an aristocratic Dutch
family. The trip was made by donkey and took over two hours.
De Forest, the heaviest and tallest member of the party, was
given the smallest donkey, and he "felt like a big ass mounted
on a little one; like a mountain taking a ride on a molehill" (7).

In Smyrna, De Forest met the Reverend Pomroy, a minister
from New England who had laid aside the usual gravity of
his vocation and assumed the buoyant spirits of youth. De Forest
admired the rational piety and the merciful religion of Reverend
Pomroy, and the young man was happy to gain the reverend's company on the trip to Beirut. That journey eventually
began on the good ship *Imperatrice*. It was filled with pilgrims
bound for the Holy Land, and most of them were ill-smelling
and unkempt. Watching them, De Forest meditated on their
dirty predecessors of long ago, innumerable hosts with vast
dreams and fanatic zeal, and he concluded that the tide of
religious enthusiasm had long passed its peak and would only
revive with another divine inspiration. For the lofty grandeur
and poesy of the crusades of the past, he asserted his admiration,
but for the folly of the pilgrimages of the present, he felt
only contempt.

Arriving at Beirut, De Forest found a dirty, shabby city filled
with the smell of rotting vegetables and decaying refuse. The
main thoroughfare was narrow and crooked, and down it ran
a gutter of running water which served no purpose and cleaned
away no dirt. Shabby, turbaned Orientals lounged in the streets
or in front of cafés; others, less disreputable, occasionally picked
their way between puddles toward an ugly public bath.

In Beirut, John stayed with Dr. De Forest and his wife
Catherine, and the three-story stone residence in which John
lived hummed with missionary activity. In the basement of the
building were the printing press and the chapel of the American
Mission. Dr. De Forest was kept constantly busy ministering
to the medical needs of the Syrians, while Catherine was hardly
less active in teaching four native girls whom the De Forests

had taken into their home and who later became the nucleus for the American Mission School for girls.

John, however, sometimes felt that he was living a life of sybaritic softness and luxury. Soon he was known as Howaja Hanna (or Gentleman John), and by March of 1846 he was gaining familiarity with Syrian life. A dinner given by friends of the Hakeem (or Dr. De Forest) so impressed John that he wrote his mother on March 11, 1846: "On arriving we had rose water dashed into our faces, were seated on cuishons [*sic*] spread on the floor, and finally smoked by incense, a cloth having first been put over our heads in order that we might loose [*sic*] nothing of the perfume.... The dinner was laid on little round tables, about six inches high, to which we sat down cross legged or in any other mode which seemed more convenient."

By May of 1846, De Forest had visited a number of the historical sites near Beirut and had spent sixteen days in and near Jerusalem. Almost everywhere he felt surrounded and annoyed by beggars and fleas. In Jerusalem he saw numerous sacred sites, but he felt hovering about them "an air of absurdity" (80) which excited in him skepticism rather than devotion. The irrational quarrels of various Christian sects made him a little contemptuous of the "church militant in action" (89). Occasionally nationalistic pride made him feel that "The American eagle soars in the face of the sun, and is not to be scared by the horsetails of a dilapidated crescent" (82). Despite these feelings, he was awed, near Jerusalem, by the purity of the atmosphere, the vastness of the view from the mountain of Jebel Kanaan, and the vistas of scarlet and yellow poppies.

A week after his arrival in Jerusalem, De Forest "witnessed the annual bathing of the pilgrims in Jordan; that great spring washing of the dirtiest of possible sheep in the dirtiest of possible rivers" (92). For De Forest, this public bath seemed comparable in its folly to the silliness of American Millerites clothed in ascension robes. The essential absurdity of the scene was not lessened by the occurrence of two serious events: the death of one old man, who was whirled away in the rapid current of the Jordan, and the birth in the thick, yellow waters of one singularly fortunate child.

The party with whom De Forest had journeyed to Jerusalem disbanded there. John returned by boat to Beirut, and then rejoined Dr. De Forest and his wife, who had moved to Bhamdun, a town of around two hundred flat-roofed, yellow-limestone houses in the Syrian highlands. Dr. De Forest had a gigantic basement and four large rooms. The floors were of hardened red earth, and John occupied a large room originally destined for use as a grand dining hall. In the basement were lodged a number of horses, and these occasionally disagreed clamorously. By far the most numerous inhabitants were the rats who "rattled and rolled through invisible galleries, like diminutive four-legged peals of thunder"(133).

Life in Bhamdun, a cool nest in the Mount Lebanon area, was uneventful but pleasant, and slowly Gentleman John became familiar with Syrian customs, conversation, folklore, and tradition. Visitors in puffy trousers and elaborate turbans were continually dropping in to see the Hakeem, and almost always someone—schoolmaster or priest or businessman—would be "cuddled upon the divan, or against the wall, his pipe sending a wreathing fragrance among the rats and swallows" (134-35). One of the most welcome of the visitors was a Syrian Protestant familiarly known as Uncle Khalil. A representative Syrian businessman, Khalil at one time proposed to John De Forest that the two enter business together, and De Forest jested that the idea was tempting: "I could have had a town house, a mountain house, a wife from some genteel Arab family, . . . a couple of blood horses, and three or four servants. . . . Not seldom since those days has the lazy sunshine of that idea lured my mind back to Syria. I sometimes feel as if it would be delightful to retire into a turban, shadow myself with tobacco smoke, and let the age drive by" (139). John's contentment with his life in Syria led him to write to his mother (July 6, 1846) that he was "turning Turk very fast. I sit cross legged . . . , smoke the argeeleh water pipe, and intend very soon to buy a little black boy who shall fill it and clean it for me." In a more serious vein, De Forest added that smoking the water pipe seemed to have medical value for his bronchial condition; he had "some hopes of being cured, or, at least, relieved, although I had long made up my mind to remain as I am for life." Partially because of medical reasons, John wrote that he had decided to stay in Syria a year longer. He defended the length of his stay by saying that he knew that he was missed at home, but he felt that he was needed by Catherine and Henry also. Both were overworked, and Henry's health was especially poor.

Not until February of 1847 did De Forest leave Syria. Dr. De Forest and Catherine were sorry to see him go, and John left a vivid impression with Catherine. She wrote to her brother:

"He [John] is one of the most truly godly men I have ever known and reminds me of what I suppose ... old worthies to have been."[14]

## III  *Youthful Scholarship: The Indians of Connecticut*

After leaving Syria, De Forest went by steamer to Malta. There he passed quarantine inspection before going on to Athens, Smyrna, Constantinople, and home. Soon after (or possibly shortly before) he reached Connecticut, his mother died. Years later De Forest may have been remembering the event when he wrote of a death-bed scene between mother and son: "a sickness of heart fell upon him, and a trembling as if his soul were being torn asunder. Yet neither wept; the Puritans and the children of the Puritans do not weep easily; they are taught not to utter but to hide their emotions. The nurse perceived no signs of unusual feeling .. [though] to him this was an hour of anguish while to her it was one of unspeakable joy."[15] His mother's death left the young man without parents; and his own invalidism and lack of vocation made the future look bleak. He had always been fond of reading, and now he did a great deal of it. Before long he decided to investigate thoroughly the history of the Indians of Connecticut; the results of his research, he decided, might make an interesting article, or even a short book.

For several months, De Forest worked in the libraries of New Haven, and then he extended his studies to Hartford, Norwich, Groton, and Stonington. In Hartford he became more and more aware of the extent of his subject. To Andrew he wrote on July 7, 1848, that his study was "a much more serious affair than I had imagined," and he asked Andrew not to emphasize his scholarly pursuits in talking to George, for it would lead to "troublesome questions and tiresome jokes." Andrew's answer apparently implied that he was more in sympathy with George's jokes than with John's ambitions, for John complained on July 31:

> You intimate that a failure in the enterprise would probably be of benefit to me in more ways than one. If it would cure my bronchitis, it certainly would be so; otherwise I cannot see how it can be of any benefit at all. As long as that continues with me, I must continue my silent mode of life; and I had certainly better occupy it in some pursuit with a determinate end, than to pass it away in little more than amusements.

During his scholarly work, De Forest rode determinedly on horseback over much of Connecticut. By 1850 he had completed a manuscript of which a mature scholar might have been proud. De Forest titled the work *History of the Indians of Connecticut,* and submitted it to the Connecticut Historical Society in hopes of gaining the approval of that august body. The society appointed a committee of three on February 5, 1850, to judge the manuscript. These men reported that the study contained "abundant evidence of labor and research, and a collection of facts which they think highly important for a full elucidation of the history of the state."[16] The study was, therefore, published with the sanction of the Connecticut Historical Society, and that body's approval helped the book to go into five editions, the last of which appeared in 1964.

In his introduction to the *History,* De Forest noted that love for his subject, not the desire to become an author, had led him to write. In the work itself, De Forest first described the Connecticut setting before the advent of the white man; then noted the manners, institutions, and populousness of the various tribes at the time when the white man came to America; and finally treated the histories of the various tribes from the earliest known period to 1849. Occasionally De Forest quarreled with recognized authorities on his subject. Most notably he differed with other scholars on the strength of the various Indian tribes, and he pointed out the tendency of such authorities as James H. Trumbull and John Winthrop to exaggerate the number of the aborigines. The rationalism with which De Forest approached his subject is implied by his objection to Winthrop's estimate of the size of Indian canoes. Winthrop felt that these craft were often capable of carrying sixty to eighty men, but De Forest noted logically and dispassionately that the size of New England trees made it unlikely, if not impossible, that any canoe could have approached such enormous size.

De Forest indicated in his study that he would emphasize two aspects of the history of the Indians of Connecticut: first, "the treatment of these tribes by the white settlers"; second, the cause of the Indians' "steady and apparently irremediable decline" (1-2). De Forest did not gloss over the injustices done to the red man. At times he indicted the savagery with which the red men were decimated, and at others he exposed the knavery of whites who by cunning or outright theft appropriated the lands of the Indians. At times, too, De Forest noted the childish and impulsive savagery of the Indians, and at others he exposed the tendency of the Indians, especially in the more recent past, to drunkenness, licentiousness, and laziness. Typically De Forest presented two viewpoints, that of the Indians and that of the conquerors; and then he attempted to reconcile the two. In discussing the campaign against the Pequots, which resulted in almost total destruction of the largest and bravest of the Connecticut tribes, De Forest first asserted the horror of the "indiscriminate butchery"; then he noted that the frightful cruelty might be "almost excused by necessity"; and finally he concluded: "My own opinion of the burning of the Pequot fort is, that it was a piece of stern policy, mingled with something of revenge, from which floods of argument could not wash out a stain of cruelty. If it receives any approval, it must be that of the intellect and not that of the heart" (139-40).

This tendency to present both sides carried over into De Forest's presentation of individuals among the aborigines. He characterizes Uncas as a constant friend of the whites but also exposes him as an unscrupulous, selfish betrayer of his own people. Similarly De Forest praises Samson Occam for his acceptance of Christianity and his intellectual achievement, but De Forest does not lose sight of objectivity in appraising the importance of Occam's achievements.

In his *History* De Forest often evinces his own religious temperament as he judges the actions of the whites and the aborigines. Commenting upon the magnanimous and unselfish role the whites played in bringing peace between the warring Pequots and Narragansetts, he asserts that religious principle often illumined the Puritan treatment of the aborigines, and his final conclusion largely absolves the whites from any great blame in the decimation of the Indians:

> Their own barbarism has destroyed them. . . . While we must admit that the white population of Connecticut has not fulfilled its responsibilities as a civilized and Christian race, we are also bound to admit that, judged by the rule of the ordinary course of human conduct, it has not, on the whole, in its behavior toward the Indians, been guilty of any peculiar degree of heedlessness, or inhumanity, or injustice (490).

Without doubt, as scholars have commented, the *History of The Indians of Connecticut* was a contribution to knowledge. More important than that, however, is the fact that it is the work of a rational, though Christian, man whose angle of vision made him capable of seeing that reality and human nature were exceedingly complex.

## IV  *European Travels*

The death of De Forest's mother brought him a legacy, considerable for the time, of $3,677.86. This money, plus what remained from his earlier inheritance, John invested as a silent partner in the new lumber business of his brother Andrew. It was a wise investment, for Andrew had been well seasoned in business in Bridgeport and New York, and it also left John free to follow his inclination to go to Europe in search of health and foreign culture. Soon after signing the contract for the publication of the *Indians* (on October 10, 1850), De Forest set out for Europe. By December 9, he was writing Lucretia De Forest, Andrew's wife, to tell her that English preaching was shallow and ineffectual and English women were "fat with big red cheeks, thin ancles [*sic*] and large feet." Soon afterward, he wrote Andrew (December 19, 1850) that he was on "a little, nasty steamboat" to France, and from there he proceeded "hurry-scurry" to Florence. There breakfast cost eight cents and dinner twenty; and for seven dollars a month, he rented two stylish rooms that were not only profusely furnished but also were paneled in handsome frescoes of gods and goddesses.

Soon after De Forest arrived in Florence, he consulted the eminent English physician Sir Charles Herbert. Sir Charles felt that the climate of Florence would benefit De Forest's bronchial ailment; therefore, De Forest remained during the winter of 1850-51. He kept largely to himself, for he felt a vague discomfort when among Italians and seldom spoke to them, but he did a good bit of studying, walking, and writing. Occasionally he enjoyed listening to the martial music of Austrian regimental bands, and at times he visited the art museums of the city. He was disappointed in the famous Titians and Rubens that he saw, and he concluded (an opinion of which he was later ashamed) that Angelica Kauffmann was a better painter than the masters he had seen.

In Florence, De Forest struck up an acquaintance with a young Virginian named George Newton, and he also met the famous sculptor Horatio Greenough. Greenough, who had recently spent eighteen months at Graefenberg, where a hydropathic sanitarium was located, was full of praise for the curative powers of cool water and wet bandages. Greenough's faith in water was as convincing as that of any of the fifty-thousand American hydropathic enthusiasts of the time who subscribed to the popular *Water-Cure Journal* and *Herald of Reform;* and in *European Acquaintance,* De Forest described his own search for health at the watering places of Europe. "Pursued by the fretting enmity of a monotonous invalidism" (5), he determined at first to search for his health at Graefenberg. George Newton joined him, and with a letter from Greenough, the two new disciples set out to meet Vincent Priessnitz, the high priest of hydropathy.

De Forest and Newton, on their way to Graefenberg, spent brief periods in Trieste and Vienna, and they passed a fortnight in Venice. In Venice, De Forest did the usual things celebrated by the conventional travel books: he rode in gondolas, gazed in awe at the many domes and colors of St. Mark's, and admired the richness of Venetian painting. He was more interested in people, however, than in sights; and, while he was in Venice, he became increasingly aware of the nationalistic ferment there. De Forest was sympathetic to the Italian dreams of unification and *la repubblica,* but he was also eminently rational. He had no misconceptions about the vast wisdom of Italian government or the total villainy of Austrian rule. He had no fancies about the future glory of Venice. Facts were facts, and decay must have been the destiny of Venice "no matter who were its rulers; for its riches and power necessarily flew away on the vanishing wings of commerce; and the Austrians are hardly more responsible for its decline than for the fall of Babylon or the death of the first Cheops" (21).

On the way to Graefenberg, De Forest and Newton (whom De Forest called Neuville in *European Acquaintance*) were joined by two other Americans. Though the four heard varying stories about Priessnitz—some people claimed he was a humbug; others, a spy; and others, a professional gambler—the companions remained inclined to smell out the sanitarium for themselves. Laboring up the high hill on which the establishment was located, the four young men came upon a fountain; at its base was the inscription: "AU GENIE DE L'EAU FROIDE." A few minutes later they met some of the disciples of hydropathy

wandering confusedly hither and thither . . . all of them shabbily attired—some in linen, as if in derision of our flannels; some bareheaded, with clipped hair, others with towels about their temples—their pockets bulging with glass cups, or their shoulders harnessed with drinking horns. Most of them carried thick canes, and raced up the eminences with the hearty-good will of Christian climbing the hill difficulty (31).

For two months in the spring of 1851, De Forest remained among these cheerfully eccentric people. His home was a rustic cabin which had formerly been a stable. His food, though plentiful, was an "insult to the palate and an injury to the stomach" (68). The health treatment he underwent was spartan. At five in the morning he arose to be packed in wet sheets and blankets "as if I were a batch of dough set away to rise" (37). Following this treatment, he was taken into "awful nether regions of wet pavements, brooks, and cisterns," and there he plunged into a freezing bath which left his body "so perfectly iced that it felt hard, smooth, and glossy, like a skin of marble" (39). After a brisk rubdown, followed by an air bath before open windows, De Forest was ready for his morning walk. This he took "nearly as thinly dressed as Adam and Eve" (41). As he wandered the woods before breakfast, he occasionally took, as the treatment demanded, a drink of water. Soon he was "choke full of water" and felt he resembled "a water-logged ship or a dropsical cucumber" (41). After the walk, De Forest was ready for a breakfast of sweet and sour milk and of rye and barley bread. De Forest and the other patients ate the simple fare in abundance.

So the day began, but it continued in much the same fashion: wet sheets, freezing baths, air baths, long walks, and simple but hearty meals. By bed time at nine o'clock, De Forest usually felt like a weary, half-drowned puppy. Repeatedly during the first chill Graefenberg nights he awoke wishing for something more to warm him than the single blanket to which the patients were restricted. Remarkably enough, however, De Forest thrived under this regimen. He soon abandoned his woolen garments and in the coldest and rainiest weather wore light linens without catching cold or being exceptionally uncomfortable.

Listening to the Graefenberg gossip, De Forest heard of remarkable cures occasioned by hydropathy. He also heard of countless treatments imitative of it. Among these were "a curd cure, in which sick people drank and were bathed in sweet and sour milk; a straw cure, in which patients drank straw tea and slept naked in straw beds; and a wine cure, in which great quantities of wine were drunk while food intake was diminished and expanded on a sliding scale" (63).

De Forest was able to smile at the eccentricity of these strange cures and at the fanaticism of those befuddled patients who believed in them. Even hydropathy he viewed cautiously; he had been made skeptical by "years of unrewarded obedience to doctors and of fruitless foragings in apothecaries' shops" (66).

He was highly pleased, therefore, when he found his health improving, and he noted that he felt so well that "I could eat not only the sour milk before me, but the cow that gave it.... To the habitual invalid... there is no sensation more glorious, more superhuman, than consciousness of abounding and sufficient strength" (67).

De Forest, however, could stand no more than two months of Graefenberg. The dreary food and the chill, rainy climate drove him to search for a more comfortable hydropathic establishment. Possibly he felt more inclined to move because his property, under Andrew's handling, had increased in value. He could not only afford to be less thrifty but could even advise his brother George to distribute $100 a year for him on religious and charitable purposes.

In the late summer of 1851, De Forest wandered for a while through the cities and the ruined castles of Rhineland. To Andrew he wrote a long, undated letter from Bonn in which he gave his impressions of the scenes he was viewing. Prague seemed to him grave, somber, and oriental, and the people who walked its streets struck him as insubstantial specters who might melt into air at any moment. Dresden was quiet and drab, despite its fine art gallery, and De Forest suspected that the ladies of the city were the ugliest in all Europe. Berlin, with its broad streets and well-kept houses, with its elegantly tasteful public buildings and its fresh, new air, approached New York in atmosphere. Brunswick was queerly old and picturesque: its streets wandered tangledly and crookedly everywhere and nowhere; and its houses, with one story jutting out over another, looked as if they had been turned upside down. Düsseldorf had some remarkable painting, and De Forest felt that Lentze's depiction of "Washington Crossing the Delaware" was one of the grandest pictures he had ever seen. Cologne's famous cathedral, despite its vast age, seemed so light and fanciful that "it might have been the magic creation of a single night."

His wanderings made De Forest feel cosmopolitan, and he began to think he understood the Europeans: "I could return to Italy [he wrote Andrew in his long letter from Bonn] and find the Italians by no means the reserved people I supposed them while I was reserved myself. That was the trouble; I was afraid to speak to them.... Oh, how impudent I am going to be all the rest of my life." Despite his new cosmopolitanism, he found it difficult to accept the curious standard of morality he found in some Europeans, and that looseness he condemned

when he saw it. He remembered it vividly in *Miss Ravenel's
Conversion from Secession to Loyalty*, for in it he reported that

> many people of high social position hold a . . . mixed moral
> creed; they allow that a gentleman may be given to expensive
> immoralities, but not to money-getting ones; that he may indulge
> in wine, women, and play, but not in swindling. All over Europe
> this curious ethical distinction prevails, and very naturally, for it
> springs out of the conditions of a hereditary aristocracy, and
> makes allowance for the vices to which they are not tempted. A
> feeble echo of it has traversed the ocean, and influenced some
> characters in America both for good and for evil (396-97).

In the autumn of 1851, De Forest set out for the hydropathic
establishment of Divonne, which was near Lake Leman and the
Swiss frontier. There De Forest "made myself conspicuous by
talking incessantly a singular jargon approaching in sound to
French" (79). With a tutor, De Forest studied French regularly;
by the time he left Divonne, he had a thorough mastery of
the language.

Many of the people at Divonne were pious Protestants with
considerable evangelical zeal. Others De Forest found less en-
thusiastic but more truly Christian, as De Forest conceived that
faith. In the distinguished minister Frederick Monod, De Forest
found an ideal example of the man of God. In Monod were
combined the spiritual and the earthly in perfect harmony. In
this he was, De Forest felt, like all true ministers, for ideally they
should be "conscious of the beauty of earth and their brotherhood with humanity, yet never forgetful of their mystic life, their
heavenly calling, the price of their redemption" (85).

In contrast to the evangelical Christians, Divonne housed
at least one religious and political radical. De Forest himself was "orthodox in religion and believed society in the shape
of the family to be the only society possible" (117). He, therefore,
could never talk to this heretic without quarreling. Often De
Forest lost his temper and made dogmatic assertions, but the
Frenchman reasoned calmly and cautiously. The shock of hearing
the Frenchman deny the fall and the redemption—De Forest had
heard such infidelity only once before—left the American naïvely
astounded. Less astonishing but still irritating were the political
ideas of the Frenchman. De Forest felt the radical's desire for
"something more humane than mere individualism" (120) was
symptomatic of the ills of a France which was "full of men
wandering blindly and anxiously up and down the steps of
socialistic platforms" (121).

Other members of the Divonne group were of the European nobility. To De Forest, these aristocrats were remarkable for their naturalness and good taste. In them he found "less haughtiness, less reserve, less affectation of superiority than in many of our [American] people. . . . Vice incomparable there may be in the soul, but on the surface only a fascinating courtesy and unpretentiousness" (192). Still others at Divonne were ardent republicans, proud of the success of the French Republic. When Louis Napoleon's *coup d'état* brought the practical end of the Republic, the Divonne republicans, like those throughout France, received the news in stupor and terror. Napoleon's pretense of free elections, by which he tried to drape his usurpation, fooled few people. So good a republican as De Forest felt that France had not only fallen low but had been made to appear ridiculous: "It was bad enough to be beaten thus like a hound; but to be forced to gambol . . . was ludicrously contemptible" (107).

Between French lessons in grammar and politics, parlor games, occasional experiments with mesmerism—the subject seemed absurd to De Forest—and the constant exigencies of the hydropathic cure, De Forest passed the fall of 1851 swiftly. With winter, however, the Divonne patients moved elsewhere, and De Forest was left with little companionship. He whiled away a good bit of time in reading such books as Eugène Sue's *Mysteries of the People,* which he wrote Andrew (December 28, 1851) was largely melodramatic trash but was, nevertheless, praiseworthy in its "democratic tendency, being written to show the sufferings which the people have in all ages suffered from the hands of the great." He learned that his book on the *Indians of Connecticut* was selling well, and that encouraged him to write some miscellaneous essays and poetry with the hope of making a publishable volume. Nevertheless, he became so lonely that at one time he spent five minutes making faces at a lone cat who was observing the solitude of the Divonne salon. De Forest became so bored that he grew a gigantic beard; but, looking in the mirror one day, he saw so frightful a vision that he had the beard trimmed off except for a trifle of hair on his upper lip and chin. The surgery, he wrote Mrs. George De Forest on March 15, 1852, left him looking "a little like the portraits of King Charles the First. . . . a good deal like a rascally Italian."

Until June of 1852, De Forest persisted in the hydropathic cure. By then he felt that pure water had raised him "to as high a degree of health as is the ordinary award of mortals" (162).

With his new health and sophistication, he kissed Vidart on the cheeks and set out to explore France and Italy again. But Divonne had been more expensive than Graefenberg, and De Forest's Puritan conscience rebelled slightly. He tried to quiet its pangs by musing, as he wrote to George (June 7, 1852), that he was "seeing the world in general and Europe in particular, learning languages, getting my health, growing immensely stout and active, making lots of first class acquaintances ... and all at the trifling expense of twelve hundred dollars. ... I have gone to dansing [sic] too." Nevertheless, De Forest decided to economize by spending the summer in the picturesque Swiss village of Bex.

On the way to his valley retreat, De Forest stayed overnight at Vevey, where an American tourist called on him. Obviously of an excellent social position, this visitor struck De Forest as typically American in the way he categorized humanity into "foreigners and Americans; the former a queer and incomprehensible set at best, the latter one huge brotherhood of fine fellows, who can never know too much of each other" (166). Listening to this garrulous chauvinist, De Forest commented that he had not spoken to an American for over nine months. When he was gently chastised, De Forest did not protest, but he meditated what folly it was to associate much with Americans while abroad; "foreign languages are not acquired, foreign character is not effectively studied. ... Now all wisdom is surely not confined by American shores, and even religion seems to have existed before the Declaration of Independence" (167). A related kind of foolishness, De Forest felt, was the American neglect of modern language study. "Of what use," he asked, "are Greek and Latin to ... our young people ... compared with French or German?" (169).

After an uneventful summer at Bex, where he added to his knowledge of European eccentrics, De Forest departed for Paris in the late summer of 1852. Early in his sojourn there, he accidentally met his friend Newton while the two were strolling down a boulevard. Taking pains not to choose establishments frequented by Americans and Englishmen, De Forest and Newton sampled the food, gossip, and atmosphere of French restaurants. For the Café-Jouffroy, near the Boulevard Poissonniere, De Forest took an especial liking. He loved to promenade of an evening near the restaurant, gaze into the windows of the elegant little shops, and hear the chatter of the loungers as they talked over *café noir* and ices.

In August, 1852, De Forest went to England to see about the prospects of publishing his verse. He received little encouragement, but through the publisher he did meet Mr. Samuel Griswold Goodrich, better known as the publisher of the Peter Parley children's tales. Mr. Goodrich encouraged De Forest to submit his work to Putnam, and by November that firm had gently refused the work. To his brother George, De Forest wrote of his conviction that prose was the future way for him, and to Andrew he wrote, on December 9th, of his "worthless stuff": "Do not show it to anyone. Do not mention it even. I would not have it published if any publisher would be found stupid enough to do such a thing. I have been reading other poetry lately; then looking over my own; and I am not such a blockhead but that I can see the difference."

As if to torment himself, De Forest told Andrew of some European writers he had met who were finding it difficult to keep from starving. Gratefully, De Forest noted the profitableness of his partnership in Andrew's business, and then he added a comment that showed he had not been totally overcome by either the rejection of his poetry or the problems of impoverished authors: the Chicago *Tribune* had asked for some travel letters, and he hoped to become a foreign correspondent. If either Andrew or George had been telling him (as they well might have) that writing was a pleasant fancy but hardly a way to make a living, this letter of John's must have made clear to them (and possibly purposely so) that his dream of authorship was vivid and irreplaceable.

From Paris, De Forest and Newton traveled to Florence, where De Forest spent most of the fall of 1853. Florence's beauty and art stole his heart completely and made him feel "as though my spirit had been born there in other centuries, and had possessed there long ago a country, a history, love, joy, sorrow, and death" (191). For a while, De Forest and Newton spent days of almost perfect indolence. They rose at ten, dressed leisurely, and finished breakfast at the Café Doney by noon. Then they walked for a while, perhaps stopping to rest inside a cool cathedral or to buy some luscious strawberries. After their afternoon walk, they smoked and read a little Italian in their rooms. By five o'clock they were ready for dinner and social conversation, a short evening ride, and possibly a concert or an opera. For De Forest the life was like that in Eden, but occasionally his Puritan conscience nagged him. The leisurely existence of the good-hearted but toadyish Florentine dandies seemed com-

parable to De Forest to the life of an amusing dog named
Burrasco, who frisked and gamboled as he begged for food.
Such a sponging existence De Forest could condone in a dog
but not in a man, no matter how charming the man might be.

Occasionally De Forest attempted to combat his indolence.
He tried to appreciate the art of Florence (and later of Rome
and Naples), but he found himself disappointed in what he saw.
Where his spirit should have soared and the past have been
rekindled, he found his imagination easily wearied and his spirit
clogged. He rationalized his failure to appreciate the achievement
of Italian art by blaming the excessive beauty and sensuousness
of the country and the climate, and he "wondered how Galileo
could have been intellectual there, how Dante and Michael
Angelo could have been sublime there" (267). No more successful were two other attempts of De Forest to quiet his conscience.
First, he attempted (with an Italian friend) an Italian translation
of *The House of Seven Gables,* but the negligence of his col-
laborator soon led De Forest to abandon the project. Next he
decided to improve his command of the Italian language. With
Newton he spent a number of days in pilgrimages to various
monasteries where they thought they might stay and learn the
language. No monastery was willing to shelter (or teach) two
such mad Americans; and, when the two friends mistook a
nunnery for a monastery and in high indignation were turned
away, they abandoned the search.

During his stay in Florence, De Forest heard that his brother
Henry was seriously ill. John's response was more pragmatic than
it might have been earlier, for he wrote Lucretia (October 28,
1853) that Henry and his wife should return home immediately:
"They have worked too hard and stayed too long. . . . The Lord
does not seem to be, by any means, so anxious to convert the
Syrians as the missionaries are."

Late in the autumn of 1853, De Forest left the flower girls,
the dandies, and the superstitions of Florence to spend the winter
in Rome and Naples. When he visited St. Peter's, the vastness of
everything there made his head swim until he felt faint with
awe. At other times he listened with American satisfaction to the
Italians' wish for a republic or a constitutional monarchy, and
he sympathized with the Romans' complaints about the foolish
priestcraft and the undemocratic papal government. The grum-
bling boded well, he felt, for the Italian future; but he doubted
that the Italian temperament would lead to swift changes.
Listening to one innkeeper tell how governmental officials were

allowed each year to kiss the foot of the Pope, De Forest was disgusted by the vanity with which his host described his own participation in the foot-kissing sport. In true Protestant and democratic style, De Forest thought it would be wiser for the Romans unanimously to "set teeth into the fat legs of their popes and cardinals . . . and they too will have their just share of the beefsteaks of Italy" (255).

While he was in Rome, De Forest learned that the business in which he and Andrew were co-partners was going badly, but he wrote Andrew (December 29, 1853) that he could not be blamed "for any speculations no matter how bad, while I am spending my time and wits in the manner I am." Despite his feeling that his present mode of life was folly, De Forest asserted in the same letter that he could for the present live no other. He planned to spend another year in Rome, and irresistibly he was drawn again to the writing of poetry. His reason, he told Andrew, was not that he especially wished to write verse but that he wasn't at the moment interested in prose. He then implied that his determination to become an author had hardened by noting that ". . . a man cannot write without being interested in his subject; unless, indeed, he is driven to it day after day by want of bread. When that time comes, if it ever does, then I will resume prose, and think that I can live by it." For the moment, however, De Forest was writing a long poem. This work, which has not survived, he described to Andrew as "a kind of fanciful drama, something in the style of Long-fellow's *Golden Legend* or Goethe's *Faust*." Added to some shorter pieces, De Forest hoped to publish this romance and have it admired. But even if the latter did not occur: "I shall at last [*sic*] have passed my time agreeably, have thought harder and studied harder than ever before, and have wrought the English language more pliant round my finger ends, in case of ever being obliged to return to prose. It is a hard thing indeed to think of wasting one's life away in seeking impossibilities; but how many people do the same and die before they find out their mistake?"

CHAPTER 2

# 'The Most Precious Reward'

## I Return to America: Authorship and Marriage

IN LATE 1854 or early 1855, John De Forest returned to America. A slim young man who liked an occasional cigar and glass of wine, he had thick brown hair, hazel eyes, a high forehead, and a classically handsome profile. He had lost much of his youthful timidity but had not, as he once had feared he might, become brash, arrogant, or dilettante. With his new sophistication, De Forest looked at New Haven with skeptical eyes. In *Miss Ravenel's Conversion* he recorded, a few years later, some of the defects he saw in New Haven. The geometrically precise, two-story, box-brick architecture of numerous New Haven homes seemed to be peculiarly suited to the stiff, angular, and moral soul of a puritanic people whose virtues did not encompass a love for the beautiful. Looking about him, De Forest saw a town full of cliques and coteries, with the peak of the social pyramid allocated to the president and the professors of Yale University.

He also saw with new vividness what might happen to the human spirit if the gracelessness and rigidity of Puritanism were not softened by human warmth. Of a typical New Haven lady he noted in *Miss Ravenel*: "Thin-lipped, hollow-cheeked, narrow-chested, with only one lung and an intermittent digestion, without a single rounded outline or graceful movement, she was a sad example of what the New England east winds can do in enfeebling and distorting the human form divine" (17). Of her male, but maidenly, counterpart, De Forest wrote in the same work: "Thin, pale and almost sallow, with pinched features surmounted by a high and roomy forehead, tall, slender, narrow-chested and fragile in form, shy, silent, and pure as the timidest of girls, he was an example of what can be done with youthful blood, muscle, mind and feeling by the studious severities of a Puritan university" (19).

By the time De Forest returned to America he had decided to attempt to earn his living by the pen. Well aware of the financial perils of such a decision, he suspected that his brothers looked with some condescension upon such a profession, but he himself tended to a youthful deification of authors and their work. Without doubt he was reproducing his own dreams and ambitions when he created the hero of *Seacliff* and had that young man proclaim that authorship had once seemed to him "The most precious reward offered to human exertion. . . . What should a Christian preacher say of a man who would rather be Byron the young than 'such an one as Paul the aged?' And yet, I have been that man" (255).

To his profession, De Forest brought more than adolescent dreams. He had already written one book; and, though it was scholarly rather than imaginative, he had shown the perseverance that authorship demands. He had read widely in English and American literature and almost as thoroughly in French and Italian (both of which he spoke and read almost as fluently as his own tongue). He had considerable knowledge of Spanish and Latin literatures, which he read in the original. He had recently savored literary favor by publishing a sympathetic portrait of Olimpia Morata, a remarkable Protestant whose harsh treatment by her native Italy convinced De Forest of the evils of Catholic tyranny and "the iron of religious despotism."[1] Perhaps most important of all, his American provincialism had been subdued by his travels, and his experience abroad provided him a subject which magazines were willing to publish.

Even while De Forest had been in Syria and in Europe, he had asked his family to preserve his letters. Now he added material to the Oriental letters, smoothed out the narrative flow, and polished the style. Soon he had published segments of his experiences in *Putnam's Magazine*, and by 1856 the complete *Oriental Acquaintance* was in the hands of the public—those few who cared to buy. De Forest had not expected to awaken famous overnight, but he had expected somewhat less moderation in public demand than he found. A trifle of pathos is mixed with rationalization in his enquiry of his publishers: "I suppose that there is not much demand for the 'Oriental Acquaintance', such is the present public excitement concerning the elections."[2]

While he was working on *Oriental Acquaintance,* De Forest spent most of his time at the New Haven House, a modest hotel; and there he met Harriet Silliman Shepard. Miss Shepard was the daughter of Dr. Charles Upham Shepard, who at the time held a dual appointment as Professor of Chemistry at Charleston Medical College and Professor of Natural History at Amherst

College. Dr. Shepard, a first cousin of Ralph Waldo Emerson, had an international reputation as a mineralogist; was recognized as an authority on meteorites; was a popular lecturer in both the North and South on the subject of "Manners"; was highly rational and strongly idealistic (the portrait of Doctor Ravenel in *Miss Ravenel's Conversion* is undoubtedly based on him); and was friendly with such well-known Americans as the scholar Lounsbury, the hymn-writer Palmer, the geologist Silliman, and the poet and scientist Percival. His daughter had a reputation for brilliance as a Classical scholar and linguist, and in addition her beauty and charm brought her many admirers of both sexes. A hint of her attractiveness is suggested by the fact that two New Haven streets, Harriet and Shepard, are reputedly named after her.

De Forest was soon attracted to Harriet, and on May 12, 1855, he copied into Harriet's commonplace book of poetry, at her request, his poem "To A Coquette" (later printed in the *Home Journal* and "addressed to so brilliant and charming a fashionable *belle*, that the inspiration is not at all wonderful"). On May 28, he gave Harriet a copy, written in his own hand, of his poem "Tableaux Vivant." The two poems suggest that De Forest's poetic skill was slight, and they also imply Harriet's fondness for Romantic verse. (Longfellow and Byron are the most oft-quoted poets in Harriet's commonplace book, while celebrations of tragic love and of youthful death, as well as lengthy praises to God, have prominent places.) "To a Coquette" possibly reveals a romanticized version of De Forest's courtship of Harriet as he saw it at the moment, for in the poem he tells of a man so enslaved to a belle that "The warning call of Christ might fall / On his heavy ear unheeded." The coquette, however, is indifferent to her victim, and De Forest tragically (and conventionally) ends his poem:

> Care not for corroded years,
> For a fallen spirit's moan;
> For a pallid face in the vale of tears,
> Which looks on thee alone.
> Leave him within his hell,
> Soar to some heaven apart,
> Forget him well as the bridal bell
> Tolls o'er his buried heart.[3]

By November, 1855, De Forest's courtship of Miss Shepard had become so serious that he followed the Shepards to Charleston when Dr. Shepard resumed his teaching duties there. The city struck De Forest as old and moldy, and it reminded him somewhat of the brick-built towns of England. Inevitably, in this heart of the South, he found himself absorbed in the subject of slavery. His first impression of the Negroes of Charleston, though it was written in cool, comparative, anthropological terms, undoubtedly echoed opinions he had recently heard. The Negroes of Charleston, he wrote Andrew on November 9, 1855, seemed smaller, more stupid, and more childish than the free-born Negroes of New Haven, and possibly the slaves were "not worth all the hullabaloo that is made about them." Continuing in this vein in later letters, he noted that Charleston's Negroes were lazy and corrupt. Their constant thefts made it necessary that everything be kept under lock and key, so that the mistress of every house with slaves had a long string of keys forever at her side. Though the Charleston Negroes were saucy, he wrote Andrew's wife Lucretia (December 31, no year), they did not as yet resemble the "turbulent" Negroes of Maryland and Virginia. In Charleston at least "Quashee has no desire as yet to eat his Missus; all he wants is his Missus' cakes and sweetmeats." De Forest's conclusion was that in a century or so the name of the Negro, the nameless race, might be written in revolutionary blood and fire. A better solution, he told Lucretia, would be "to have slavery melt into serfage, and serfage gradually rarify into freedom. This would take ... six generations, a period not at all too long."

Despite the tinge of Southern thought in his reflections, De Forest was hardly converted to faith in slavery. In the same letter to Lucretia, he reflected more orthodox New Haven opinions. Looking at the continual gaiety and "sniggering" of the younger Charleston Negroes, he felt disposed to quarrel with them for being happy, especially when he saw the deplorable, woebegone condition of the older Negroes who could not work and whose masters therefore no longer cared for their health and welfare. The vast fortunes made out of slavery (much of the wealth accumulated by Northerners and Europeans) appalled him; and he did not admire those apostate Northerners who came South, bought slaves, and then became apologists for slavery in order "to quiet their consciences; and like all apostates, they are apt to be worse than the original sinners themselves. I have heard a New Englander abuse New England, declaring that it was governed by the 'almighty dollar,' while I knew that he was governed by the 'almighty nigger.'"

Despite such New Haven orthodoxy, De Forest's family—especially his brother Henry—was disconcerted by some of John's comments about slavery. To family warnings that he should not be seduced by Southern immorality, De Forest wrote Mrs. George De Forest (December 16, 1855) that he had been merely looking at a side of slavery that was seldom reported in New Haven. He needed no strengthening in his dislike for that institution: "I am stiff as far as the politics of the matter are concerned, as well as on the remote question of justice or injustice. I believe in Free Soil, Kansas Squatters, Sharp's rifles, and Mr. Seward." With purposeful irony, De Forest then pointed out another virtue of slavery: it tended to elevate the character of the Irish immigrants by giving them someone to whom they could feel superior. The "elevation" of Irish waitresses De Forest illustrated by anecdotes of "Bridget" lording it over "Mulatto Sam."

While he was courting Miss Shepard in New Haven and Charleston, De Forest did not neglect his writing. In December, 1855, his novel *Witching Times* began to appear serially in *Putnam's Magazine.* The acceptance of the novel may well have encouraged him to believe that he could actually make his livelihood through literature, and it is likely (though the date is not certain) that it was at about this time that he sold his lumber interests to his brother Andrew. In addition his confidence in his literary abilities may have seemed to him to justify a new step. At any rate he and Harriet Silliman Shepard were married on June 15, 1856, in New Haven's Trinity Episcopal Church. Though Harriet's health was weakened by bronchial trouble through much of her married life, the marriage was at first a happy one. Undoubtedly one reason was De Forest's initial adoration of his beloved, but perhaps another was his idealization of women. Typically Victorian in his attitude, De Forest despised what he considered the foolishness of some women, especially their giddy chatter and flirting and feminism; but woman at her most "womanly" he saw in noble terms. In *Miss Ravenel's Conversion* he made a religious doctrine out of his belief that woman's role

> . . . is passive obedience and uncomplaining suffering, while through her the ends of life are accomplished. . . . Like Jesus of Nazareth she agonizes that others may live; but, unlike him, she is impelled to it by a will higher than her own. At the same time, a loving spirit is given to her, so that she is consoled in her own anguish, and does not seriously desire that the cup may pass from her before she has drunk it to the dregs (372).

After spending the summer and fall in New Haven, De Forest and his new bride returned to Charleston for the winter of 1857. On February 23, De Forest's only son, Louis Shepard De Forest, was born. For the next few years, De Forest lived in New Haven and devoted himself to his writing. In various magazines he published reviews, short stories, poems, and travel articles. In addition, his second volume of travels, *European Acquaintance,* was published in 1858, and his novel *Seacliff* appeared in book form in 1859. His confidence in his own merits is implied in the tone he took with his publishers. To Harper and Brothers he wrote (April 27, 1857) on submitting *European Acquaintance*: "I offer the Mss. for book publication, and want a good bargain, as this is not my first launch, nor will be my last. . . . I hate that very common phrase in a publishing agreement, 'after all expenses are fully reimbursed and repaid,' and would rather have a clean offer at a less percentage."

To the request of the publishing firm of F. H. Underwood that he write an introduction to *Seacliff* eulogizing his own merits, De Forest responded sharply on April 26, 1859: "As for a preface, or other 'harp, sackbut and psaltery' prelude to my own honor, I do not feel inspired to that labor." His confidence in his abilities must have been strengthened by *The Atlantic's* review of *Seacliff*: "A novel evincing so much intellectual labor, written in a style of such careful elaboration, and exhibiting so much skill in the development of the story, can scarcely fail of a success commensurate with its merits."[4] To give academic sanction to De Forest's contribution to letters, Amherst College, undoubtedly inspired by Professor Shepard, granted De Forest an honorary Master of Arts degree in 1859. The future could hardly have seemed other than bright.

## II  *Travel Books and Short Fiction*

Between 1856 and 1860 De Forest published two travel volumes, half a dozen short stories, and two novels. The two travel books, *Oriental Acquaintance* and *European Acquaintance,* were unostentatious works. The former conspicuously omitted the appeals to the exotic, the sensuous, and the mysterious that had made George William Curtis' *Nile Notes of a Howadji* (1851) sell so well. The latter avoided the Transcendental idealism that had permeated C. A. Bartol's *Pictures of Europe, Framed in Ideas* (1855); ignored the passages through royal society and fashionable drawing rooms of Mrs. Stowe's *Sunny Memories of*

*Foreign Lands* (1854); omitted the adolescent shrieks of rapture and enthusiasm that filled Bayard Taylor's immensely popular *Views Afoot* (1846); and made no attempt to capture the social milieu and national character that Emerson's *English Traits* (1855) had depicted so keenly and profoundly. Quite deliberately, De Forest also avoided the popular travel-book formula in which the traveler first told of the humor of his ocean voyage; moved from that to a description and historical sketch, largely inspired by Murray's guides, of a number of hallowed literary shrines; intimated and occasionally dramatized the peril of travel in mysterious settings; and spiced the whole with what the writer fondly hoped was eloquence and sentiment.

Of the travel works published earlier than his own, De Forest's work, in its natural, chatty, gossipy tone, was most closely related to Nathaniel Parker Willis' *Pencillings by The Way* (1841). Of travel volumes published soon after his own, De Forest's work most closely resembles, in its concern for the trivial but meaningful detail and its preoccupation with the ordinary everyday life, Howells' *Venetian Life* (1866) and *Italian Journeys* (1867). In *Oriental Acquaintance* De Forest notes he is unconcerned with the grand and marvelous, for his subject is "chit-chat about travelling companions and adventures" (81); and in the conclusion of *European Acquaintance* he makes the same confession:

> my forte is tittle-tattle
> Concerning living men, the motley throng
> Which greets the lazy observation
> In street and shop, and coach and railway station (275).

To cling to his unpretentious tone, De Forest ignored the great religious and literary monuments of Europe and the Orient. In *Oriental Acquaintance*, when he does depict monuments, he describes ruins that are almost forgotten. He felt no necessity, however, to take a humble tone toward either these magnificent piles or this antique world; and at times he showed, though without jingoism, his pride in his republican country and in the Protestant religion. He also viewed the dirty, impoverished pilgrims to Jerusalem with scorn, for he felt that the ruins he saw mocked the Orient and ridiculed the impotence of a people far declined from true power and real religion. Iconoclastically, he saw only comedy and "hocus pocus" in the ceremonial of the Miracle of the Holy Fire that took place in the Church of the Holy Sepulchre in Jerusalem:

Everybody had a taper in his hand, passing fingers, beard, and face through its flames, and pretending to purify his very garments by its sacred unconsuming heat. "It won't burn! It won't burn!" shrieked an old Greek *papa* by my side. . . . I tried to make him hold his fingers in the blaze but the old fellow dodged them through dexterously, and to my disappointment, got off without a scorch (108).

In a similar way in *European Acquaintance,* De Forest occasionally mocked, though without the acidity of Twain's *Innocents Abroad* (1869), "Romantic" old Europe and sentimental reactions to it. He puts commonplace, sunburnt peasant girls, "more frail than fair" (55) in "sylvan scenes"; explains haunted houses by ordinary facts; and is contemptuous of a young man who becomes ashamed of his feelings that the Alps are "confoundedly small" (71) and hopes someday to acquire the proper Romantic awe.

Wherever De Forest traveled in the Orient or in Europe, he found eccentric characters. The water sanitariums of Europe were apparently among the habitats of quaint humanity, and in *European Acquaintance,* De Forest wittily captured some of these human oddities. At Graefenberg, De Forest's bathman Franz looked as if "he would slice up cold and juicy, like a melon or a tomato" (46). A Hungarian who liked to walk alone and to play melodies on the cane he put to his lips seemed to De Forest like "Orpheus, who, it will be remembered was in the cold water line and had a fancy for playing airs to rocks, fishes, and other dumb creatures" (40). According to De Forest, one man who was escorted to the nether regions of the baths fell on his knees and cried, "Oh sir, remember that I have a wife and children" (48). At the Graefenberg dances, De Forest noted a little man in black who invariably coupled himself with the tallest woman present and "maneuvered her about the hall with the helpless jerkings of a jollyboat trying to tow a frigate" (56). It must have been passages similar to these, totally free of the excessively fine writing that sometimes afflicts De Forest's travel books, that one anonymous reviewer had in mind when he referred to De Forest's "quiet humor . . . intense and sweet like Lamb's."[5] It is also in passages like these, which show an obvious fascination with people, that De Forest prophesied his future work as a novelist.

Among the minor works De Forest wrote during this period were also five short stories. These early tales, though derivative, are interesting because they reveal interests and attitudes that

De Forest explored throughout his writing career. "The Hasheesh Eater" shows De Quincy's influence and suggests in its surrealistic nightmare the fascination that delusions and deluded mentalities had for De Forest.[6] "The Isle of the Puritans" sketches a number of anecdotes, in the vein of Irving's supernatural folklore, about a ghostly island whose spectral inhabitants are the varied saints of Puritanism who have "been heated white hot in the furnace of affliction and then quenched in heavenly resignation."[7] "The Baby Exterminator" is indebted to Bunyan for its allegorical technique, and is told with a satirical tone that seems traceable to such tales of Hawthorne as "The Celestial Railroad." The central character of De Forest's intriguing tale is the learned, cultured, and amiable Reverend Armageddon. The Reverend's one flaw is that children, with their squalling and squirming, annoy him. When the Peppergrass family moves near the good Reverend, he invents a contraption, a baby exterminator, which captures and strangles the youthful innocents. The narrator is amused by the device, but his friend Mr. Punch Punner loses his respect for the commercial possibilities of the contraption—it would have a great sale, he thinks, among unmarried men—when he himself becomes snarled in its coils. The story ends happily, at least for the Reverend, when Mr. Peppergrass, after the loss of six of his children, moves to the country. De Forest's allegory obviously implies that victory or defeat in each man's private battle of Armageddon rests on the success with which he tolerates his fellow beings. However, the narrator counsels a minister in the story "against this insidious system of turning plain facts into tinkling symbols....I beg you to believe...that what I have stated...is the very gravest and exactest reality."[8] The warning suggests the inability of some men, the narrator included, to see beyond their noses; but at the same time De Forest seems to be mocking the Puritan tendency to see everything in terms of symbols. Excesses in either direction may lead to partial blindness.

Another of these early tales is "Henry Gilbert," a conventional piece of sentimental magazine fiction about a young Southerner who can't control his desires for an insensitive young flirt. The story begins and ends on a high moral tone and has more than its share of fine writing, but it does have some interest because it foreshadows the novel *Kate Beaumont*. The setting (South Carolina) in the two works is the same; the heroine in both is named Kate; the father of both Kates is a fiery, irascible high-toned gentleman burdened with arthritis; and in both works an idealistic young man fires in the air rather than shoot at his opponent in a duel. The most important similarity is that De Forest indicts with vigorous irony the *code duello* as a barbaric habit of Southern "civilized" society.

The last of these early tales, "My Neighbor, The Prophet," is an amusing and well-constructed satire of glossolalia, unreason, and fanaticism. The "Prophet" is the Reverend Potter, who convinces a number of his congregation that the truly reverent can see miracles even in nineteenth-century America. When a young man named Riley appears in Reverend Potter's church and begins to babble a strange tongue and make expressive gestures, the congregation, persuaded by the minister, is convinced that it has heard a revelation. The narrator of the story, a scientist and a rationalist, attempts to persuade the "Prophet" that the unreason of his sect pleases only those "who hate the true revelation" and love to "see it mocked and caricatured by those who profess and mean to honor it."[9] Dr. Potter's cult of Dispensationists, however, continues to hold Dispensaries, or meetings, filled with babbling, weeping, and convulsions until the police reveal that Riley, the original babbler, is an escaped lunatic. De Forest's intimation that such sects as the Dispensationists made true, rational religion, as well as its parodies, laughable to the skeptical explains in part De Forest's later attacks upon irrational beliefs.

## III  Witching Times

In his *Indians of Connecticut* and in his two travel books De Forest showed a mind hostile to romanticization of history and contemptuous of the irrational wherever he found it. In his first novel, *Witching Times*, he dramatized the horrors that may spring from the loss of reason. For his subject he chose the Salem witch trials, and this work, according to one recent critic, is the first "fictional treatment which covers the entire period of the Salem distresses and provides a comprehensive and psychological account of actors, scenes, and motives in that mad delusion."[10] To do justice to his setting, De Forest supplemented his knowledge of Mather's *Wonders of the Invisible World* (1693) with Joseph Felt's *Annals of Salem* (1854) and with Robert Calef's *More Wonders of the Invisible World* (1700). With the aid of such books, and influenced by the example of Balzac, he drew a concrete, localized picture of seventeenth-century Salem. His world he filled with verisimilitude of detail ranging from the architecture of Salem's shops and houses to the furnishings inside them, from the precise salaries of some of the Salem ministers to the pious Puritan custom of sending children from the table before the dessert because "our sensible ancestors thought it unwise to expose the little people to the temptations of strong liquors and rich pastry."[11]

To people his world, De Forest drew freely upon such historical figures as Elder Parris, Elder Noyes, George Burroughs, Cotton Mather, Martha Carrier, and Giles Corey. For the dramatic incidents of his tale—among them the pressing of Giles Corey, the trial of Goody Bishop, and the trial of Rachel More (the latter of which is based on the historic trials of Martha Corey and Rebecca Nurse)—De Forest leaned heavily upon his sources. His debt to Calef's rationalist attack on Mather's *Wonders* is especially clear in the parallels between Calef's description of Elder Parris' sermon on the text "Have I not chosen you twelve, and one of you is a devil?" and in De Forest's use of the same sermon in the same situation and with the same results in the fourth chapter of *Witching Times*.

In *Witching Times*, De Forest weaves, with moderate success, two slightly related strands of plot. The first of these, which is relatively convincing in its illusion of reality, tells of the heroic struggle of Henry More against the forces of unreason in Salem, and that narrative ends well before the novel does with the execution of More. The second strand, largely Romantic in tone, is a conventional courtship triangle. The hero and heroine are Mark Stanton and Rachel More; the villain is Elder Noyes; and the love tale ends happily with the heroine's rescue from a jail cell where she is awaiting execution as a witch.

This kind of double plot is suggestive of the Romantic-Realistic dichotomy of much of De Forest's art, from his first novel to his final book of poems; but his greatest strength—his unidealized characters, his natural, colloquial American diction, and his exploration of Realistic settings—is usually in the subordinate, less popularized narrative. The hero of that thread in *Witching Times* is Henry More, an aristocratic spokesman for the author. The prototype of the historic George Burroughs and endowed with Burroughs' almost superhuman strength, More is a religious man; but he is also a cosmopolitan and rational one. His breadth of education and travel makes him believe in the Classic ideals of balance and moderation, and he constantly espouses the virtues of a sound mind in a healthy body. When some of the children of Salem are "possessed" by witches, More tests the

extent of their bewitchment and finds that a few threats and
a little punishment bring the young devils swiftly back to sanity.
When one of the children of Elder Parris has a fit and claims
to have been tormented and bitten by Sarah Cloyse, More wants
to examine the marks on the child's arm, for they hardly look
like tooth marks to him. As the village becomes increasingly
irrational, More struggles stubbornly and tactlessly against the
hysterical rash of accusations and confessions.

While others pamper their clergymen, More quarrels with
such sacred doctrines as original sin and infant damnation, and
he offends the ministry even more with his outspoken feeling
that "A country priest-governed is a country ill-governed" (IX,
192). His imprisonment and execution, despite the inexorable
logic of a defense similar in tone and argument to that of the
historic Burroughs', are inevitable; but even in his final moments,
he is trying to assert truth over the drum-rolls that purposefully
keep his voice from the multitude. He dies unheard, and yet the
voice of reason cannot be forever stifled. New protest against
the Salem Juggernaut arises, and the excesses that stem from its
irrationalism eventually doom it. Even cautious Elder Hale
protests the slaughter when his own wife is accused of witchcraft.
In an authorial aside De Forest sardonically praises the sensible
Elder "for setting store by Mrs. Hale's neck; and only wish
that he had been equally careful not to dress chokers for other
people's windpipes" (IX, 524).

In his tale, De Forest probes for the grounds of the Salem
hysteria and through four characters he dramatizes these causes.
One reason is illustrated through Cotton Mather. A calm, stately,
authoritative young man, he is also cold, rational, and vain.
More an occasional visitor to the action of the novel than a
participant in it, Mather exists to make a point as important to
De Forest as it was to the rational historian Robert Calef. Like
Calef, De Forest asserts that Mather's ambition was one of the
causes for the continuation of the Juggernaut. Mather, De Forest
implies, had little belief in the supernatural causes of the "en-
chantments," and he could have stopped the slaughter if he had
wished. However, his ambition to see a theocracy established
in New England and his desire "for the destruction of those who
love not the reign of the Lord's ministers" (IX, 516) kept him
from ending the hysteria. In him, De Forest might have
created a memorable character, but he attempted only an outline with AMBITION writ large upon its breast, and he
created no more.

De Forest achieves his greatest success with Elder Noyes, who plays important roles both in the Realistic, historical narrative and in the Romantic, courtship plot. Where Mather passively accepts the Salem hysteria out of ambition, Noyes, in the historical narrative, actively encourages the progress of the Juggernaut because of his physical desire to possess Rachel More. To the courtship narrative, Noyes adds a psychological depth lacking in the idealized figures of the pure, innocent, and beautiful Rachel and in the brave, honest, and loyal Mark. Because of his lust, Noyes struggles between physical and spiritual desires. In torments reminiscent of those of the Reverend Dimmesdale, whom Noyes also resembles in his sensitivity, introspectiveness, and hypocrisy, Noyes succumbs to the devil. Noyes's inordinate passion leads him ever downward until he believes that possibly he has committed the unpardonable sin. After unsuccessfully trying to force Rachel to marry him by threatening that her decision will mean the salvation or destruction of her father, Noyes descends even deeper into sin by instigating the trial of Rachel for witchcraft. He persuades ignorant and half-mad creatures to testify against Rachel; and, as his plot against her nears success, he becomes merry and frenzied. He drinks and laughs continually, he seems to be listening to voices over his shoulder, and he becomes skeptical of ethics and theology. Rachel's escape from jail drives him to near insanity, and he raves about his study in "bedlamite malignity" (X, 229). At this point he seems a good but weak man destroyed by a tragic flaw.

De Forest, however, ends Noyes's spiritual testing not with a bang but a whimper. When the hysteria of Salem ceases, Noyes returns in relative placidity to his Bible and to orthodoxy. Undoubtedly De Forest had in mind the heroic, if not melodramatic, public confession of the Reverend Dimmesdale when he wrote of Noyes's more commonplace fate: "What a shabby, feeble, inane termination to that tragedy of soul which he had passed through; ... such was his coward mind that he could not inflict any terrible punishment upon himself; dared not become a warning to mankind by openly bearing the cross of utter condemnation" (X, 230).

A third character whom De Forest indicts for his part in the witchcraft trials is Elder Parris. A caricature reminiscent of Uriah Heep, Parris is an envious hypocrite who dreams of acclaim and is dominated by simple hatred of anyone who opposes his desires. De Forest condemns him by authorial asides and charged descriptions; he makes a fool of him by giving him an illiterate wife, by making him a glutton, and by having him mouth ridiculous, nasal speeches in ranting cockney language. Trying to browbeat a confession out of Goody Cory, Parris illogically roars: "Are you not a Witch of Endor? How dare you thus deny the scriptures? If you deny them, you make yourself a liar, and have your part in the lake of fire and brimstone. Will you tell me there is no such lake? I tell you there is. Woe to you for an infidel and an atheist" (IX, 310).

It is hard to believe that such a simplified man as Parris, even though he may have the oratorical powers with which De Forest endows him, could have originated the Salem hysteria; and, in letting Parris play that role De Forest shows—at least for our time—ineffectual artistry as well as intellectual naïveté. The former charge De Forest would readily have granted, at least later in his life when he commented that *Witching Times* was one of "two very poor things" that he had "scribbled . . . just for practice."[12] On the other hand, De Forest would have rejected the latter indictment. Certainly in *Witching Times*, De Forest himself asks how any intelligent human being, in the days of Salem, could have believed the lies and antics of neurotic children; and he answers quite simply by saying that men, supposedly intelligent, *were* deceived and *did* believe. Emotion, fear, caution—these overpowered reason, and men assented to unreason.

Nor, claims De Forest, is this reaction unusual. Insistently in *Witching Times* he draws parallels, in moralizing Thackerayan asides, between the irrationality of the provincial Salemites and the unreason of the supposedly sophisticated nineteenth century. The latter period, he notes, "gabbles not a little about Stratford mysteries, Rochester knockings, and universal table turnings" (VIII, 578); and a good many people are still fond of going occasionally "to roast a Negro" or to wander "to midnight church yards in white robes, to be in at the resurrection" (IX, 404). The only difference between the unreason of the seventeenth century and that of the nineteenth, or so De Forest insists, is that the drama of Salem had tragic intensity while the follies of the nineteenth century are piddling affairs without crisis or heroism or philosophy. As an artist, De Forest saw advantages in the earlier time; as a rationalist, he foresaw a time when superstition would disappear completely. Ideally, however, he preferred a time of balance, one in which wonder remained but reason was also respected. This moderateness he implied when he wrote of the century he had been condemning

so harshly: "perhaps . . . we ought not to be too hard on an
earnest sincere age which was willing to write out its contritions
in its own blood. Is humanity to be allowed no faith, no wonders?
. . . Are the chambers of the supernatural to be scoured forever . . . by those terrible housemaids, the sciences? Forbid it,
Jupiter, forbid it Isis and Tammuz, and all ye helpless gods of
the decayed past" (IX, 404).

In Mather, Noyes, and Parris, De Forest dramatized how the
lack of a healthy balance in man's desires and emotions caused
and perpetuated the Salem hysteria. Yet, he insists, one other
thing was needed to allow the Juggernaut to do its work:
the near deification of the clergy by a narrow and provincial
populace. The results were vain ministers with inordinate expectations on the one hand and timid men with excessive fears on
the other. A typical representative in some ways of the ordinary
man of Salem is Deacon Bowson. The brother-in-law of Henry
More, Bowson is, at the beginning of the novel, a kind, cheerful,
humble, and charitable man. The progress of the Juggernaut,
however, changes him from a man to a foolish caricature of one.
He becomes a cowering ruin, "a mere dog" who "wagged his tail
or barked as he [Noyes] directed" (IX, 521). As Bowson's
mind becomes ever weaker, he abuses all those who oppose the
hysteria. In nightmares he sees the devil and his witches.
Eventually the mist of superstition and fear so envelops him
that he dreams he and the devil have made a compact. Bedeviled
by this delusion, he forces a stock-Irish comic servant to an
imaginary witches' council, and the two ride (or rather run)
through town on their witches' broomsticks. In the forest beyond,
they get uproariously drunk; and their insane clamor, plus that
of a stereotyped howling dog, thoroughly frightens the more
timid townspeople. Finally some of the braver ones venture into
the forest, capture "this important hellish brood" (X, 66), and
consign the two humans to jail.

The satirical conclusion of Deacon Bowson's hysteria is probably directed at such tales of the supernatural as "Young Good-
man Brown," and De Forest is obviously implying that a man
becomes a caricature when he loses his reason. These are points
worth making, and yet it would be untrue to say that De
Forest makes them successfully through Bowson. The portrayal
fails because it ultimately becomes too permeated with De
Forest's contempt for the unreasoning simpleton he is drawing
and too lacking in artistic understanding of, and sympathy for,
that fool. Most of all, however, the treatment of Deacon Bowson

fails because it lacks congruity: it becomes too saturated in the mood of burlesque for a work of artistic seriousness.

*Witching Times* is obviously a book of many faults. The attempt to utilize both a tragic and burlesque tone jars artistic unity and decorum. The shift from relatively Realistic actions and portrayals to thoroughly conventional and Romantic ones is unsuccessful. At times, as in the melodramatic yet comic-opera rescue of Rachel More, the narrative sounds like Fenimore Cooper at his worst. The beginning of the novel, probably influenced by Hawthorne's rose-bush imagery in the opening chapter of *The Scarlet Letter,* lacks the functionalism of Hawthorne's use of nature and manages only to suggest the ornate fine writing that De Forest was capable of: "That opulent Santaclaus, the sun, hurried over the whole country, looking up . . . all the . . . big and little children of nature's family, to rejoice them with new gifts of life and beauty" (VIII, 570).

To say these things, however, is not to condemn the novel completely. In some of his characters De Forest creates people of psychological depth. At times he conjures up with the concreteness of Balzac, who undoubtedly influenced him, the locale and the atmosphere of a world gone mad. In addition his subject of "an age of false accusers and fabricated conspiracies" (IX, 412) is a worthy one, for possibly the Salem hysteria did foreshadow in America, as Henry More asserts, "a new style of wickedness, which . . . has become our national sin and will, some day, work out its peculiar national judgment" (IX, 412). Today, beset by the fantasies of American Birchites, the judgment of More seems pertinent; and no less relevant is the counsel of the venerable Elder Higginson which De Forest recalls at the end of his novel: "If there is any lesson to be drawn from this book, it is that, even in such a trinity as faith, hope, and charity, the greatest and most beautiful thing of all is charity" (X, 404). In asserting these things, *Witching Times* reveals as much about the mentality of De Forest as any novel he was ever to write. Possibly that alone makes Edmund Wilson's feeling that *Witching Times* deserves resurrection by some university press[13] a shrewder judgment than Gordon Haight's opinion that "De Forest judged wisely in not reprinting the story."[14]

## IV  Seacliff

From the exploration of the American past, De Forest turned in *Seacliff* or *The Mystery of the Westervelts* to an investigation of contemporary American society. Chatty and digressive, the book is full of the kind of wit that led the New York *Times* to compare its treatment of American social life to that of such English transcribers of the "froth and foam of social life" as Disraeli and Bulwer-Lytton.[15] Typical of this flippant tone is De Forest's mock-apology for writing of petty events rather than of grand adventures: "After all, is it my fault that I live in a degenerate age, when there are no dragons. . . . and when fathers do not immure their recusant daughters in sloppy dungeons" (341). Or this incidental comment on a woman who possessed a high temper: "She rather thought it a convenient thing to have; and even, when not using it, she often kept it in sight and *in terrorem*, like a bully's bowie-knife peeping from his bosom" (105). Or this passing remark: "Many a sensible man . . . has saved up all his weakness for his choice of a wife" (236). Or, finally, this prick at a common habit: "The American is the only man who knows what to do with the small of his back. He sits on it. No other nation has made this discovery" (229).

*Seacliff* also reveals a well-read author youthfully determined to show his literary sophistication. A partial list of the authors to which De Forest swiftly alludes (usually by reference to an event or character in their works) includes Dante, Ariosto, Cervantes, Plato, Cicero, Milton, Byron, Irving, Swift, Fielding, Charlotte Brontë, Tennyson, various Southwestern American humorists, Lovelace, Ruskin, Virgil, De Quincy, Dumas, Scott, Dickens, Herodotus, Sappho, Chesterfield, Rousseau, Rochefoucauld, and Voltaire. In addition there are numerous allusions to *The Arabian Nights*, the Bible, and Greek mythology, as well as half a dozen or so references to Bunyan and Thackeray. Considering De Forest's later fondness for science, the absence of all scientific allusions is revelatory of the contrast between De Forest's youthful and mature interests.

The really significant literary debts *Seacliff* shows are those to Dickens and Thackeray (though De Forest was also vaguely inspired by Balzac's panorama of French society [*La Comédie humaine*] to see himself as a social historian of contemporary society). De Forest continued to be indebted to Dickens for a concept of character in which exaggeration was a fundamental technique, eccentricity of personality was insistently emphasized, and reiteration of peculiar words and phrases in individualized dialogue was prominent. De Forest's greatest debt, however, was to Thackeray, and undoubtedly in *Seacliff* he attempted to write a novel of manners in the Thackerayan mold. At the same time, De Forest obviously hoped to gain a popular audience for his work by adding to his social comedy a melodramatic mystery story. Though the latter is far from as well done as Poe's earlier short tales of ratiocination, it is worth noting that *Seacliff* is probably the first extended American assay at a mystery tale which involves rational investigation and detection. Not until 1860, a year after the appearance of *Seacliff*, did Wilkie Collins publish *Woman in White*, the work usually considered the first English mystery novel of rational detection.

*Seacliff* opens with Louis Fitz Hugh, the narrator of the work, calling on the Westervelts, a Connecticut family of some means whom he had met while in Europe. Fitz Hugh wishes to renew the acquaintance because of his admiration for the two Westervelt daughters. Pausing outside the Westervelt home, he sees a pastoral green landscape on which intrudes a snobbish dwelling suggestive of the gaucherie of upper-class American tastes and manners. After he has given his card to the maid, Fitz Hugh walks to the other end of the long parlor, where a number of pictures are hanging. One of the pictures is a madonna reminiscent of Mary Westervelt. Another, a copy of Guido's beautiful but grief-stricken Beatrice Cenci, reminds Fitz Hugh of Genevieve Westervelt, the younger of the two sisters. Musing on the pictures (and the sisters), Fitz Hugh hears a masculine voice from a nearby room. The voice proclaims, "I tell you I have no pity!" and then Fitz Hugh hears indistinctly a tearful, womanish voice. In answer there comes the retort: "Quick then! or I will expose you and myself together" (13)! Thinking that he should not be eavesdropping, Fitz Hugh retreats to the other end of the parlor; but, as he does so, he ponders the mystery in the family and thinks how unwise it would be to marry into it.

So *Seacliff* begins, and the plot of the novel entwines mystery and courtship. Neither the mystery (who is blackmailing whom and for what cause?) nor the romance (who will Fitz Hugh court and with what success?) is successful as narration, for there is little conflict in the courtship, and the solution to much of the mystery is clear early in the novel. De Forest's weakness in, or contempt for, narrative inventiveness in the courtship plot is implied by the way in which he has his hero win the love of the heroine (by rescuing her from a runaway horse) and by the manner in which the villain plans to win the heroine (by forcing himself into her room and compromising her by remaining there for the night). In the mystery strand of the plot the same kind of narrative inadequacy is apparent; for, though De Forest has his hero investigate the mystery, Fitz Hugh's inquiries lead nowhere and his ratiocination solves nothing. It is chance that reveals the existence of an enigma to Fitz Hugh, and accident (the overheard word, the fortuitous sight) carries the mystery onward in its unraveling and solution.

What makes *Seacliff* readable is the gallery of portraits the author draws. That De Forest himself valued these is evident within the novel, for the narrator Fitz Hugh is a neophyte writer who occasionally muses upon his craft. At one time, after mocking a Byronic romance he has been composing, Fitz Hugh concludes that Realistic portrayal of character is the dominant quality that places the novel "among those kingly gifts that the world rejoices to receive" (270). This Realism of character, Fitz Hugh realizes, is difficult to attain. For the young writer who knows little about humanity such perceptiveness is almost impossible. This lack, says Fitz Hugh, leads the young writer of talent, but not genius, to borrow Romantic materials—just as Fitz Hugh himself has unconsciously plagiarized from De Quincy and Byron. The neophyte writer hopes that these borrowings will veil the inadequacies in portraiture, but such imitativeness soon leads the writer into the clouds of fantasy. From the moment he depends for inspiration on other literary works, instead of the truth about people, he is doomed to fail as an artist.

In his insistence that "just analysis of human nature ... is the gem which lends practical value to a romance, gives it the power of fact under the grace of fiction" (270), Fitz Hugh is obviously not only a spokesman for a limited kind of Realism but also a mouthpiece for De Forest himself. That is not to say that De Forest was consistently successful as a Realistic analyst of human nature. Despite his theory, he still leaned heavily in the portraiture of *Seacliff* on caricature, convention, and idealization. Moreover, he continually showed his Victorian inclinations by numerous moral asides in which he praised the virtues and condemned the vices of his creations. Such traits weaken, in the usually accepted sense, De Forest's "Realism" of character, but they do not alter the fact that De Forest was, above all, in *Seacliff* attempting to illuminate the mainsprings of human nature.

Notable among the portraits is that of Louis Fitz Hugh, whose background and ambitions are similar to those of De Forest. Somewhat polished by travel but neither arrogant nor brash, Fitz Hugh is a man of common sense and conventional beliefs who compares himself to Thackeray's very human but highly honorable man of letters, Arthur Pendennis. Though Fitz Hugh feels that authorship is "the most precious reward offered to human exertion" (255), he disdains the romances he has read because the miraculous happenings in such books seldom happen to people of his acquaintance. Totally lacking in bohemian impulses and somewhat suspicious of those who have them, he firmly believes in the sexes keeping to their proper spheres, is properly worshipful of the female sex as long as it remains "female," and is acceptably, though not deeply, religious. Not a complex man, he is still neither one of De Forest's caricatures nor one of his conventionally idealized lovers. At times he is sharp, snappish, and thoroughly ungallant with women; at others he displays more curiosity than a Victorian gentleman should; and at others he is prone to such slightly cynical thoughts as "the gentlest of us have something Vampyric [*sic*] in our nature" (458); or, "It is not the great temptations that ruin us; it is the little ones" (4); or "It is a matter of much satisfaction and gratitude with me to observe how heroically most of us endure the misfortunes of other people" (425).

In delineating the people who live in the mysterious house of Seacliff, De Forest manages to say a good deal about human goodness, folly, weakness, and depravity among those who neither toil nor spin. He also examines some domestic relations of the relatively well-to-do; and, though he has nothing profound to say, he does reveal a good deal of common sense, as well as some Puritan and Victorian attitudes.

In his depiction of Mary Westervelt, De Forest implies his concept of the ideal woman. Unobtrusively intelligent but never intellectual, amateurishly devoted to art, uniformly placid, submissive, and retiring, and constantly kind, charitable, and gentle, Mary Westervelt is never exciting; but neither is she ever common. She is a natural lady, despite the shallowness of her stepmother and the neglect of her father, and she demands in her feminine submissiveness no loud acknowledgment of her merit. After Fitz Hugh has married her, he realizes he can never praise her adequately and yet show proper gentlemanly reserve, and so he decides not to "prate of her," for "she prefers to shine only in the quiet of my heart" (466).

Less idealized is Genevieve Westervelt. More exciting than her sister, she is also more prone to dangerous desires and impulses. Where her sister is blonde and passive, Genevieve is a brunette who, in her non-conformity and passion, reflects Hawthorne's influence. Witty, snappish, moody, and independent, Genevieve has the temperament of a fast girl; and her lack of parental guidance gives her opportunity for folly. For a while she is attracted toward a liaison with the civilized villain Somerville, but she has the good sense to recognize danger when her sister points it out. Fitz Hugh is pleased to learn that she is not the mysterious blackmail victim whom he had suspected her of being (primarily because of her remarkable, but "red-herring," physical similarity to Beatrice Cenci). By the end of the novel Genevieve has matured in femininity, and Fitz Hugh is gratified to see that she is "no longer positive, dictatorial, quick-tempered and impertinently sarcastic but possessed of that most useful talent of womanhood, gentleness" (463-64). Her new femininity implies that she is well on the way to making her own life, as well as that of some future husband, a happy one.

Among the guests of the Westervelts are Bob and Henry Van Leer, Mrs. Henry Van Leer, and Mrs. Van Leer's collegiate, but rusticated, brother Hunter. Though the dullness, churlishness, and boorishness of the parvenu Van Leer brothers, both of whom typify the stolid, sports-loving American male, are partially redeemed by the warmth of their hearts, De Forest finds little reason to condone what he calls the "parvenudity" of Mrs. Van Leer and her posturing, sophomoric, "skipping-jack" brother. These latter two are lively, vain, and shallow creatures, and both need authoritarian restraint and guidance. Of the two Mrs. Van Leer is the more fully presented. A bubbling, soda-water creature, she combines in her person the flirt and the feminist, both of which types De Forest was to satirize often. Constantly she speaks in affected ways that she considers fashionable—"Oh! That's deli—cious! That's superb!" (86); wears tantalizingly low-cut dresses; flirts outrageously; chases men in plain sight of her dull-witted husband; and talks nonsense, or what Fitz Hugh conceives to be nonsense, about woman's equality with man.

What makes her worse is that beneath her façade of bravery and independence, she is a coward and a hypocrite. Fitz Hugh exposes her as a flirt when he lures her into the woods and pretends to take seriously her coquetry. By so doing, he frightens Mrs. Van Leer into womanly prudishness; but, when she is out of danger, she again becomes flighty and frivolous. Soon she is cackling like a boisterous rooster over Fitz Hugh's "naughtiness and . . . discomfiture, flinging bravadoes . . . of lively scorn at me because I had wanted to be so saucy, but dared not" (267). Even more hypocritical is her feminist gabble, for when she is given a chance toward the end of the novel to prove how strong-minded and independent she can be, she does not have the courage to seize her opportunity. Instead, she quails at her husband's fury at the thought that she might have been unfaithful, and she meekly begs forgiveness. So affected is she that she even learns something; she grows less of a silly animal (and animal imagery clusters around De Forest's descriptions of her) and gains more of the feminine graces. She is "no more a knight-errant in search of amorous advances . . . and running risk every day of being swooped upon by the wicked magician, Scandal" (465). The new authoritarianism of her husband makes him a wiser man and her a better and happier woman. The change in their relationship shows the end of Henry Van Leer's marital blindness and the beginning of conjugal common sense, and De Forest was not talking solely of the marriage of the Van Leers.

De Forest also explores the domestic relationships of the Westervelt family. In doing so, he emphasizes the need for love and understanding between father and son and husband and wife, and he implies that an excessive fondness for either business or money tends to destroy the natural affections. To make his point, De Forest first contrasts the older Westervelt, the grand-father of Mary and Genevieve Westervelt, to the younger Wester-velt. The elder man is a business tycoon, crafty, blunt, and strong; his son is a weak man with little business sense. Molded of "Quincy granite from top to toe" (359), the father has little understanding of his son's weakness, and the elder man's contempt for the mercantile foolishness of his son makes him unwilling to allow the younger Westervelt any responsibility in the Westervelt enterprises.

From this father and son estrangement flow numerous con-sequences. One is that the younger Westervelt, in order to keep up fashionable appearances, needs money constantly. A second is that, beset by money worries, the younger Westervelt spends his time in New York and has little time or love to spare to his family. Constantly harassed by his needs, he gambles irrespon-sibly on the stock market, borrows from whoever is unwary enough to lend him money, and is more than willing to sell his daughters in marriage to those to whom he owes money and from whom he hopes to borrow more. His need for money makes him totally self-centered, and he pouts childishly when his daughter Mary accepts the marriage proposal of Fitz Hugh,

JOHN WILLIAM DE FOREST

a poor source for borrowing, rather than that of the wealthy parvenu Bob Van Leer.

In his egoism, the younger Westervelt is blind to the fact that his wife is being blackmailed by Somerville, and in his weakness Westervelt offers his wife no solid structure on which to lean. Her insoluble dilemma leads Mrs. Westervelt to fear, panic, madness, murder, and suicide; and De Forest suggests that her tragic fate is the result of a collaboration, a tangled web of people and circumstances. She herself is responsible because the excessive love she once had for the vanities of life made her submit to Somerville's plan to cheat her brothers out of their just inheritance. Somerville is obviously responsible. The younger Westervelt's failure as husband makes him bear part of the blame. And even the elder Westervelt is indirectly at fault, for his son is what he is, at least partially, because of his father's harshness. The elder Westervelt shows that he realizes his role in the tragedy when he vows to try to understand his son better, to judge him with more love, and to allow him to assume more responsibility in the Westervelt empire. Most at fault, however, in the Westervelt tragedy is the excessive desire for money. Though De Forest offers no real alternative to a society dominated by monetary values, he does insist that in the family one should find a world of order (founded on masculine authority and strength) and one of love. Out of these come security and happiness for both man and woman.

Another major character is the blackmailer Somerville, in some ways the most original character in the work. A man in his middle thirties, traveled and suave, full of drawing-room wit, Somerville has dissipated through most of his life; but he is "as fresh, as unwrinkled, as graceful ... as if Father Time had just brought him to the full perfection of manhood" (20). This contrast between Somerville's external beauty and internal depravity is everywhere present, but no place more so than in the antithesis between the moral sentiments he mouths on appropriate occasions and the vampiric nature he shows by his symbolic, fanglike teeth. Ironically, however, one can learn from Lucifer himself, and Somerville teaches Fitz Hugh that "A gentleman in manners ... no matter how vicious is a civilizer.... An importation of Chesterfields ... would be an immense benefit to our society of hoydens and counter-jumpers.... Great is urbanity, great is decorum, and almost worthy of being classed among the moralities" (319-20). The natural grace of Somerville is an obvious contrast to both the dull churlishness of the Van

Leer brothers and the artificial fashionableness of Mrs. Van Leer and her sophomoric brother, and the point of the comparison is obvious: The true gentleman (or lady) combines manners and morals, external beauty and internal warmth.

Once the mask is torn from Somerville's face, *Seacliff* becomes melodrama filled with moralizing. Mrs. Westervelt admits her sin, goes mad, stabs Somerville to the heart in an eerie moonlight scene, and then commits suicide. When the father of Somerville comes to claim his son's body, the elderly man proves to be a good, religious man who is aware of, and appalled by, his son's nature. The purity of the father leads Fitz Hugh to affirm that innate depravity, as well as environmental influence, does exist. Somerville is one of those rare intelligent beings "who choose the broad road with a full consciousness of its evil ... and for such there is rarely passion of repentance ..." (445). To Fitz Hugh, the lack of morality of such a creature makes him less than human, as De Forest has implied through the continual beast-like imagery surrounding Somerville; and Fitz Hugh recalls for the second time Dante's tale of Branca Doria wherein a demon steals the form of a human being.

In addition to his full-scale portraits of the relatively well-to-do, De Forest sketches representatives from a more modest level of society. Among these are a gossip columnist with literary talent who replies to Fitz Hugh's indictment of his shoddy trade by admitting that "it is the Satanic Press that I work for" (135) but who also maintains that American indifference to meritorious literature forces him to do the hack work he does; a pair of middle-class rustics, Ma and Pa Treat, whose Dickensian idiosyncracies De Forest repeatedly illustrates, so that Ma Treat seems to be continually mouthing vestigial Puritan doctrines, which she clinches with fictitious biblical references, while her Yankee husband is forever searching for words which he does not find, except in moments of danger, so that his rare conversational moments are spiced with numerous "thingumabobs" and "thingamajigs"; and the impoverished family of Warners, forever testy, lazy, and drunken, continually bringing unwanted children into the world, and constantly whimpering about their supposed bad luck. For the "hereditary vice and worthlessness" (349) of the Warners, these nineteenth-century Jukes and Kallikaks, De Forest had no sympathy. His picture of their world compares in its grossness, though without the implications of the moral failure of society and religion, to the environment Stephen Crane was later to draw in *Maggie*.

For any serious student of De Forest, *Seacliff* is a novel worth reading despite its score of faults. An exuberant, youthful work, it shows a mind fascinated by the humors of people. The worst flaws of the work are its weakness as narrative (a weakness De Forest seldom overcame in his novels), its tendency to caricature some characters and idealize others, its fondness toward the end for romantic clichés of action and language, and its lack of artistic concentration and control. The latter fault is especially apparent in the novel's ineffectual focusing of theme and its continual shifts in tone; these flaws the reviewer of the New York *Times* must have had in mind when he criticized *Seacliff* for not being sufficiently serious in tone, and then indicted De Forest for not "having entire faith in the truth and importance of his own narrative."[16] De Forest himself noted early in *Seacliff* that a tendency of the embryonic novelist is, when he runs out of inspiration, to substitute fantastic action for depth of character. This is exactly what De Forest does in the latter third of the novel. The final result is that the Dickensian, Thackerayan, and melodramatic elements of *Seacliff* do not jell effectively. Some parts of the novel, however, suggest that the author may one day grow beyond imitation—may even learn to focus his theme and unify his tone.

### CHAPTER 3

# A Union Officer in War
# and Reconstruction

## I  *The Writer Goes to War*

THE PROMISING LITERARY CAREER of De Forest was interrupted by the Civil War. This dominating event of his life was foreshadowed by a trip to Charleston, where his wife had spent the winter of 1860-61. He reached the city on January 19, 1861, scarcely a month after South Carolina had adopted, in Charleston, the South's first "Ordinance of Secession." Because the President-elect, that "Black Republican" Lincoln, had not as yet clearly announced his intentions toward Fort Sumter and "peaceable secession," the citizens of Charleston could talk of little else. In his article "Charleston Under Arms," De Forest found the people and the city more shabby, tense, sober, and troubled than when he had been in Charleston some four years earlier. He found considerable fear of Negro insurrections, and he surmised that one minor cause for secession was the desire of white Southerners to show the Negro that Lincoln's forthcoming inauguration did not mean that the Negro could expect to be freed.

With his usual objectivity, De Forest respected what he felt was the moral purity and fearless honesty of "a persuaded, self-poised community, strikingly like its negative pole on the Slavery Question, Massachusetts."[1] At the same time he saw clearly that the certainties of the Charlestonians made it impossible to reason with them because "they see but one side of the shield,—which is quite different, as we know, from the custom of the rest of mankind."[2] The ironic phrase *as we know* points out clearly De Forest's awareness that blind unreason on both North and South made inevitable the future war. Though he blamed no single individual for the hostile stance that existed, he agreed with the Carolinians in their contempt for the wavering policy of President Buchanan; and De Forest exclaimed that "The man who could explain Mr. Buchanan would have a better title than Daniel Webster to be called The Great Expounder."[3]

After six days in Charleston, De Forest boarded the *Columbia* to return North, but the ship ran aground on Sullivan's Island and De Forest and the other passengers returned to Charleston. Not until four days later did De Forest manage to sail for New York on the *James Adger*. Family legend has it that De Forest and his wife returned on the last boat that left Charleston before Fort Sumter was fired upon;[4] but, since it was not until April 12 that "Sister Caroline" took that warlike action, the family story seems a romantic exaggeration. On the other hand, a family belief that De Forest was in Europe when war was declared seems possible, though Louis Effingham De Forest, John's grandson, notes in a chronology prepared by him and corrected by his father: "if De Forest did not leave Charleston until April 1861, and had enrolled a company before January 1, 1862, it seems unlikely he was in Europe."[5] Where Louis's mistake undoubtedly occurred is in his assumption that John did not leave Charleston until April. "Charleston Under Arms" and a letter of January 29, 1861, to Andrew De Forest (both of which apparently were unfamiliar to De Forest's son and grandson) show that De Forest arrived in Charleston on January 19 and left on either January 29 or January 30.

Whether or not De Forest spent the spring of 1861 in Europe, he felt no urgency to join the Union Army even after Fort Sumter was fired upon. Like most Americans, he was confident that the North would be swiftly victorious, and not until after the debacle of Bull Run did he begin to believe in the possibility of a long war. The humiliation and the tragedy of that first defeat affected him deeply, and undoubtedly he was remembering his own response to Bull Run when he made Colburne, the hero of *Miss Ravenel*, cry out at the news: "Oh! it's horrible—horrible. I don't believe it. I can't believe it. . . . It's too much to bear. . . . It makes me too sick to talk" (60).

In September, 1861, Major General Benjamin F. Butler, already known for demagoguery but not yet notorious as "Beast" Butler, was authorized to raise a special division consisting of a regiment from each of the New England states. In hopes of gaining a commission in the Charter Oak regiment, De Forest began recruiting a company of volunteers. Such a task was necessary because the governor's appointive power extended down to unit officers, and regiment commissions were determined largely by the ability of potential officers to attract volunteers. For

De Forest, recruiting was discouraging work. The frantic war hysteria immediately following the firing on Fort Sumter (at which time regiments had been raised in a single day) had been replaced by calmer second thoughts, and Bull Run had made the danger of war evident to those who earlier had seen enlistment as an opportunity for three months of fun and adventure. In *Miss Ravenel,* De Forest drew upon personal experience to depict the shy and studious Colburne's difficulties in luring recruits: "not having belonged to a fire company or militia company nor even kept a bar or billiard-saloon, he had no retainers nor shopmates to call upon, no rummy customers whom he could engage in the war-dance on condition of unlimited whiskey.... For a time he remained almost ... solitary in his office" ... (74).

Eventually De Forest was given an examination to determine his military qualifications. The questioning struck him as genial, shallow, and irrelevant. On January 1, 1862, however, De Forest was officially commissioned a captain of Company I of the Twelfth Connecticut, and on February 24 the regiment left Hartford for New York. Three days later, on board the steam-transport *Fulton,* the regiment set sail southerly, destination unknown.

Toward the end of his life, De Forest summed up the most memorable years of his life: "Counting service in war and in peace, I was six and a half years under the colors. I was in three storming parties, six days of field engagements, and thirty-seven days of siege duty, making forty-six days under fire."[6] His experiences in war De Forest described at the time in letters to his wife and brothers, as well as in articles published from 1864 to 1868 in *Harper's New Monthly Magazine* and *The Galaxy.* Much of this material he combined in his later years into a manuscript which he planned to make the first in a two-volume work to be called *Military Life.* It was not until 1946, however, that James H. Croushore edited for Yale University Press De Forest's *A Volunteer's Adventures.*

## II  A Volunteer's Adventures

*A Volunteer's Adventures* is interesting to a student of De Forest. One reason is that the work is autobiographical, and De Forest's best novel, *Miss Ravenel's Conversion,* is a fictional reworking of much of the same materials. In addition, *A Volunteer's Adventures* has psychological interest, for it shows in some detail the inward changes that occur in men under the impact of war. Finally, De Forest depicts the physical facts of war with thorough Realism, and he does so in a prose style lacking ornateness or artifice and yet filled with a peculiarly wry and appropriate humor.

For De Forest, close involvement in actual warfare began at Ship Island, near New Orleans and the Mississippi Sound. On Ship Island he met General Butler for the first time; and, though he found him less porcine than the illustrated weeklies depicted him and more alert and ingratiating than De Forest had expected, still "he seemed less like a major general than like a politician who was coaxing for votes."[7] More to De Forest's taste was Brigadier General John W. Phelps, a sardonic Vermont Yankee, a hard-core abolitionist, and an expert drillmaster.

One of the Union successes of the winter and spring of 1862 was Admiral Farragut's naval conquest of New Orleans, and the Twelfth Connecticut was among the troops assigned to occupy an embittered and impoverished New Orleans. After a few days bivouac in New Orleans, the Twelfth moved to Camp Parapet, a few miles removed from New Orleans. There De Forest drilled his troops under the broiling Louisiana sun. For a while he was relieved of this duty by an appointment as president of a court-martial court. It was not a job he liked, for almost everyone that was tried pleaded guilty, and almost everyone, including De Forest's own pet sergeant, was guilty because he had been drunk. This fact led De Forest to conclude that "an army of teetotalers would be one-fourth more reliable and effective than an army containing the usual proportion of hard drinkers" (30). After condemning such poor devils to ball and chain, De Forest returned to his drilling gladly, but soon he became feverish and was sent for a week's sick leave to the breezes, what there were of them, of Lake Pontchartrain. His wife wrote telling him of her desire to join him in Louisiana, but he advised against it. When she begged him to come home on furlough, he wrote that he could not, and would not if he could. His regiment was terribly depleted from illness, discharges for physical disability, furloughs given soldiers who pretended illness, and desertion.

What had happened to his regiment was not unique, and De Forest drew two conclusions he felt even a politician should be able to understand: it would be wiser to fill up old regiments, where there were mature officers who could teach discipline, than to raise new ones with green officers at their heads; and it was time for the North, like the South, to resort to conscription. Somewhat later, De Forest came to another political conclusion. Seeing the Negro "contraband" all around him, he also saw how aptly the Negroes took to drilling when given a chance. Remembering the reports of how gallantly the Negroes had picked up and fought with the rifles of the wounded at Baton Rouge, he agreed with General Phelps that the "darkies" should be allowed to enlist.

With the fall of 1862 came the humid torture of malarious Louisiana, scorching and drenching the strength away from Union soldiers. For the men (and a few of the officers) there was some alleviation of the monotony and the climate by continual drunkenness and incessant profanity. Some relief came for De Forest when he was detailed in mid-September to general court-martial duty in New Orleans. Though he usually returned to his regiment in the evening, he occasionally stayed overnight in New Orleans. On one such occasion he met a "new race" (47) —he called its members "white Negroes" in *Miss Ravenel*—at a wealthy Negro's home. Composed of men and women of mixed black and white blood, these sophisticated, well-to-do people were loyal Unionists. Most of them had been educated in France, some spoke only French, and all had little physical resemblance to the Negroes De Forest knew. Their desire to find some decent footing in human society had De Forest's sympathy, and he was gratified at the opportunity to talk to an attractive, intelligent, and civil woman.

On another social evening, De Forest stayed in the luxurious, requisitioned quarters of an officer of the Thirteenth Connecticut, and the comfortable bed and clean sheets felt so unusual he could not sleep. Elsewhere, too, De Forest noted the sybaritic living of these garrison troops, and its softness, compared to the stick-in-the-mud existence of the field troops, disgusted him. In typical soldier-fashion, De Forest griped that even lieutenants and adjutants in New Orleans lived in treasure-box houses, had former chefs preparing their meals, and served exquisite Sauterne for breakfast. Many of these officers sent home costly treasures taken from their requisitioned quarters, while others plundered private wine cellars such as that of the jurist Soulé. De Forest thought General Butler's toleration of such looting was outrageous; that strict old abolitionist General Phelps would have arranged things differently, for he "would not take a private house for himself and fretted over the theft of a sweet potato" (50).

On August 22, 1862, General Butler made an effort to cope with the growing problem of the "contraband" clustered around Union camps. He appealed to the free Negroes of Louisiana to enlist in the Union Army, and before long four Negro regiments were being formed. During the fall, De Forest considered applying for a colonelcy in one of the Negro regiments. The advice of De Forest's senior officer, Colonel Deming, was urgently against such an experiment, and De Forest decided to continue on, despite the poor prospects of promotion, with the Twelfth. Undoubtedly the dominant reason for this decision, as he noted in *Miss Ravenel*, was that he longed to do his fighting under his own State flag and at the head of the men whom he had himself raised and drilled for the battlefield.[8]

While De Forest was on court-martial duty in New Orleans, the Twelfth was transferred from its status as a regiment in the First Brigade to duty in a Reserve Brigade (the name was deliberately deceptive) under Brigadier General Godfrey Weitzel. After being unable to confuse his new regiment in drill maneuvers, General Weitzel pronounced himself content with it and the Twelfth soon went on the war path—to use De Forest's term. On October 27, in the stagnant alligator-ridden Bayou Lafourche, De Forest for the first time came under fire, and for the first time he saw a man wounded in war: "a ghastly sufferer, his knee crushed by a shot, his torn trousers soaked with a dirty crimson, his eyes full of the agony of death" (59).

After this baptism, De Forest's regiment had little combat duty, though it had a great deal of marching and drilling, until the regiment joined the forces of General Banks in laying siege to Port Hudson. During the siege, De Forest and his company took part in the assault of May 27, the night attack of June 10, and the storming party of June 14. In addition they took part in some forty days and nights of trench duty, in which the men's clothes grew stiff with mud and dirt, and their bodies became swamps of lice and festering sores. Though the sharpshooting during trench duty was continuous, the life was as monotonous as it was perilous. To relieve the dreariness, many of the men played cards, and some of the officers tried sharpshooting. De Forest, however, "could never bring myself to what seemed like taking human life in pure gayety, and I had not yet learned to play euchre" (144). Instead he read old newspapers and took an occasional perilous walk. On one such jaunt, he received a flesh wound, but, since it did not disable him, he reported it neither to the medical corps nor to his wife.

He did suffer considerable mental anguish, however, for Sergeant Weber told him innocently of a folk tale which said that such a wound foreshadowed another that was fatal. Not until the attack of June 14 was over did De Forest feel that he had thwarted destiny.

The eventual victory at Port Hudson on July 8 followed even greater Union conquests at Vicksburg on July 4, and at Gettysburg on July 1. Optimistically, De Forest hoped for a furlough, but it was long in coming. First, the Louisiana campaign against Confederate General Richard Taylor had to be fought, a campaign in which De Forest was often near starvation, while large numbers of his men died of swamp fever. Not until January 30, 1864, did De Forest and those of his men who had re-enlisted sail for home.

On furlough, the Twelfth recruited new strength, and De Forest stored up memories of the wife and son he had not seen for over two years. In New Haven, he heard the news of Banks's disastrous Red River campaign in Louisiana. With his wife he rejoiced at the word that a competent fighting man, Ulysses S. Grant, had become the Union commander. In this period also he probably wrote his article "First Time Under Fire," which appeared in *Harper's* in September, 1864.

When De Forest's furlough ended in mid-April of 1864, the Twelfth sailed again for Louisiana. After a few weeks' encampment at Carrollton, it was hurried back to help defend Washington, which was being threatened by the forces of General Jubal A. Early. During the late summer of 1864, De Forest served again as field officer, tramping from place to place in Virginia, West Virginia, and Maryland while he mused: "Of course the general understands it all, and perhaps Omniscience does, but nobody else" (167). The climate was superior to that of Louisiana, but De Forest, who had brought insufficient bedding, soon caught a hacking cold; the marching and the eternal dirt were, however, just as wearing. Worst of all was the desperate struggle against starvation. Often De Forest's men were reduced to rations of crackers and coffee, while De Forest and the other officers managed to survive as best they could on green apples and green corn. De Forest emphasized these hardships to his wife, who dreamt foolishly of somehow joining her husband; and to his brother he wrote bitterly:

> we shall starve in our coming campaigns unless we get our funds. The Army Regulations will neither furnish an officer with rations nor trust him; he must pay cash down, or he can have

no food. In addition many of the commissaries are scamps, who
charge us a profit over and above the government price for the
articles. I have known the same article to vary in price, during
the same day, from fifty cents to fifteen. . . . I cannot help
suspecting that some generals share with the commissaries in this
kind of plunder.[9]

By the fall of 1864, the higher military circles, with considerable cause, exuded confidence that the war would be over
by Christmas. Such optimism made De Forest think seriously of
whether he should re-enlist when his time was up in December.
He did not like the idea of another three-year hitch, especially
since the chances of promotion were so slim; but he wondered
where in civilian life he would be paid the $1500 a year he
now earned. At times he regretted that he had not accepted a
colonelcy in a Negro regiment when it had been offered him.

In early October, De Forest was appointed an aide to Major
General Emory. He reported soon after the battles of Winchester
and of Fisher's Hill, in both of which he participated with
distinction; and he was wearing the ragged outfit of a common
soldier. When he apologized for his clothes, General Emory
responded: "I am not very well dressed myself . . . I think you
will do" (197). De Forest now became more an observer than a
participant in warfare—or so at least he reassured his wife. In all
likelihood, his new appointment was a consequence of the
publication of his article "The First Time Under Fire," for part
of his new duty was to publish accounts of the actions of the
Nineteenth Corps. His new viewpoint deepened his knowledge
that most battles were fought in confusion and chaos, that
victory was achieved as much by chance as by plan; but he
also re-learned another lesson: "Tolstoi is right in maintaining that
it is largely 'the spirit of the army' which wins victories" (218).

The last battle in which De Forest participated was that of
Cedar Creek, a victory memorialized by General Sheridan's
romantic last-minute ride. The victory destroyed effective Confederate resistance in the Shenandoah Valley, and it played a
considerable part in ensuring the re-election of Lincoln in
November, 1864. To an objective eye, the war seemed all but
over, and De Forest felt justified in accepting his discharge on
December 2, 1864, the end of his period of enlistment. Nevertheless, he must have felt proud of the commendation of Major
General Weitzel, who urged De Forest to stay on in the army
and who promised him the finest field position that Weitzel
could command for him: "it shall be a majority, at the least," De

Forest reported Weitzel as saying. "I consider you one of the best volunteer officers that I had under me."[10]

Many years later De Forest remembered that he "went home with what then seemed a totally ruined constitution."[11] In *Miss Ravenel's Conversion,* De Forest reported the return home of his hero Colburne in much the same way: "He was ... quite feeble, his eyes underscored with line of blueish yellow, his face sallow and features sharpened. The eyes themselves were heavy and dull with the effects of the opium which he had taken to enable him to undergo the day's journey. Besides his long brown mustache, which had become ragged with want of care, he had on a beard of three weeks' growth ..." (424). In the war, the hero of *Miss Ravenel* learned courage, resignation, obedience, and stoicism. At the age of thirty-eight, De Forest had been taught those virtues in the same school.

Beyond its interest as autobiography, *A Volunteer's Adventures* is memorable for its vivid depiction of the emotional states of men at war. Quite possibly, as Professor Thomas O'Donnell has suggested,[12] De Forest's magazine articles were sources for Stephen Crane's painting of the psychological changes in the young soldier of *The Red Badge of Courage* (1894), but De Forest's narrative is far more concerned with the ordinary day-to-day drudgery of the soldier's existence.

Early in *A Volunteer's Adventures* De Forest suggests the callow innocence of the soldier, his bitterness at the "healthy, monotonous, stupid life," and his desire "to go somewhere even at the risk of being shot" (7). Under fire for the first time, De Forest notes that though he was bitterly angry at the enemy for shooting at him, he had no fear. However, the reason for his bravery did not stem from any superior virtue in him. Instead, he felt his courage was founded on the facts that he was ignorant of the real danger of battle and that he was caught up in the excitement of action. De Forest concluded that "A regiment of well-drilled greenhorns, if neatly brought into action can charge as brilliantly as veterans" (59).

In the battles in which he participated, De Forest saw incredible acts of bravery by both Union and Confederate soldiers, and their heroic deeds De Forest and his comrades impartially admired. At times De Forest met habitual cowards and malingerers. For them, he felt only contempt; and, like his comrades, he was inclined to greet the death of a coward with an emotion approaching pleasure. On the other hand De Forest could sympathize with the instinctive urge toward self-preservation that might lead a raw recruit, in his first engagement, to march rearward, naturally and without fright, as if only "resolved to get out of danger . . . [his] was the simplest and most persuaded countenance imaginable" (63). Watching his comrades' reactions to battle, De Forest concluded that officers were usually braver than their men, and he theorized that the cause was the fact that the officer "partially forgets his own peril. His whole soul is occupied with the task of keeping his ranks in order" (75).

Often De Forest experienced personally the emotions of battle. At Port Hudson he witnessed the slaughter of brave men without flinching, but once, as he recollected shamefacedly, he became "faint in battle and had to draw long breaths to steady myself" (104). Occasionally during attacks at Port Hudson, De Forest's men were not being butchered in futile attacks but were firing back at the enemy, and this return fire De Forest found "wonderfully consolatory and sustaining" (112). At such moments De Forest felt the intoxication of battle, and he fought "shouting with enthusiasm, cheering my men with jokes and laughter . . . and running about regardless of exposure" (112). He made no claims, however, to being a war lover; for, unlike the marine propagandists he despised, he knew that war "is just tolerable; you can put up with it; but you can't honestly praise it. Bating a few flashes of elation . . . it is much like being in a rich cholera district in the height of the season" (123).

Only once did De Forest experience real panic during battle. During the initial retreat of the Battle at Cedar Creek, he personally felt "that strange depressing epidemic which the ancients attributed to a god; it seemed to me that the whole army was scared" (216). This mass fear De Forest explained by the fact that men and officers had "got out of their places in the military machine" (220). This loss of group unity and mass identity, De Forest felt, turned soldiers into "bummers" and "sneaks," and for a time threatened the complete rout of the Union forces.

Over the course of time, De Forest felt a moral degeneration in the men of his command. In Louisiana most of the men and officers foraged without conscience. The well-disciplined Twelfth had three men shot trying to run the guard, but in the callous atmosphere the deaths aroused practically no interest. With the passage of time De Forest's men even seemed contented with the coarseness of army life; however, they were "not so good as they were once; they drink harder and swear more and gamble deeper. De Quincy is right in his statement that if homicide is habitually indulged in, it leads to immorality" (85). Looking at his men before an attack on Port Hudson, De Forest realized suddenly that they retained not the slightest vestige of their earlier innocence and pacifism; instead they resembled "bulldogs and bloodhounds held in leash" (108). Despite this moral change, De Forest had no doubts about the merit of his comrades. Their patient self-sacrifice, the heroism with which they bore not only battles but sickness and hunger, made De Forest feel at times that the worthy soldier deserved a place "on a level with the martyrs" (151).

A Volunteer's Adventures is memorable for a third reason. In a plain and idiomatic style, far removed from the poetic impressionism of Crane's The Red Badge of Courage (1894) and even more distant from the surrealistic exaggerations of Bierce's war tales, De Forest treats the facts and appearances of war. Like Howells and Hemingway, De Forest may have hoped that, if he caught appearances perfectly, he might capture as a by-product something approaching Truth, but he was not striving for Truth; he was not eternally comparing, as the great American Romantics had done, superficial appearances to a greater reality; he was not constantly attempting to pierce beyond the cardboard mask. What he wanted to show was truth, with a small t. If, as Howells later maintained, "Realism is nothing more and nothing less than the truthful treatment of material,"[13] De Forest became in A Volunteer's Adventures more than a precursor of Realism; with the work he intimated, though in non-fiction, that he was— as Professor Haight has claimed—"The first American writer to deserve the name of realist."[14]

One aspect of De Forest's Realism in A Volunteer's Adventures is the wry humor, intimately related to common sense and far removed from sentimentality, with which his narrative is permeated. He wrote his wife fully of the absurd and pretentious spectacle of turning out the guard, and he ironically concluded: "This ceremony must be performed twice a day, or the nation would go to the bowwoys" (12). In the middle of the malaria season in Louisiana, he reported: "Two funerals yesterday, and as many today, but none of them mine" (152). After listening to an officer who outranked him show his incompetence, De Forest restrained his contempt, for, as he stated, "It is part of a man's business in the army to obey and respect his inferiors" (82). Once, as part of a deceptive maneuver, De Forest's company poured a steady fire into an empty woodlands, and De

Forest noted "The squirrels and stray pigs must have wondered what we had against them" (195).

Among the facts of war were its sheer horror, and De Forest did not neglect such details. In New Orleans he heard respectable citizens begging for regimental garbage, and he also listened to Southern ladies assert their patriotism by screaming and cursing at Northern soldiers. On the battlefield he saw bodies putrefying, limbs cut clean away, eyes dangling from eyelids, blood streaming from gigantic wounds, and guts oozing from dark caverns. When one brave, carefree young lad was shot through the head, De Forest remembered seeing "two ghastly orifices through which the blood and brains exuded, mingling with his auburn curls" (117).

It is the everyday facts, however, that De Forest captures most superbly. Of General Phelps's frustrations in molding his recruits into soldiers, De Forest wrote:

Two days ago he fell afoul of a gawky lieutenant who was lately promoted from a sergeantcy. The lieutenant, dressed in trousers and a red shirt, and barefoot, was seated on the head of a barrel, eating an apple and gossiping with a sentry. The general, who was taking a stroll, halted in front of him and glared at him. The lieutenant, without rising, and still munching his apple, saluted.

"Who are *you*?" snarled the general.

The lieutenant gave his name, title, company and regiment.

"What business had you talking to a guard? What are you dressed in that style for? Don't you know any better?"

The lieutenant dismounted from his barrel and tremulously entered upon a defence of his costume and behavior.

. . . with an expression of disgusted despair the general stalked away. . . . "I wouldn't have been so mad with that fool lieutenant," he afterwards explained, "if he hadn't saluted me with his apple core" (23-24).

Describing the everyday existence of his men in Louisiana, De Forest noted:

The night air is as heavy and dank as that of a swamp, and at daybreak the rotten odor of the earth is sickening. It is a land, moreover, of vermin, at least in this season. The evening resounds with mosquitoes; a tent hums with them like a beehive, audible rods away. . . .

Tiny millers and soft green insects get in my eyes, stick to my perspiring face, and perish by scores in the flames of my candle. Various kinds of brilliant bugs drop on my paper, where they are

slain and devoured by gangs of large red ants. These ants rum-
mage my whole habitation for rations, crawl inside my clothing
and under my blanket at night, and try to eat me alive (38).

Of the torment of the blistered feet which accompanied one
of his company's innumerable forced marches, De Forest
remembered:

> When you stand, you seem to be on red-hot iron plates; when
> you walk, you make grimaces at every step. In the morning the
> whole regiment starts limping, and by noon the best soldiers
> become nearly mutinous with suffering. They snarl and swear at
> each other; they curse the general for ordering such marching;
> they curse the enemy for running away instead of fighting; they
> fling themselves down in the dust, refusing to move a step
> further (92).

Such writing extends the truthful treatment of materials beyond
the world of the "Divine Jane" who, Howells proclaimed, "was
the first and the last of the English novelists to treat material
with entire Truthfulness,"[15] but that is less a flaw in De Forest's
honesty than a limitation of Howells' vision of Realism.

## III  A Union Officer in the Reconstruction

De Forest spent the Christmas of 1864 with his wife and
young son, but he decided after two months of recuperation to
re-enlist in the army. His reasons for this action are ambiguous,
but undoubtedly an important cause was his fear of being
unable in civilian life to make a comfortable living for his
family. At any rate, he took a physical examination on January
25, 1865, for entrance into the Invalid Corps of the U. S. Army.
The purpose of the Corps was to relieve able-bodied men for
strenuous service, and the doctor that examined De Forest
found that the chronic diarrhea which he had incurred while in
service had made De Forest "unfit for active field duty ... but ...
fit for garrison duty."[16] On May 7, 1865, De Forest received his
official commission as captain of the Veteran Reserve Corps
(formerly the Invalid Corps) with the rank to date from
February 10.

After a few months of service in Washington as a captain of
Company I, 14th Regiment, De Forest was assigned to duty on
September 13 as Acting Assistant Adjutant General in command
of the Veteran Reserve Corps branch of the Provost Marshal
General's office. In this post he supervised nine clerks and was

responsible for keeping current the records of enlistments and transfers into the Corps. His most imposing task was to prepare a history and a defense of the Veteran Reserve Corps. The practical purpose of the essay, which was eventually published in the *War of the Rebellion, Official Records,* was to justify the continued existence of the Corps, but even while De Forest was writing, he foresaw that General Grant's opposition to the Corps meant its gradual dissolution. Because of the uncertainty of his tenure in Washington, De Forest decided against bringing his wife and son to the city. Instead, he lived with the family of his brother-in-law, Charles Pinckney James, a Harvard graduate who had studied law at Georgetown, become a well-known Cincinnati jurist, and then, in 1864, migrated to Washington to try his legal fortunes in a less rugged atmosphere than that of the West. De Forest's military tasks in Washington could not have been arduous; for he completed while there a number of short stories and articles and his finest novel, *Miss Ravenel's Conversion.*

The political climate of post Civil-War Washington was troubled by the contradictory impulses of vengefulness toward the South and forgiveness of it. In his humanitarian feelings, De Forest followed the lead of Lincoln and Grant. Even after the murder of Lincoln, De Forest opposed radical Republicanism and preached the doctrines of leniency and compassion. These feelings, as well as financial necessity, made De Forest amenable to Reconstruction service with the Freedmen's Bureau, and in July of 1866 he was transferred to that arm of service. For another two months, he served in Washington on a board which revised the regulations and increased the responsibilities of the Bureau, and on October 2 he became the Freedmen's Bureau agent in the sub-district of Northwestern South Carolina. His capital was located in Greenville, a town of some fifteen-hundred whites and one thousand Negroes, and his territory was one of the more orderly ones undergoing Reconstruction. The officer whom De Forest relieved proclaimed that De Forest's post was the best in South Carolina, but he added that the poverty was extreme and the widows and orphans numerous and pitiful.

Using his experience as a Bureau Major, De Forest published (in *Harper's, The Atlantic,* and *Putnam's Magazine*) nine Reconstruction articles between 1868 and 1869, and in the later years of his life he fused these into a chronological narrative. This he wished to publish as the second volume of his work entitled *Military Life,* but not until 1948 did this second volume

find publication as *A Union Officer in the Reconstruction.* Like
*A Volunteer's Adventures, A Union Officer* is interesting for its
autobiographical facts, for its realistic honesty, and for its humor;
but in addition the work has such sociological perception that a
recent commentator on the South in American literature claims
De Forest's work "constitute[s] one of the shrewdest appraisals
of Southern character ever written."[17]

De Forest's satrapy, as he called it, consisted of the counties
of Greenville and Pickens (and was later enlarged by the addition
of Anderson county), and in his domain of approximately three
thousand square miles there lived some eighty thousand
black and white citizens. Almost all of these were confused by
the new status occasioned by the defeat of a society and by the
enfranchisement of a race, and one of De Forest's tasks was to
clarify these novel relationships. Essentially his duty was to
protect the rights and lives of the Union loyalists and the new
freedmen in his territory; but insofar as possible he was supposed
to do this without encroaching on the powers of either civil
officials or military government. Since both the civil and military
authorities were themselves inadequately defined, the duties of
a Freedmen Bureau official demanded considerable tact.

In addition to diplomacy, a bureau official needed compassion,
industry, and wisdom. To serve as judge between white employer
and Negro employee (neither of whom was remotely aware of
the duties and limitations of his new role), to allot transportation,
and to allocate relief supplies for indigent Negroes and Unionist
refugees, to prevent violence between Negroes and "unrecon-
structed" whites, to assure justice to Negroes and Union loyalists
in Southern courts, to promote and supervise Negro education,
and to administer the entire program through the red tape and
endless forms of military routine—such a variety of tasks might
have discouraged Solomon and challenged Hercules. To do
such duties without field aid, clerical staff, or sufficient supplies,
as De Forest was forced to, inevitably meant imperfect perform-
ance. A less rational or more humanitarian man than De Forest
might well have agonized endlessly over his inability to alleviate
adequately the suffering around him. De Forest did his job as
best he could, but he seems to have suffered no great distress
at his impotence to do a better one, and at times he demonstrated
a moral chilliness that is hard to applaud. He seems, for instance,
too much the Benthamite philosopher who loves man in general
and too little the Christian who loves man the individual, when

he notes his objections to a distribution of food and then concludes:

> Thus I remained a general principle, merciless toward the few for the good of the many, refusing to feed the suffering lest I should encourage the lazy. If I had drawn rations for thirty old Negroes whose decrepitude could not be questioned, three hundred other old Negroes, whose claims were almost equally as good, would have presented themselves. The watchword of "draw day" would have spread like a fiery cross . . . bringing into Greenville many hundreds of people who otherwise might remain at work.[18]

Such an attitude undoubtedly reflected De Forest's commercial backgrounds (where feeding at the public trough was at least a minor sin), and so also did the thrifty way in which De Forest guarded the public purse and discouraged corruption in public servants. One of these officials, who suggested a joint peculation to De Forest, soon found himself cursing man's ingratitude from a prison cell.

For fifteen months De Forest worked and lived in Greenville, and it must have been a lonely life. One reason was that he preferred not to subject his loved ones to the uncertainty, turmoil, and even danger of his new environment and so left his wife and child in New England near the security of his brothers and Professor Shepard. Another cause was De Forest's feeling that his authoritative position made it unwise for him to fraternize with the natives of the city. Still another was the attitude of some of the Greenville citizens, especially patriotic females, that the war was still on and that the Freedmen Bureau man was the leader of the enemy. Though De Forest attended a number of the entertainments of Greenville and even became a member of a literary club, he was seldom allowed to forget that "to my native infamy as a Yankee I added the turpitude of being a United States military officer and the misdemeanor of being a sub-assistant commissioner of the Freedmen's Bureau" (187).

Though lonely, De Forest's life was not uneventful. On his first day in sole charge of the Greenville district, De Forest was awakened by a persistent rapping at his hotel door. He found there a Negro named Cato Allums, who told him that some white bushwhackers had tried to break down the door of his home and kill him. In self-defense, according to his story, Cato had shot one of the bushwhackers and then had run for the protection of the Bureau Major. Believing Cato, De Forest felt the bushwhackers should be brought to justice, but he also felt "that my first duty lay in raising the blacks and restoring the whites of my district to a confidence in civil law" (5). After consulting with the foremost citizen of Greenville, former Governor Benjamin F. Perry, De Forest advised Cato to return home and to make a complaint to the civil authorities against his attackers. To Cato's lament that he would get arrested and not those who had molested him, De Forest's answer was that the forms of law must be obeyed and that Cato would be wise to try to get justice while the Yankees were in South Carolina to protect his rights. Cato agreed; but, after he had left, De Forest feared that he had sent a man to certain death—if not at the hands of bushwhackers, then at those of a mob incensed at the killing of a white by a Negro. Luckily, De Forest's fears proved unjustified. After being jailed for a while, Cato was freed because none of the bushwhackers would chance coming to court to testify.

To De Forest, the history of Cato Allums was a triumph in proving the right of the Negro to defend himself, but "the great point gained was that the Southerners had of their own accord come to this decision" (13-14). From the beginning until the end of his administration, De Forest continued to allow Southern citizens and Southern courts to act without interference until he was convinced they would not act with justice. Such training in responsible, self-sufficient citizenship was dangerous, and in a less law-abiding district might have led to chaos, but in De Forest's district it worked well. De Forest reported only six outrages of whites against Negroes or of Negroes against whites in the period he was in Greenville.

A typical day for De Forest at this time began somewhere between eight and ten o'clock, the hour growing later the longer De Forest remained at Greenville. He first ate a breakfast of beefsteak, bacon, eggs, and hominy; then he smoked his pipe and read the Charleston papers. Since his hotel, the Mansion House, faced the courthouse where his office was located, he was able to observe when any of his constituents needed him. When he saw one of the freedmen or the poor whites "looking up and down the street with an air of patient, blank expectation" (26), De Forest strode to his office. There he might be met by the request of a Negro woman for transportation to see her daughter, to join her husband, or to see a famous doctor. Because the Negroes were constantly wanting transportation, usually for frivolous causes, and because he disapproved of this form of charity even more than others, De Forest soon became curt and sharp to such requests. In transportation, as in other matters,

De Forest felt each individual should pay his own way, Negro as much so as white; and De Forest tried continually "to convince the Negroes of the fact that the object of the government was not to do them favors, but justice" (38).

Next, De Forest might have a call from some of the impoverished whites of his territory. These poor white trash, especially the "pore, lone wimmen," pestered De Forest continually; and, "tryin' to git," they forced him unwillingly into such dialogues as this:

"Mornin'. How you git'n 'long? Got anything for the poor folks?"
"Nothing at all. Not a solitary thing."
"Got any corn?"
"No."
"Got any shoes?"
"No."
"Got any close?"
"No."
"Ha'nt got anythin'?"
"No. I told you so at first."
"Didn't know but you had *somethin'*. I thought I'd name it to you" (67-68).

This scene might be followed by the visit of a mulatto with a tale of impoverished gentry, sick, unable to work, and starving. One such aged gentlewoman, formerly the owner of 650 acres on one of the richest of the South Carolina sea islands, lived in a shanty with most of the windows broken, slept on a mattress on the floor, did the most menial of tasks, and begged her food from friends hardly better off than she. Undoubtedly De Forest remembered those like her when he began *The Bloody Chasm*.

On this typical day, De Forest closed his office at around two o'clock. Then for a brief while he might do the paper work which so annoyed him but about which he could still joke: "I decided that the Romans conquered the world because they had no paper" (87-88). Next he would eat a substantial and well-prepared dinner at the Mansion House and then saunter out to observe the capital of his domain. In the streets of Greenville, he would see cows foraging into market wagons for food; would observe (if it were shortly after pay day) a number of noisy, drunken, and quarrelsome soldiers staggering about; would notice the pipe-smoking, narrow-hipped, low-down women strolling about with their mannish gaits; and would pass quietly by the tall, handsome, respectable young ladies of the town. Beyond the city, De Forest would find a pleasantly hilly and varied countryside, and there he would walk alone for from three to eight miles. He might have liked an occasional companion, but, as he noted, "no young man would like to be seen much in my company; the Southerner so forgetting himself would not be smiled upon by woman" (46).

After his walk, De Forest went to the Mansion House for tea. Then, if the Baptist Church were not sponsoring a fair or a magic-lantern show or a Gyascatus exhibition (at which an incredible chained "beast" howled fearsomely and thereby delighted the freedmen) or if his duties did not lead him to some Negro entertainment, De Forest would repair to his room. There, drawing upon his experiences of war, Washington, or Greenville, De Forest did a good bit of writing.

Possibly, before his typical day ended, De Forest worked on his novel *The Senator.* Though no such work has ever been published, De Forest undoubtedly spent much time on it in Greenville. In March, 1867, he wrote to *The Galaxy* to tell the editors that he had lost seventy chapters of *The Senator* and to request that he be advised if any such work was submitted to the magazine. A year later, on March 9, 1868, De Forest was issued a copyright, dated in the District of Connecticut, for a novel entitled *The Senator: A Romance.* The difference in time between De Forest's letter to *The Galaxy* and his grant of copyright may, perhaps, be accounted for by the lapse between the request of copyright and the grant of one; but the copyright and letter together leave no doubt that De Forest wrote and lost *The Senator.* Possibly the work may have been a precursor of *Honest John Vane,* but that exposure of Washington corruption could hardly be called "A Romance."

In his day-to-day life in Greenville, De Forest came to know the people of his district well. He was besieged in his official capacity by the unfortunate, the indolent, and the quarrelsome; and this circumstance, as he was aware, could easily have given him a jaundiced view of Southern society and manners. Instead, he remained as coolly objective as was humanly possible for a Yankee reared to honor in equal measure the dogmas of Calvin and of Poor Richard. In a number of vivid anecdotes and sketches, De Forest depicted the new man and brother (the Negro),[19] the low-down people (the poor white trash), the semi-chivalrous Southrons (the small farmers of the mountains who remained Union supporters during the war), and the chivalrous Southrons (the plantation aristocrats).[20] To numerous

Southerners, De Forest's portraits seemed less than truth, and his satirical treatment of certain aspects of Southern character seemed exaggerated and offensive. The *Southern Review* spoke in July, 1869, for such Southerners when it accused De Forest of attempting to ridicule and "Northernize" the South.[21] Undoubtedly De Forest was annoying in pointing out the haughty provincialism of a planter who proclaimed: "I go first for Greenville, then for Greenville District, then for the up-country, then for South Carolina, then for the South, then for the United States; and after that I don't go for a thing" (177); or a high-toned Southerner who went to New York and discovered: "I can't respect myself when I am run against a dozen times a day by Irishmen, Jews, Yankees, and all kinds of busy people.... I must go South again ... go where I can make myself known" (174-75). Despite the *Southern Review*, however, De Forest consciously avoided sensationalism, stereotypes, and political partisanship, and he portrayed the four Southern classes with a sociological depth and a literary Realism that was unique in his time and is rare in ours.

In his portraits De Forest insisted upon the fact that environment maketh the man, and occasionally he showed his recent reading in Darwin by speculating upon whether natural selection would ensure the survival or destruction of one of the Southern classes as it then existed. The Negro was what he was, De Forest asserted, because of his years of irresponsible African savagery and American servitude. These had made him a strange child—one who was prone to drunkenness, frivolity, and theft, yet ambitious for education; one who was generous, affectionate, and gregarious, yet dishonest, adulterous, and shiftless. His emancipation, De Forest felt, paradoxically enough, was a blessing to the whites; but for the Negro the responsibilities of the future were as menacing as they were hopeful. Whether the race would survive was difficult for De Forest to decide, but he was convinced that the challenge of the Negro's future would "terribly test his vitality" (134).

The chivalrous Southron was also what he was—brave but unthinking, proud and individualistic to extremes, convinced of his superior masculine virility, quick to defend his "honor," and exaggeratedly generous, sensitive, and courteous—because of a background which had induced these qualities. Whether he would survive, in all his provincialism and instructiveness, was no question at all for De Forest. Soon the chivalrous Southron would be "as dead as the slavery that created him" (204). A

worthy Southern novelist, De Forest advised, might well shift
from the former aims of most Southern writers (to praise
Southern gentility and to mold some dainty prose) and strive
for higher ones. Such a novelist might, if he could forget provincialism and prettiness, create a true picture of the chivalrous
Southron and so "furnish us vast amusement and some instruc-
tion" (204). The Southern novelist, as De Forest implied in his
essay "The High-Toned Gentleman," might even treat the
chivalrous Southron so that Northerners might learn from him
some virtues almost forgotten in their cold climate: "that politics
deserve the care of the best and highest; that social courtesy is
a necessity of the highest civilization; that respectable humanity
claims its own respect."[22]

Of the four classes De Forest came to know well in Greenville,
he admired the low-down people the least and the semi-
chivalrous Southrons the most. In the "mean whites," whom he
was certain would soon find "sure and deserved oblivion" (130),
De Forest could find only one real virtue: their temperance in
drink. Even this he attributed to their preference of laziness
to liquor. The other qualities of the "poor white folksy"—their
improvidence, immorality, pugnacity, and social degradation—
disgusted De Forest; and he sketched these foul sluts and grasp-
ing brawlers with such memorableness that a recent commentator
has noted that De Forest provides "not only the finest glimpses
we have of the poor-white in Reconstruction, but also the keenest
and most complete comment upon them."[23] One typical portrait
is of a mother and daughter:

> The mother was forty-three, looking sixty, short and broadly
> built, haggard, wrinkled, filthy, with desperate gray eyes and
> unkempt gray hair. The daughter, fifteen years old, with a white,
> freckled face and yellow hair, had but one garment, a ragged
> frock of cotton homespun, unbleached, uncolored, and foul with
> long wearing. Not large enough to meet in front, it was tied with
> twine in a loose fashion, exposing entirely one of her breasts.
> This child had in her arms another child, a wretched-looking
> baby of six weeks old, tied up in an old rag of carpet, her own
> illegitimate offspring. Her first words were, "How you git'n 'long?"
> Her next, "Got anythin' for the lone wimmen?" (50).

Though De Forest's depiction of the semi-chivalrous Southrons
has not been so highly praised—perhaps because no Faulkner
or Caldwell has celebrated these independent mountaineers—
De Forest caught with only slightly less vividness the horse-
sense, pugnacity, moral vigor, and stubbornness of these Union

loyalists. In portraying the latter characteristic, De Forest tells of a Unionist widow whose husband refused to fight for the rebels and who was then, because of the Confederate conscription act, shot in his own yard as a Confederate deserter. The widow haunted the Bureau Major's office with her plea for justice, a cry that De Forest remembered when he wrote his story "Fate Ferguston," but De Forest doubted if the case would ever be tried. He felt that it was better that it not be: "let us bury the bloody past as deep as we can; the present has better and more pressing work on hand than vengeance" (170).

De Forest's stay in Greenville was hardly a pleasant one, but he did get a good deal of creative work done, and he did gain materials which he would use in such other works as *Kate Beaumont* and *The Bloody Chasm*. In late 1867, however, De Forest received a Freedmen's Bureau order which notified him that district officials of the Bureau would be expected in the future to travel more and to do more to correct local disorders at the place where they originated. Such travel, De Forest felt, would be not only time-consuming but purposeless, and it would have left little possibility for writing. De Forest welcomed, therefore, an order of late 1867 mustering all volunteer officers out of Freedmen's Bureau service. Declining a civilian appointment, he completed his term of service on January 1, 1868, and for the second time he attempted to pick up the threads of civilian and family life. No longer innocent of the dangers ahead of him, he intended to earn his bread solely by his pen.

## IV  *Minor Fiction: 1863-67*

During his career as soldier and military administrator De Forest managed to write, in addition to his essays upon war and reconstruction, a number of short stories. Some of these tales were mediocre formula fiction, a type of writing De Forest was to attempt often in the future but never to write well. One of these is *Dr. Hawley*, a trivial *nouvelle* which satirizes a Yankee lout who comes into a fortune and then brutishly drinks himself to death. The story is weakened by its continual moral asides to "dear reader," its constant authorial comment "Such is life," its caricature of the Yankee Ezekiah Hull, its idealization of Dr. Hawley, and its convenient happy ending. Another example of formula fiction is "Tom Mallory's Revenge," a tale about a young man who vows revenge after a girl rejects his offer of marriage. When, however, years later, he does win her heart and so makes her vulnerable, he finds that his evil passion has been transformed into real love. With its plot of a Southern girl and a Northern boy torn apart by war but finding love anew at war's end, "Rum Creeters is Women" also fits the pattern of formula fiction. Platitudes fill the writing, for De Forest insists on asserting (as he often did in other tales) that love for man is but part of life, while 'tis woman's whole existence; that women love men first and country second; that women, through tears, gain their ways with men; and that women often proclaim one thing and wish another. Despite the dependence on such a bromidic plot and such clichés of expression, "Rum Creeters is Women" does have some merit. The platitudes are at times cleverly stated, and the story does show some of the stark realities of war. The cold-blooded murder of captured prisoners by both Northern and Southern forces is dramatized in a way that might well have turned weak stomachs; and the hero is less (or more) than a feminine audience expected when he tells his beloved that he has just killed her cousin and then turns coldly on his heel and leaves her.

In two stories during this period De Forest showed that he had not remained untouched by the influence of Howells' Divine Jane. In these domestic tales of the commonplace, De Forest wittily contrasted the common sense of Mr. Pullet with the foolishness of his scatterbrained wife. "Mrs. Pullet's Perversion" satirizes Mrs. Pullet's desire to become a member of fashionable society and its humiliating consequences. In "Mr. Pullet's Mistake" De Forest shows that even the sensible Mr. Pullet can make an error, for Mr. Pullet's infatuation with a married woman leaves him feeling so small that "Barnum would have paid thousands to get him for his museum."[24] Both the humiliation of Mr. and Mrs. Pullet are good for them, De Forest suggests: such lessons may lead even the scatterbrained and the lovesick to the beginnings of wisdom.

One of De Forest's better stories of this period is "Visit to the Isle of the Puritans," a satirical allegory in which De Forest envisions a visit by some representative Americans of his day to the sanctuary of the ghostly heroes of Puritanism. The consequences for the visitors imply De Forest's sympathy with the contempt of Bunyan and Hawthorne for easy Christianity. Mr. Cockayne is caught kissing a Puritan maiden and is soon under the whip of a red-breeched Puritan; Reverend Armaggedon is caught sleeping at sermons and is knocked on the sconce by the Puritan tithing man; Major Slick is caught smoking and is escorted to the pillory; Mr. Punch Punner, after being condemned for drunkenness, is shorn of his hair; and Mrs. Milyun and Miss Schottische are jailed for the indecent exposure of their evening dresses. Even the gentle and reverent Henry Howard, who sees the saintliness of the old Puritans, agrees with the conclusion that "This generation and that couldn't get along together nohow... men of one century hain't no kind of business in another century."[25] Thanking Heaven, therefore, for their escape, the worshipers of Vanity Fair leave the ghostly island and "the forefathers of whom we were not worthy."[26]

The best of the stories of this period is "Fate Ferguston." Told by a Bureau Major in South Carolina in 1866, the tale seems more case history than fiction. The story opens with the father and fiancée of Fate Ferguston asking the Bureau Major to see that justice is done for the murder of Fate. The Bureau Major then seeks the facts about the life and death of Fate Ferguston and peers at the same time into the social history of a time, a place, and a breed of men. Fate Ferguston was one of the rugged mountaineers of South Carolina who were at first, during the Civil War, Union Loyalists; then they became marauders using the War to justify their robbery and destruction; and finally they became hardened buccaneers robbing and killing without fear of man or God. The tale, much of which dramatizes Fate Ferguston's execution by his own gang, is told with a complete lack of moralizing and sentimentality; and the rational Bureau Major, looking for facts alone, eventually concludes his case by reporting that he does not feel justified in searching further for the slayers of a loyalist who used the war as a justification for murder.

The language of the report in "Fate Ferguston" echoed that of other reports that Greenville's Bureau Major was making at the time. Possibly De Forest felt some guilt at exploiting the pitiful lives of the people of his territory. At any rate, he wrote on February of 1867 to The Galaxy to insist upon higher pay for his work, specifically for "Fate Ferguston." He noted that "I am so far from civilization that I have to beg favors, as well as so light in purse as to feel no shame in bargaining"; and he concluded by saying that, if the magazine could not pay his price, he would publish elsewhere.[27] The magazine responded by sending an additional thirty dollars for "Fate Ferguston," but not without commenting that De Forest had been paid the usual price for manuscripts. The reply appeased De Forest, but he wrote The Galaxy that "the price of blood" was on some of his pieces, and he thought it only right that he be paid a premium rate.[28]

## V  Miss Ravenel's Conversion

During these destructive, yet fertile, years of war and reconstruction De Forest wrote and published *Miss Ravenel's Conversion from Secession to Loyalty.* He began the work during the two-month interval in 1864 and 1865 between his military discharge and his re-enlistment, and the novel must have almost written itself. By October, 1865, Harper's offered De Forest one thousand dollars for all publication rights to *Miss Ravenel.* At first De Forest balked at such terms, but in late December he accepted $1250 for all publication rights to the novel. The agreement was that *Miss Ravenel* would be published serially, and illustrated copiously, in *Harper's New Monthly Magazine.* Then, at the pleasure of Harper's, it would be reprinted or not in book form. In accepting these terms, De Forest noted: "I make no objection to your reform of the story. If it goes into the *Monthly* of course it ought to be made proper for families. Only I think it ought to be understood, for the sake of *vraisemblance,* that the Colonel did frequently swear and that the Louisiana lady was not quite as good as she should be."[29]

Such comments implied the hesitation which the Messrs. Harper were beginning to feel about publishing *Miss Ravenel* in a family magazine, and eventually their fears led to a new contract which De Forest signed in October, 1866. In it, Harper's agreed to publish *Miss Ravenel* in book form, and De Forest accepted the money paid earlier as an advance in royalties. If the novel earned less in three years than $1250 in author's royalties, De Forest promised to pay the difference, plus interest, to the publishers. Under this agreement, *Miss Ravenel* was published in May, 1867. It came out as a 521-page, brown-cloth, duodecimo volume full of typographical mistakes. Many of these errors were apparently occasioned by the compositor's inability to distinguish the difference between De Forest's *n*'s and *u*'s and his *l*'s and *b*'s (Lillie, for example, often came out Libbie), and few were caught by a proofreader. De Forest's bitterness at the incompetent job done by America's largest publisher remained with him for many years. Attempting in 1887 to persuade Harper's to assign him the publishing rights to *Miss Ravenel,* he commented: "The plates of *Miss Ravenel* are almost the worst I ever saw . . . These *Ravenel* proofs, by the way were never sent me; it was understood that Guernsey would correct them; I was at the South on army duty."[30]

At times De Forest attempted to rationalize the poor sale of the book (1608 copies of the slim first edition were still un-sold in 1884) by blaming the publisher. A more likely cause for *Miss Ravenel's* initial small audience was advanced by Mr. J. H. Harper, some years after the novel's publication, when he noted "the public was tired of reading about the war."[31] Still another reason, one advanced by Howells in his *Heroines of Fiction* and accepted in the 1939 edition of *Miss Ravenel* edited by Professor Haight, is that the Realism of De Forest made it inevitable that feminine novel-readers would avert their delicate eyes. Finally Alexander Cowie and Edward Wagenknecht agree that the portrait of Lillie Ravenel, especially in her marriage to the sexually magnetic and casually immoral Colonel Carter, might have sullied her in the eyes of feminine readers of the time.[32]

Whatever the cause, *Miss Ravenel* sold poorly on its initial publication, despite laudatory reviews in *The Atlantic* and in *Harper's*; and it was virtually ignored from that time until 1939 when a small edition of fifteen hundred copies was published. Not until 1955 did *Miss Ravenel,* as one of the Rinehart editions, reach a wide audience. Ironically, the small 1939 edition follows the revisions and deletions De Forest made in his later life to the original manuscript, while the 1955 edition duplicates, save for minor mechanical corrections, the original 1867 edition.

Fundamentally, *Miss Ravenel* is a "biography" of its heroine; secondarily, it is a novel of a nation at war with itself. Binding these two aspects of the novel together is De Forest's insistence that Miss Ravenel's conversion to Unionism, Democracy, and Christianity reflects the transformation of America into one unified, democratic, and Christian nation. Using Darwinian doctrines of evolution as his justification, De Forest asserts that the Union victory was inevitable, for the Civil War was a Holy War, and its results were foreordained by Heaven and justified by Heaven's evolutionary laws.

For the dominant action of his novel, De Forest drew upon the sexual triangle: "the only kind of plot a writer could get the public interested in."[33] The merit of *Miss Ravenel,* however, lies in its plain, military prose—Hemingway's suspicion of the adjective was foreshadowed by De Forest—and the lack of romanticization and idealization with which De Forest treats the characters of his triangle. That De Forest himself felt the difference between *Miss Ravenel* and his earlier novels is suggested by a comment he made many years after the publication of *Miss Ravenel*:

In that book for the first time . . . I came to know the value of personal knowledge of one's subject and the art of drawing upon life for one's characters. In my younger days everything was romance. A writer was praised very highly when it was said of him that he had· a great imagination. . . . From *Miss Ravenel* on I have written from life and have been a realist.[34]

At the apex of the triangle of the novel is Miss Lillie Ravenel, a character who owes a good deal to De Forest's wife and a somewhat lesser amount to Thackeray's Amelia Sedley. The corners of the triangle are occupied by Edward Colburne, undoubtedly drawn in part from De Forest's image of himself and in part from Thackeray's Colonel Dobbin; and by Colonel Carter, who bears resemblances, in differing ways, to De Forest's own commanders, Colonels Colburne and Deming, and who has considerable similarity as well to Thackeray's George Osborne.

The "biography" of Miss Ravenel, as De Forest often describes the novel, begins immediately preceding the Civil War when Dr. Ravenel and his daughter flee secessionist New Orleans. After they arrive in the New England stronghold of Puritanism, a college town which strikingly resembles New Haven but which De Forest satirizes under the name New Boston, Miss Ravenel makes little attempt to disguise her Southern loyalties. She irritates a number of the maidenly college widows and New Boston Puritans, and she cannot see the higher and broader ethic her father asserts when he satirizes her provincialism by proclaiming: "Suppose I had the misfortune of being born in the Isle of Pines; would you have me therefore be the apologist of piracy? I do hope that I am perfectly free from the prejudices and trammels of geographical morality. My body was born amidst slavery, but my conscience soon found the underground railroad" (51).

Though she is a charming young girl at the opening of the novel, it is obvious that Miss Ravenel is also a superficial and a frivolous one. Because she is so completely feminine, a creature of heart and not of head, a girl who does not act but is acted upon, her "biography" emphasizes the part the three men in her life play in making her a Unionist—and a Christian. The first man is her father, an amiable and witty Southerner but, far more important, an ideal cosmopolite. In one personality he combines the manners and courtesies of the Southern high-toned gentleman and the deep morality of the New Boston Puritan. When he and his daughter return to New Orleans during its occupation by Union forces, they are ostracized by their former friends and Dr. Ravenel is attacked on a dark street by one of the Southern "patriots." To both events Miss Ravenel reacts with feminine emotionalism, and the wounds of her father make her see, more than could hours of logical argument, "that secession was indefensible, and that the American Union should be preserved" (144).

A second man in Miss Ravenel's life is the forcefully masculine Colonel Carter. Miss Ravenel meets Carter in New Boston, where he has come to recruit a regiment, and their acquaintance deepens into love when the two meet again in New Orleans. Despite Dr. Ravenel's dislike for Colonel Carter, whom he recognizes as a man of the world with the peculiar code of "honor" of the high-toned Virginia gentleman, Dr. Ravenel finally accepts the engagement and marriage of Lillie and the Colonel. The marriage brings Lillie closer to the Union for whom her husband is fighting; and, even more important, it brings her closer to Christianity. When her father decides to aid the Southern Negro by supervising a plantation of laboring Negro freedmen, Lillie accepts the responsibility of teaching reading to the former slaves. She does it, however, "for Carter's sake; she had not yet learned to do it for Jesus Christ's sake" (239).

Colonel Carter also contributes to the maturity of Miss Ravenel in another way. After his marriage he abandons for a while his drinking and his casual sexual alliances, but on a trip to Washington, where he has gone in search of promotion, he is lured into unfaithfulness by a New Orleans widow, Mrs. Larue. Later on, Lillie's agony in childbirth leads to the end of Carter's affair. After Carter returns to battle, however, Lillie accidentally learns of his affair, goes through paroxysms of agony at her humiliation as a wife, and returns to New Boston with her father. The death of her husband in battle brings her, despite her separation, another trial which she bears in much the same fashion as Thackeray's Amelia Sedley. She turns worshipfully to her child and shows increasing, though highly personal, devotional tendencies; she prays nightly for those near to her, though "It is possible that she may have forgotten the heathen, the Jews, and the negroes" (436). She has journeyed from girl to woman and has not only survived but has been made better by the pilgrimage.

The third man in Lillie's "biography" is Edward Colburne. Though Miss Ravenel is attracted to him when they first meet in New Boston, he lacks the obvious virility of the swaggering,

mustachioed Carter. Miss Ravenel explains the difference in the
two men by saying that Colburne is not "magnetic," but what
she obviously feels is sexual desire for Carter. (The implication,
of course, is that she, as Bunyanesque pilgrim, must journey
beyond the Vanity Fair of animal sensation before she can find
conversion and salvation.[35]) Later on, in New Orleans, Colburne
further weakens his suit for Lillie. He admits attending parties
given by New Orleans' Creole Negroes (or "white Negroes"), and
he is too much a gentleman to reveal that Colonel Carter has
also attended these occasions. In his defense of his actions, Colburne offends the dignity of the immature Lillie; and when
Colburne leaves her home, "The pride of race, the prejudices
of her education, would not permit her to be cordial" (171).
It is not until after she has grown toward Christianity and
beyond prejudice, until she has experienced the twin agonies
of the birth of her child and the death of her husband, until
she has grown selfless and shows it in her devotion to her child—
it is not until she has been spiritualized by the trials of life that
she is able to recognize the selfless love of her Dobbinesque
admirer Colburne. In doing so, she is fulfilling, in a rather
Freudian way, a part of God's plan, based on the "despotic
instinct" of sex. "Do you believe," asks De Forest, "that
conscience, sense of duty, philanthropy would ... save the race
from extinction? Strike out the affection of sex for sex and earth
would be first a hell, then a desert. God is not very far from
every one of us. The nation was not more certainly guided
by the hand of Providence in overthrowing slavery than was
this man in loving this woman" (462). Miss Ravenel's conversion
is complete when she accepts Colburne and tells him that she
prefers to live in the North after they are married. After her
comment, De Forest notes: "She was willing at all times now to
make confession of her conversion" (480).

*Miss Ravenel* is a love story, but it is intertwined with a war
story, and the three men in Miss Ravenel's life play important
roles in this Holy War. Dr. Ravenel is an Abolitionist, "plotting the
benefit of the human race" (227); and, as the civilized cosmopolite whose values transcend time and place, as the philosopher
who sees the truth behind appearances, as the Christian visionary
who sees the workings of God's will in the inevitable progress
of mankind toward a better world—as all these things he
serves as a kind of chorus, moral and witty and epigrammatic, to
the novel. Because he is the civilized man, he preaches courtesy
to all; and, out of his conviction that "Politeness is a part of

piety" (238), he condemns both Southern ruffianism and Northern chilliness and ungraciousness. Because he is a Christian with strong Puritan leanings, he sees the war as a struggle between "Heaven fighting with Hell" (461), and he indicts the South as a nineteenth-century Babylon, a modern Sodom and Gomorrah.

Because he is a philosopher, he can see the guilt of both the North and the South—the North in its desire to profit financially from slavery and the South in its obliviousness to Christian morality—and he can insist that the common guilt means that "None of us ought to get off easily, and therefore I conclude that we shall not" (123). Finally, because he is a Christian visionary, he can proclaim that the Civil War is "the fifth act in the grand drama of human liberty. First, the Christian Revelation. Second, the Protestant Reformation. Third, the War of American Independence. Fourth, the French Revolution. Fifth, the struggle for the freedom of all men without distinction of race or color" (460). As the visionary, he can go even further. For him the agony of the war is God's punishment for the American sin of slavery; but, like Milton, whom he is fond of quoting, Dr. Ravenel sees a benevolent purpose in God's ways.

As a scientist, Dr. Ravenel sees this benevolence working through Darwinistic evolution. He welcomes change as the source of man's progress from barbarism, and he sees the Civil War as part of God's Darwinian plan. For Dr. Ravenel, the warring, slave-owning planters are justly doomed to extinction because "The world had got too intelligent for them. They could not live without retarding the progress of civilization" (233-34). The North's victory he views as the triumph of a just, democratic system of labor and government over a tyrannical, aristocratic one. In Dr. Ravenel's eyes the Darwinian struggle for survival becomes a Divine plan, and, like Lincoln, he feels that right makes might: "In that sense 'The hand of God' is identical with 'the heaviest battalions'" (461).

Though he is an enthusiast and a visionary, Dr. Ravenel is also, in the highest view, a practical man. He is willing, though fumblingly, to take up arms to defend his convictions. He puts his theories about free labor into practice, and they work: the "Doctor's negroes did more work ... than double their number by the agency of a white overseer, drivers, whips, and paddles" (244). When his views and the facts conflict, Dr. Ravenel is able to abandon his theories, as is apparent when he discovers that the Uncle Tom he had once believed might exist is founded on fancy. Pragmatically, he learns that education is indispensable to religious exaltation—"Renewing a man's heart is only a partial reformation, unless you illuminate his mind" (248)—and out of the same practical wisdom he preaches the wisest way to treat the South after the North has achieved victory. In one of his typical anecdotes he notes: "For instance, you hear a man talking treason; you look at him and say, 'It is that poor fool, Cracker.' But all the while it is Planter, who, being stronger minded than Cracker, dwells in him and blasphemes out of his windows. . . . I say, hang Planter and tell Cracker to get to work. Planter gone, some better man will occupy Cracker and make him speak and live virtuously" (462).

Captain Colburne also plays an important part in the Holy War. Though he has been brought up in the morally and esthetically confining atmosphere of New Boston, he is quite different from such contemporaries as John Whitewood, Jr., a sallow and puritanic parody of manhood. Instead, Colburne at the beginning of the novel is an example of New Boston manhood at its best. He is merry, frank, and healthy, somewhat unpolished in his manners, rather uncertain of his own virtues and powers, somewhat morally prim though not quite priggish, and relatively narrow in experience. When he goes to war, he becomes the citizen soldier who fights from conviction and not by profession; for him the war is a test of manhood by the fires of reality. On the battlefield and elsewhere he sees scenes of unparalled horror, as for instance when he watches his comrade Lt. Van Zandt wander drunkenly around a field hospital:

> In the centre of this mass of suffering stood several operating tables, each burdened by a grievously wounded man and surrounded by surgeons and their assistants. Underneath were great pools of clotted blood, amidst which lay amputated fingers, hands, arms, feet, and legs. . . . The surgeons, who never ceased their awful labor, were daubed with blood to the elbows; and a smell of blood drenched the stifling air, overpowering even the pungent odor of chloroform. . . .
> "Come up and see them butcher, Captain," said the iron-nerved Van Zandt, . . . glaring at the process of an amputation with an eager smile of interest much like the grin of a bulldog who watches the cutting up of a piece of beef. . . . From table to table, from sufferer to sufferer he followed the surgeon of the tenth, slapping him on the back violently and shouting, "Doctor give me some whiskey. . . . Hand over your whiskey, damn you!" (269-71).

In addition Captain Colburne sees political corruption intrude upon the effective prosecution of the war, and he sees military merit ignored. He sees those who deserve promotion neglected, and he watches the saloon-keeper and politician Gazaway enter the army at an undeserved rank and then, despite his cowardice, rise higher and higher until he becomes a Lt. Colonel feathering his nest by allowing bounty jumpers to escape the army. Finally, in New Orleans, Captain Colburne sees even good men succumb to the temptations of easy living and easier virtue.

In this world of the reality of war and Vanity Fair, Captain Colburne's moral New Boston background serves him well. He does not succumb to the temptations of drink, of gambling, or of the widow Mrs. Larue; and he emerges from his testing a more authoritative, masculine, tolerant, democratic, and Christian person than he had earlier been. Like Dr. Ravenel, he sees the war as part of God's Darwinian plan, and to his future wife he asserts his selfless convictions:

> There are ten thousand blossoms on an apple tree, but not five hundred of them mature into fruit. So it is with us human beings. . . . It is a part of the method of God. . . . What right have we to demand that we shall be happy? That is a condition that we have no right and no power to make with the Creator. . . . Our desire should be that we might be enabled to make others happy (463).

Out of the war he has learned obedience, resignation, and stoicism. "Like the nation," De Forest asserts, "he has developed and learned his powers. . . . It is in millions of such men that the strength of the Republic consists" (484-85).

Where Captain Colburne is a representative of the New Boston Puritan who becomes the citizen soldier, Colonel Carter embodies the Southerner trained as a professional soldier. A West Point graduate, he conceives of himself as "a born Virginia gentleman" (148), and De Forest notes (in the 1867 edition but not in the revised 1939 edition) that Carter "was only in political matters . . . false to his birthplace. . . . In his mixture in short of gentility and barbarism he was a true child of his class and state" (149). Though Carter is a poised, charming, and virile son of the South, he, like the section he represents, is deficient in moral virtue. Primarily a creature of body, he is largely self-centered. Where Colburne is gentle with those weaker than himself, Carter is often brutal. In New Orleans he easily succumbs to drink and sybaritism. When Mrs. Larue offers herself to him, he does not have the moral fiber, though he has no great passion for her, to resist her advances. When his luxurious manner of living immerses him at first in debt and then in ruinous financial speculation (in which he uses government funds), he is forced to defraud the government in order to avoid public exposure and the loss of his army commission.

Ironically, Colonel Carter's moral perceptions are so confused that he seldom has any doubts that he is a virtuous man, "honorable even in his vices" (183). By such logic he can, before his marriage, convince himself that an illicit affair he is having is justifiable because it is helping him to forget Miss Ravenel and thereby helping both of them escape a penurious marriage. After his affair with Mrs. Larue, he is penitent; but it is a "penitence without fruit, a self-reproach without self control" (351). Even after he knows that his wife has been in agony because she has learned of his misconduct, he can, at first, forget her pain by getting drunk, and then, the next morning, justify himself by thinking "such affairs were altogether too common to be made so much of" (418). About only one thing—"The only ungentlemanly act of my life" (396)—does Carter feel really ashamed: his betrayal and defrauding of the government. The reason is that his behavior violates his military oath, the only code of "honor" which he respects; and De Forest insistently dramatizes the fact that "Professionally if not personally, as a soldier if not as a man, he had an imperious conscience" (105). Because of this professional integrity Carter objects to the moral compromises of the Governor of Barataria—who appoints ward politicians to high military rank because they control the votes necessary for political success—and resents the necessity that he bow down to congressional wire-pullers in order to gain a brigadier general's star.

In truth, Carter, a strange mixture, can be blamed for his conduct no more than Major Scott, the Negro whose marital infidelity disillusions Dr. Ravenel about the possibility of the existence of an Uncle Tom among the Southern Negroes. A man can know only what he is taught—and De Forest's references to Balzac in *Miss Ravenel* imply where he gained this attitude—and Carter's Cavalier and military backgrounds have instilled in him no morality higher than his military oath. The point is made most clearly when, as he is dying, Carter rejects the plea of the chaplain that he think on Jesus Christ. Carter replies, "Don't bother—where is the brigade?" (424). The Surgeon, as

Carter dies, proclaims that Carter has died with the same logic
as he had lived, but De Forest insists that the Surgeon does not
know "the tenderness which existed at the bottom of that passionate nature. With another education Carter might have been a
James Brainard or a St. Vincent de Paul" (425).

In addition to his major characters, De Forest creates a
number of memorable minor ones in *Miss Ravenel*. One is Lt. Van
Zandt, the hard-gambling, hard-drinking, hard-swearing soldier
who is so boastfully proud of the fact he comes from old
Knickerbocker stock and is a graduate of Columbia College.
Another is the old Negro, Major Scott, who loves the forms of
military command almost as much as he loves the Bible he quotes
so constantly and understands so imperfectly. Most unforget-
table of all, however, is the French Creole widow Mrs. Larue. Of
her, Howells confessed, "I cannot think without shuddering,"[36]
and even today she is chillingly alive. Her perfect selfishness
and complete hypocrisy; her coquettish rhapsodies from Balzac
and her siren songs of *le saint passion de l'amour* and *divin
sens du génésique;* her madonnaesque, nun-like appearance and
her inward amorality as "the child ... of Balzac's moral philosophy" (384); her chameleon agreeableness that makes her all
things to all men; her instinctive animal nature and yet her
prudence in the matter of forms—all these create an example
of well-nigh perfect corruption. What makes her most coldly
plausible, however, is De Forest's insistence that she is not the
embodiment of evil. She does not really desire to hurt anyone
—only to enjoy her own pleasures—and she can even momentarily
suffer remorse over her affair with Colonel Carter. She is
perfectly suited to the world of Vanity Fair; and, like the Becky
Sharp whom she so much resembles, she is adept at using people
for her own gratification. Poetic justice fails to bring her any
punishment, just as it neglects to bring Captain Colburne any
promotion; and eventually she preserves her financial fortunes by
trading special favors for a "curious billet doux [that] she sold
to a New York speculator for fifteen thousand dollars" (412).

Without doubt, *Miss Ravenel* is the best novel De Forest ever
wrote. In it he employed the aphorisms he could coin so tell-
ingly—as, for instance, when he tells of Colburne's letters to Dr.
Ravenel and notes that each one "was a sly carom on the father,
with the intention of pocketing the daughter" (114); when he
allows Dr. Ravenel, after he has been injured by a Southern
"patriot," to comment, "I knew I was in New Orleans when I was
hit, just as the shipwrecked man knew he was in a Christian

country when he saw a gallows" (142); or when he comments of Colonel Carter, "As we say of some fiery wines, there was a great deal of body to him" (165).

In *Miss Ravenel,* De Forest also used with good effect the Thackerayan authorial intrusion. Most often he used it for such moralistic statements as: "Balzac says that very corrupt people are generally very agreeable. . . . they love nothing, hate nothing, and are as easy to wear as old slippers. The strict moralist and pietist, on the other hand, is as hard and unyielding as a book. . . . you must conform to his model, or he will conscientiously pinch your moral corns" (92). Occasionally, he intruded to laugh at Romantic writing, as when he described the renewed acquaintance of Miss Ravenel and Captain Colburne: "Of course it would be agreeable to have. . . . some burning words to tell, some thrilling looks to describe. . . . But they behaved in a most disappointingly well-bred manner. . . . This is not the way heroes and heroines meet on the boards or in some romances; but in actual society they frequently balk our expectations in just this manner. Melodramatically considered real life is frequently a failure" (137).

Most of all, however, *Miss Ravenel* is De Forest's finest novel because it is consistently realistic in both plot and character. Deliberately De Forest eschewed the more Romantic portions of his army career (as, for instance, his participation in the Battle of Winchester), and just as conscientiously he created characters and localities with mixtures of vice and virtue. Though Dr. Ravenel and Captain Colburne may be idealized a trifle, no character is unbelievable and none is a caricature. If the characters resemble in some ways those of *Vanity Fair* and in others the types of *Pilgrim's Progress,* they are at the same time as deeply American as the conflict through which they live—or die. Returning from abroad soon after the publication of *Miss Ravenel,* William Dean Howells felt deeply the power and the nationalism of the novel, and years later he acknowledged the novel's impact, as well as De Forest's authorial fate, when he commented:

"Miss Ravenel's Conversion" . . . was one of the best American novels I had known, and was of an advanced realism before realism was known by name. I had a passion for that book, and for all the books of that author; and if I have not been able to make the public care for them as much as I did it has not been for want of trying.[37]

Undoubtedly De Forest was aware that *Miss Ravenel* was a better work than much of what he had written; and, because of his desire to gain for it a larger audience than it received in 1867, he spent a good bit of time in his later life in revising the work. In the revisions he cut out a good bit of repetitive material. Probably for personal reasons he eliminated the long passage at the end of Chapter VI in which he treated the death of Captain Colburne's mother. In an attempt at the kind of Realism espoused by James and Howells, he eliminated a number of the authorial, moral intrusions (among them a long diatribe against liquor); and, where he could, he avoided the first person pronoun. For the same reason he rejected such gaudy passages as the description of Mrs. Larue's eyes: "They were beautiful spiders, weaving quite visible webs of entanglement, the threads of which were rays of dazzling light and subtle sentiment" (202). In an attempt at greater subtlety, he cut a number of the passages that pointed toward his theme of a Holy War for Christianity and Democracy, and he eliminated the summarizing end in which he prophesied the future of Lillie and Colburne. Finally, to appease the taste of a female audience, he eliminated some passages he felt might be offensive—among them the scathing comment upon Colonel Carter, "To make him love it was necessary to have a woman in pretty close personal propinquity" (109). In some ways, De Forest improved *Miss Ravenel;* in others, he weakened it. In either version, however, *Miss Ravenel* is undoubtedly one of the greatest, perhaps the greatest, of the novels to be created out of the agony of the American nation's rebirth of freedom.

CHAPTER *4*

# Magazinist

## I  *The Life: 1868-81*

ON HIS DISCHARGE from army service, De Forest accepted an invitation of Charles Wyllys Elliot, a writer for *The Galaxy,* to visit him in New York City. With a slender erect figure, De Forest at the time had straight, thin lips over the tops and sides of which straggled a luxurious military mustache; penetrating eyes with pouchy overhanging brows; and thick, brown hair which he brushed straight back from a triangular point high on his forehead. Often De Forest sallied out, cane in hand, to explore the city; and, if *The Wetherel Affair* is any indication, he must have done a good bit of walking along the docks and other less savory parts of New York. Before long the roughness and discourtesy, the excessive democracy, of the city began to annoy him. Watching the exploitation of the city by Tammany Hall and the Tweed Ring, he grew daily more disillusioned with government by the common herd for the benefit of the corrupt politician. Each passing day made De Forest more confident that New York's extension of the vote to nontaxpayers, most of them illiterate foreigners unacquainted with American customs and ideals, bred the buying and selling of elections and political offices. He was equally certain of the mediocrity of any government that had as its symbol the ward politician and which depended for its power on the lowest ranks of society. New York, he felt, was forgetting the gentlemanly ideal; and, though he knew that concept could be carried to nonsensical extremes, he also felt that democracy could be degraded to ruffianism. The problem was to combine somehow the virtues of the gentlemanly and democratic theories. In New York no such perfect union was taking place, and De Forest satirically suggested in "The High-Toned Gentleman," an article that he wrote for *The Nation* (March 12, 1868), that maybe the *code duello* might be a cure for some of the ruffianism so prevalent in New York.

While he was in New York, De Forest published a number of articles, most of them dealing with his Reconstruction experiences, and at least two short stories. One of his articles appeared in *The Nation* (January 9, 1868), and in its title, "The Great American Novel," he coined for the first time a phrase that is still familiar. The essay effectively suggests some of De Forest's attitudes as a critic and his dreams as a writer. De Forest begins by noting that a "friend" of his who had fought in the Civil War, aided in Reconstruction, and written some "experiments" and trivia constantly returns to his fixed idea of writing the great American novel. This work he sees as presenting "the picture of ordinary emotions and manners of American existence —The American 'Newcomes' or 'Miserables.'" De Forest, who asks if his friend will produce such a novel, answers that the immense obstacles make success doubtful. He looks down the roll of American writers who might have gained the prize. Irving was "too cautious to make the trial." Cooper "produced something less natural than the wax figures in Barnum's old museum" and Simms "is nearly as good as Cooper." Paulding, Brown, and Kennedy "are ghosts, and they wrote about ghosts, and the ghosts have vanished utterly."

In his own time, De Forest continues, there is Hawthorne, "the greatest of imaginations," but his romances are "characterized by only a vague consciousness of this life and his people belong to the wide realms of art rather than nationality." Oliver Wendell Holmes has done some remarkable work as the Autocrat, but his novels lack the genius of his essays. (De Forest's voluminous reading apparently did not include *Moby Dick*, which had appeared in 1851, or for that matter any of the works of Melville.) Probably the closest approximation to the great American novel, or so De Forest asserts, is *Uncle Tom's Cabin* (1852). Though the plot is defective and the characters are sometimes drawn in too simple black and white coloring, there is "a national breadth to the picture ... natural speaking, and plenty of strong feeling."

Why, De Forest wondered, had no one produced the great American novel? One reason, he found, was a fallacious popular taste which accepted "Headley as a Tacitus ... and Dr. Holland as a Vergil." A second cause was the lack of an international copyright law, so that the works of established foreign authors could be sold more cheaply than the books of unknown Americans. The disparity in cost meant poor sales of American books and extreme poverty for native authors, and all too often the talented writer disgustedly stopped writing before he had really learned his trade.

A third reason the American writer found it difficult to produce the great American novel, asserted De Forest, was the lack of a mature literary culture. Often the reason for the difference between a neophyte English and American writer was not one of native talent but one of literary climate, for "the power of an author is frequently, if not generally, no more than the expression of the community which produced him." A fourth difficulty in creating the great American novel was the variety of the subject and the diversity of the audience. In England and France the subject remained constant, and the aristocratic audience had much the "same lives . . . the same ideas and tastes." However, the kaleidoscopic changeableness of America and the fact that it was largely a nation of provinces made the American writer's task comparable to the painting of a falling star. Only the writers of a few foreign countries struggling toward national unity knew any similar situation, and Manzoni's *I promessi sposi* was the only work that had succeeded in capturing a national portrait. Such a novel, however, had taken half a lifetime and all the talent of a great poet. Whether there would soon arise an American Manzoni was doubtful. Wait, De Forest ended his essay, wait.

Living in New York, De Forest made a bare living at best from his writing. For almost the first time since childhood, he found himself without income from either job or investments. He worried a good deal about money, and sometimes his concern showed itself in strange and even humorous ways. In his article "Two Girls," which appeared in *The Nation* (February 6, 1868), he discussed the modern girl, and in all likelihood he cast his wife in some particulars of the role. The girl De Forest envisioned was living in New Haven and was the daughter of a college professor. She was healthy, pretty, pious, well educated in Greek and Latin, and had some understanding of French, German, and Italian. In addition she was able to speak of Darwin and such subjects, and capable of choosing music with taste and playing the piano passably.

Despite her intelligence and good taste, however, the modern girl was a clothes-worshiper, and De Forest was sure that to her mission of dressing "she had given meditation of which men know neither the anxiety nor the gladness." Even before Veblen, De Forest suggested that conspicious consumption, which madame had learned from unwise men, was the essential cause of the feminine worship of clothes. De Forest also knew that the preoccupation with trimmings was no feminine monopoly; insecure men also confused external appearance with the inward man. The fact that pretension was an occasional masculine sin did not, however, lessen De Forest's fear of bankruptcy, and he proposed half in jest, half in earnest, two correctives of ruinous female ostentation. From these two remedies—which were the dowry and female labor—would flow moral and pecuniary benefits to both sexes. If, for instance, the American girl had to work to pay her own way, she would be a better woman; and, when she came to marry "a poor man . . . she would share his burden rather than crush him with it."

The essay "Two Girls," as well as De Forest's continuing post-war separation from his wife, intimates that some coolness may have sprung up between the couple, and this conjecture gains additional credence by some of the verse De Forest wrote about this time.[1] In "Separation," which he noted was imitated from the French of Sully-Prudhomme, De Forest wrote of his despair at never seeing "her" while continuing to love "her" and then concluded:

> To see from day to day clearer
> She blights both hope and endeavor;
> Yet absolve her, bless her, revere her,
> Yet love her forever.
>
> Never to see her nor hear her,
> To speak her name aloud never;
> To hold her always the dearer,
> To love her forever.[2]

In "The Lottery Valentine," De Forest seems to be questioning whether some "jest" of a marriage will endure to prophesy either the bitterness or the sweetness of heaven or hell. This poem is less derivative and more natural than most of De Forest's verse, and it still conveys emotion:

> By chance allotted as the mate
> Of one you neither love nor know,
> Who brings you neither joy nor woe,
> What mockery is this of fate!
>
> .   .   .   .   .   .   .   .   .
>
> And yet the fragile jest may live,
> A prophecy of something sure,
> Of something bitter to endure,
> Or sweet as Paradise can give.[3]

Any disagreement between De Forest and his wife must have been smoothed over by September, 1868. By then De Forest had leased a house for his family (and the cats De Forest so loved) at 188 Temple Street, New Haven. From that address he wrote his first letter in a memorable correspondence with a young assistant editor of *The Atlantic.* In his note De Forest thanked William Dean Howells for requesting more of his work; expressed his gratitude for Howells' praise of "The Man and Brother" and *Miss Ravenel's Conversion;* and asserted that, when he had sufficient leisure, he would write more Southern tales for *The Atlantic.*[4]

Save for a short visit to Europe around 1875, De Forest remained in New Haven for the next fifteen years, first living at the house on Temple Street, then at more substantial homes at 75 Compton Street and 19 Compton Street. The latter house was especially imposing, and among its sixteen rooms was a pleasant library, with high-beamed ceilings, two noble fireplaces, and a view overlooking a pleasant court. In this setting De Forest did the bulk of his work from 1878 to 1883.

Until 1881 De Forest wrote voluminously, but the living he made was a precarious one, as he intimated in *The Wetherel Affair* through the magazinist Lehming: "A magazinist with talent, who works hard and gives all his time to his work, can average twelve or perhaps fifteen hundred dollars a year. In other words he can earn something more than a common carpenter, and a good deal less than an expert machinist."[5] To find a more profitable and less perilous mode of existence, De Forest half-heartedly tried in 1870 to find a position as editor of a magazine, but his belief that he "could do such work acceptably"[6] aroused no interest, and he continued to spend long hours at his writing. His favorite outlets for his work were *Harper's, The Atlantic,* and *The Galaxy,* but his fiction, poetry, and essays appeared in numerous other reputable and popular magazines of the time. Much of the fiction, poetry, and occasional essays he wrote during the period was mediocre, and it would be absurd to attempt any detailed critical analysis of most of this work. However, in three novels—(*Kate Beaumont, Honest John Vane,* and *Playing The Mischief*)—and in half-a-dozen short stories he added to his legitimate claim to a respectable place in American literature.

Undoubtedly something unfortunate happened to much of De Forest's work after he had completed his Reconstruction essays. Much of his fiction, despite his avowal otherwise in his later years, became more "romantic," more "popular," and less "realistic" than it earlier had been. It also became less interesting, less important, and less meritorious. The inevitable question is why, once he had found the direction most suited to his talent, he wavered so often away from it, returned to it, and then strayed from it again.

The answer undoubtedly has something to do with the vigorous influence that the Dickens of farce, melodrama, and eccentricity exerted upon the mind of De Forest; but the central cause for his wavering probably lies in the public reception given *Miss Ravenel's Conversion* and to De Forest's Civil War and Reconstruction essays. Though the novel had received high critical praise, it had sold only moderately; the essays received little praise and were ignored by book publishers. In each of these works De Forest had striven successfully to depict character honestly and dialogue accurately, and in each he had avoided exaggeration, prettiness, and sentimentality. In *Miss Ravenel* he had written a truly Realistic novel in which he had gone so far as to suggest that the nature of man was not simply good or evil but mixed. In his war essays he had shown the dullness of war as well as its excitement, and at times he had probed the fear, hatred, heroism, and emptiness of the soldier's mind. In his Reconstruction articles, he had caught, through simple anecdotes of commonplace events and ordinary people, the tenor of Southern life and character in South Carolina.

In varying degrees De Forest had practiced the Realism of character of Thackeray and the social Realism of Balzac; he had foreshadowed the Realism of the commonplace which Howells was soon to champion so ardently; and he had gone further than Howells would ever go in treating some of the less smiling aspects of existence. He had written as he had by preference, for until 1867 he had had either an independent income or a vocation which provided him with a livelihood. Now, however, De Forest had a fundamental problem. His works had to sell if his family were to eat, and the obvious truth, as he saw it, was that the public was less interested in Realism than in Romance, less attracted to the commonplace than to the sentimental, strange, and eccentric.

As a reasonable man, De Forest knew what he must do if he were to continue writing, and far too often he remembered the public during his fifteen-year career as a magazinist. This is not to say that he constantly tried to propitiate The Young Girl, but it is to say that he often wavered from the wisest path for his art and was especially lured by the temptations of Romance, allegory, and caricature. In the fall of 1869, when *The Galaxy* objected to one of De Forest's romantic tales and implied that it might be unwise to publish the work, De Forest wrote a letter to express his conviction that "the story of ordinary life no longer excites remark, no matter how well done. The day for easy success of commonplace subjects and good writing is over. What I try to do is to sketch realistic characters and put them through a series of extraordinary and even grotesque circumstances. Such things excite remark, . . . and that brings readers."[7]

With a lesser writer, or a greater one, this recurrent concern for the public might have made little difference; but De Forest's vision and talent were realistic and satiric. When he strayed from what he had seen, heard, known, or laughed at, his work collapsed artistically. He was unable to effect successively the compromise he so often attempted between Romance and Realism, between public taste and artistic merit; and he might well have complained with Melville: "Dollars damn me. . . . What I feel most moved to write, that is banned—it will not pay. Yet, altogether, write the *other* way I cannot. So the product is a final hash, and all my books are botches."[8] De Forest vaguely recognized the artistic weakness and he clearly saw the financial failure of much of his later work, and these facts he tended to rationalize, with some justification, by tirades against public taste and the lack of international copyright law. His complaints, however, brought no solution to his dilemma; and, like Melville, he gradually let his pen lie still.

In outward event, De Forest's fifteen years as a professional magazinist were placid ones. Undoubtedly his vanity was tickled when a critical survey of his work until 1873 appeared in *The Atlantic*. Written by Clarence Gordon and undoubtedly inspired by W. D. Howells, the article is memorable not only because it praises De Forest's work but also because the critique is the only attempt during De Forest's lifetime to survey at any length his work as a whole. Calling De Forest's work after the Civil War that of a "Hogarth of the pen," Gordon asserts that De Forest's art has value for any future historian of the manners and thought of nineteenth-century America. He concludes, as one might expect in an article inspired by Howells, by praising De Forest's "breadth, strength, and movement, wonderful honesty, freedom from prejudice, no affectation, very little exaggeration, and an entire absence of sentimentality. . . . His plane is that broad, difficult one trodden by average humanity."[9]

During this period, De Forest, ever a wide reader, probed into religious, military, scientific, and ethnological subjects; and occasionally he put the knowledge he acquired to professional use. In a series of four articles on the Roman Catholic Church he revealed considerable historical erudition and some contemporary prejudice concerning "Giant Pope."[10] In three articles on the military adventures of the Turks in Europe, he evinced his admiration for Turkish bravery, while at the same time clinging to his conviction that the Turks were infidel barbarians who had learned nothing from their exposure to European culture and religion and who were, therefore, best expelled for all time from any portion of European soil.[11] In an article on "The Cradle of the Human Race," he asserted his feeling that there is considerable reason to believe in the European origins of the Aryan Asiatic races, while "there is no solid basis for the popular theory that the European races came from ... some ... Asiatic centre of creation."[12] Combined, the articles give an impression of a mind thoroughly at home in scholarly subjects and methods, but of one that also seems to be hardening in conservative molds.

During these years when De Forest was a magazinist, Mrs. De Forest's continuing poor health meant a modicum of social life and a maximum of time for her husband to work; and this regimen was only altered in 1875 or 1876 when De Forest went abroad. His intention was to write a history of the Huguenots, but he found it impossible to work in Europe and returned in a few months. The time he spent in Britain and Edinburgh, however, did leave him with some rather smug, nationalistic, and moralistic impressions. He was annoyed by the ramshackle dirtiness of London, irritated by the British worship of royalty, and shocked by the innumerable pubs. This latter "hydra," he felt, was responsible for intensifying British pugnacity; and, though he could rationalize that the Briton's love both of drink and of fights came from England's chill climate, he still moralized that an infant brought up on a "fiery ration" could hardly "fail to grow up a drunkard, and beat his mother, if she lives long enough."[13] Nor in Edinburgh did De Forest find any earthly paradise, Presbyterian or otherwise. On a tour of the less sightly parts of town, he found an inferno of violence and drunkenness. The area was presided over by an alderman, the owner of three grog-shops, and his Herculean limbs and rolled-up shirt sleeves made De Forest meditate, "I need not have left my privileged native land to find such a city father."[14]

Occasionally during these years as a magazinist, De Forest

visited his brother-in-law Charles Pinckney James in Washington, and undoubtedly he and James often discussed the political corruption that permeated the Grant administration. In all probability James's increasing legal and political prominence (which culminated in 1879 with his appointment as Associate Justice of the Supreme Court of the District of Columbia) gave De Forest the opportunity to view at close range the American congressman—a species that had fascinated De Forest ever since he had gained his first glimpse of General Ben Butler, that adroit politician in soldier's garb.

The graft and fraud and chicanery De Forest saw in Washington made him think of himself as a political independent, but his sympathies remained with the Grand Old Party. When *The Nation* avowed in 1876 that the Republican Party should be defeated at the polls because of its toleration of Negro misrule and Northern carpetbaggery in the South, De Forest wrote to express his opposition. Without excusing the recent Republican demagoguery and venality, De Forest preferred to vote for Hayes, not Tilden. A victory for the Democratic Party would be "to enthrone the South at Washington," and such an exaltation not only would be a betrayal of the Northern soldiers of the Civil War but also would lead to the peril of inflation. The self-respect of the North, concluded De Forest, demanded the defeat of a Southern-dominated Democratic Party.[15]

The success of Hayes at the polls induced De Forest, in March of 1877, to write to Howells and the Reverend Theodore D. Woolsey, asking that they write the incoming President about De Forest's qualifications for a diplomatic or consular post. Among his qualifications, as he noted to Woolsey, were his knowledge of French, Italian, and Spanish; his military and literary experience; and his advocacy of the Republican cause in the late elections.[16] To Howells, he wrote that he wished a governmental appointment for various reasons: "sanitary, financial, a desire to revive my languages, a need of new scenes to awaken my wits."[17] In pursuit of his goal, De Forest spent a month or so in Washington, but job-seekers were legion and no appointment was forthcoming. De Forest remembered his experiences in *Justine's Lovers,* and the contempt he shows in it for governmental bureaucrats intimates the discourtesy which he must have received from official Washington. It is quite likely that the humiliation which he experienced brought him a full measure of despair and led him to pour his feelings of that time into those of a fictional character who also failed in seeking political appointment from the Hayes administration: "The Bible was the one and only book which could occupy me. I wandered through it ... for hours every day.... It was much as if I had met, for the first time in many years, some beloved guardian of my childhood.... it is a home of healing and refuge, compared with which all other asylums are bleak deserts, windblown and haunted by simoons."[18] Undoubtedly it was also during this year, and the two or three following, that De Forest wrote most of the biblical translations which he eventually published in *Medley and Palestina.* For him, this return to the Bible and to verse had therapeutic value, but the verses have little artistic merit.

Soon after De Forest returned to New Haven, he met real tragedy. On March 29, 1878, Mrs. De Forest died. At the time she was with her father in Charleston, and her death was unexpected. After the death of his wife, the flood of De Forest's literary productivity became a quiet stream, and after 1881 that diminished to a slow trickle. Occasionally he wondered why his work had made so little impression, and when Howells wrote flatteringly of his merit, he responded: "Your appreciation thaws out a heart frozen by neglect.... I don't understand why you and I havn't [sic] sold monstrously except on the theory that our novel-reading public is mainly female or a very juvenile public and wants something nearer its own mark of intellect and taste, as, for instance, 'Helen's Babies' and 'That Husband of Mine.'"[19]

This theory Howells repeated, and others echoed, when he wrote in *Heroines of Fiction* that De Forest's masculinity offended feminine sensibilities and made neglect inevitable in his time. Undoubtedly there is some truth in the idea, but just as surely it is an oversimplification. In much of De Forest's fiction he made concessions to female readers. This fact is made ironically clear by the contrast between his complaint about the novel-reading public and the novel he was publishing simultaneously in *The Atlantic.* The work was a romantic mixture of virtue, religion, and exotic adventure. De Forest called it *Irene The Missionary* and suggested to Howells that it might be advertised in the religious papers because "there is a large public which is interested in missions. I hope that I shall be guessed at as a returned missionary, or a lady."[20] De Forest may have been smiling as he wrote, but the truth is that *Irene* might quite suitably have been advertised in the *Missionary Herald.* Yet *Irene* sold no better than such realistic works' as *Miss Ravenel* and *Playing The Mischief* or as such mixtures of Realism and Romance as *The Wetherel Affair, The Bloody Chasm,* and *Justine's Lovers.* The irony of De Forest's fate is that in much of his work he made his sacrifice to the Iron Maiden, the American girl, and gained absolutely nothing in return. What he lost in these works was his art.

## II  *In Search of a Popular Audience*

Though the periods overlap, it is essentially true that De Forest's years as a magazinist can be divided into three periods. During the first, which covers the years from 1868 to 1871, he seems to be a writer desperate for an audience; he turns frantically from subject to subject, from Romantic foolishness to shallow social commentary, from basically Realistic situations and characters to implausible incidents and eccentric buffoons, from straightforward narration to Victorian intrusiveness, and from ironic indictments of folly to sentimental rhapsodizing over the beauty of love and self-sacrifice. This productive period of trivia, De Forest follows with one of meritorious work, and from 1871 to 1878 he explores, with a variety of artistic tones, the weaknesses of the social milieu of his day. The third period, from 1879 to 1881, is one of weakening artistic powers, and its slight productivity is the prelude to the almost total silence of De Forest's later years.

In the first period, De Forest published three novels and numerous short stories. Most of the stories are embarrassingly bad. De Forest was never at home with this form, and during this period especially he leaned upon mechanical plots full of coincidences and implausibilities. These tales he filled with fair, religious heroes; sturdy (though sometimes free-thinking) heroes; old, gnarled Puritans; and sour, warped old-maids. In such stories as "The Taillefer Bell-Ringings," "The Drummer Ghost," and "Lt. Barker's Ghost Story," De Forest depends heavily upon the supernatural for his plot effects, but at the same time he either mocks the irrational or finds rational reasons for supposedly supernatural events.

In a number of other tales De Forest drew upon his past. "Love in Mount Lebanon" and "Captain Horsfall's Romance" contrast—without bowing to American nationalistic pride—American and Moslem manners. "Marcus and Hildegarde" displays De Forest's knowledge of military strategy (though the tale is set in Roman times) and asserts his conviction that the nationalistic spirit of race, and its corollaries of pride and hatred, has worked much good but even more evil in civilization, and such racism might well be replaced by some nobler, more Christian mode of behavior. In "The Duchesne Estate," "A Night at Sea," "Parole D'Honneur," and "A Gentleman of the Old School," De Forest draws upon his knowledge of Southern character and setting, and though the narratives are inept in various ways—in construction, in dependence on sentimentality, in the depiction of monkey-like Negro stereotypes named Jumboloro and Chloe and Cato—the stories do have some interest because of De Forest's attempt to cope with the complex, and sometimes ironic, manifestations of the high-toned Southerner's concept of "honor." "Parole D'Honneur" is especially pertinent to De Forest's conviction that the willingness of the high-toned gentleman to keep his word, even when to do so violates his other Southern instincts, gives hope for the reformation of Southern society.

To this period also belongs a number of miscellaneous tales and a group of three allegories. Among the former are "The Story of a Handkerchief," an absurd anecdote about a young married woman who stumbles into a strange man's room; "The Oversoul of Manse Roseborough," which tells, with Emersonian overtones, of a bohemian dandy's transformation, at least temporarily, through the power of love; "The Lauson Tragedy," in which De Forest amateurishly entwines a love story and a murder mystery; "Chanet," a sentimental tale about the self-sacrifice of an old-maid for a German artist; and "The Hungry Heart," in which De Forest dramatizes somewhat melodramatically the story of a female bigamist. To the group of allegories belong three stories. In the first, "A Strange Arrival," De Forest allows the yarn-spinning Yankee Captain Phineas Glover to tell a tale flavored with salty dialect and mystical overtones about the weird crew and mysterious fate of the ship *The Flying Dutchman.* In "A Queen of Society" a woman sells her soul to a Mr. Heller in exchange for social success but manages to escape eternal damnation by a final self-sacrificial act. In "The City of Brass" De Forest uses allegory to satirize intemperate reformers.

The best of the stories of this period are "Captain Horsfall's Romance," "The Hungry Heart," and "The City of Brass." The first of these satirizes with real humor an American type: the vulgarian as tourist. This particular ignoramus is a garrulous South Carolinian who is usually full of liquor and always filled with bigotry, arrogance, biblical misreadings and illogic, foolish chivalry, and fine sentiments based on poetic doggerel, provin-

cialism, ignorance, and romanticism. Through Captain Horsfall's
infatuation with a Moslem woman, whose husband the Captain
feels is abusing her, De Forest explores the insensitivity to local
mores of such boozy, romantic vulgarians.

"The Hungry Heart" is the story of a young woman, Mrs.
Alice Duvernois, who marries two men. The cause of her crime
is her incompatible first marriage, one which De Forest compares
to "a beating heart united with a skeleton."[21] With her cold,
imperturbable, exceedingly rational first husband, Alice's warm,
emotional nature withers and grows harsh; near the man she
loves, Alice blooms with health and kindness. The situation of a
woman with two natures, De Forest tells his readers, is Hawthornean. The conclusion, in which Alice drowns herself because
of her fear of discovery and scorn, also has echoes of Hawthorne,
as does the concept of the excessively rational man, more statue
than human. Less indebted to Hawthorne is De Forest's suggestion that Alice herself might have had more of the rational
to go with her simple, emotional nature. If she had been less
a child and more a mature woman, she might have been able to
ask other, and wiser, questions than, "Oh, how can a ruined
woman defend herself but by dying?"[22]

De Forest's allegory "The City of Brass" begins by recalling
the Mohammedan tale of the Afreet imprisoned by Solomon.
With this episode as his folk-source, De Forest tells of a Boston
reformer named Harrison who has set out on an expedition to
free the Afreet (for slavery should be abolished everywhere) as
well as innumerable other Marids and lesser worshipers of pagan
gods. Before long the reformer has not only freed these once-
enchanted devils, but in the land to which he has come he is
preaching universal suffrage, is publishing a radical newspaper,
and is insisting that for the sake of freedom there be opposition
to his governmental policies. To insure dissent, he does unwise
things. Soon his subjects have grievances, and Harrison is
happy; but by then "although we were in the full reign of human-
itarianism, starvation threatened."[23] To a friend's complaints that
something should be done for the populace, Harrison can only
say that since everyone is free and has the suffrage, everyone
should be happy and things should work themselves out. The
friend and narrator's reflections are also undoubtedly those of De
Forest: "it struck me that an individual greatly in advance
of his age may be as much of a nuisance as an individual
greatly behind his age."[24] The story is obviously an indictment
of Northern idealists like Harrison: "a philanthropist by instinct

and a follower of isms by religion."[25] Too often, De Forest asserts, these philosophers forget ultimate consequences. Because of this lack of foresight, many idealists had fought for abolition and universal suffrage, turned the world topsy-turvy, and then turned their backs and expected everything to work out well automatically because abstract right had been done. From his experiences as Bureau Major in the South, De Forest knew that things were not that simple.

In addition to his short stories, De Forest published, during this first period of his career as a magazinist, three novels—none of them good. In *Della or The Wild Girl,* a novel published serially in *Hearth and Home* in early 1870 (and wisely never published in book form), De Forest attempted a portrait of a young girl, Della Steenwyck, in the grip of insanity. This St. Cecilia, who has turned into a Faustina, manifests the clouding of her reason and the loss of her spirituality by drinking, smoking, sexual looseness, and feminist proclamations: "'Give us women an even start. Take the blinders off our eyes and the bits out of our mouths. I protest against the doctrine that what is right in one sex is wrong in the other. . . . I want smoking cars and drinking saloons and gambling halls for women. . . . When we come to vote, you will see what follows.'"[26] Such talk, De Forest notes, is proof of Della's irrationality, for "It is not in the nature of the healthy female creature to . . . reject the regulations of her kind. . . . No independence for her—rather the clinging of the parasite plant."[27]

Eventually Della's desires for greater freedom lead to mental aberrations that cause her to make secret rendezvous, to begin calling herself Mr. Steenwyck, and to start dressing in men's clothing. One day, so appareled, she goes for a walk that exacerbates a cold. Near death, she returns to sanity and femininity. The resurrection of the Christian maiden in her causes her to desire to marry a good man. In her sentimentalized death-bed scene, she marries a youth of pure heart and gentle temper, and she feels that her life as a woman has not been a complete failure.

As a study of either insanity or lesbianism, *Della* is unbelievable at best and farcical at worst, but it does show clearly De Forest's inability to comprehend the possible sanity of feminist notions. In addition *Della* dramatizes anew De Forest's contempt for the fashionable society woman. Della's mother is such a hypocritical egoist: a creature who judges the merit of all things in proportion to how much pleasure they give her. With ease she can reconcile the irreconcilable, so that "she drove tranquilly from matinées to church services; she petted with an equal hand wild young gallants and serious old clergymen; she prattled about the conversion of the Jews, and conversed gravely about the latest bonnets."[28] When the desire of this woman of the world for the pleasure of society leads her to refuse to allow Della to be institutionalized and possibly saved, De Forest asks: "How are we to draw the boundary between the scarcely known wilderness of insanity and that almost equally known wilderness of sanity?"[29] The question is as sophisticated as the lesbian suggestiveness of the novel was in advance of its time; but such worldliness seems out of place amidst the prevailing melodrama and sentiment of *Della,* in which the tone is suggested by the fact that the bohemian villain Wolverton comes to Della's funeral to confess: "I am here as a penitent fiend."[30]

Probably the most chaotic novel De Forest ever wrote was *Annie Howard,* which appeared in *Hearth and Home* in the spring of 1870 and was never republished. Filled with irrelevant plot digressions and overflowing with peculiar Dickensian characters, the novel is set in New York City and essentially dramatizes the satiric contrast between the truly feminine woman and the foolish, Quixotic female. The first of these is Annie Howard. When she loses a legacy, she sets out as cheerfully as possible to earn her own living by running a boardinghouse. This action De Forest heartily applauds, and like Hawthorne, though less wittily and gracefully, he condemns the notion that it is somehow unladylike for a woman to support herself. In contrast to Annie is feminist Aunt Maria Stanley, who is full of wild dreams, philanthropic obsessions, and hypocritical ranting—all of which become most clear when she leads her intimates on a fantastic treasure hunt but is brashly insistent on her "feminine" right to have the men do all the work. Though there are occasional funny patches in the novel, as, for instance, when De Forest describes some of the Bloomer girls in attendance at a meeting of the "Society of United Philanthropists," the general level of the humor is that of inept burlesque. A typical example of the vein of humor which De Forest mines is a project of Aunt Maria in which she and a number of odd-duck abolitionists steal a Negro out of slavery, only to discover that the vermin-ridden creature is a half-wit being transported South because of the kindness of his owner.

The desperation with which De Forest was seeking an audience during this period is dramatized most fully by his novel

*Overland.* In part the work was probably inspired by Robert
T. S. Lowell's *The New Priest of Conception Bay* (1858). That
novel De Forest had praised in 1867 as having "the best
landscape pictures ever done by an American unless we except
Thoreau,"[31] and certainly in *Overland* De Forest tried to outdo
Lowell. A more obvious incentive for the work may have been
the recent popular success of works about the West, among them
Twain's "The Celebrated Jumping Frog of Calaveras County"
(1865) and Harte's "The Luck of Roaring Camp" (1867).

Set in the Far West (which De Forest had never seen)
*Overland* overflows with travelogue description of the buttes
and plains of the great desert of North America; of the agri-
cultural plateau civilization of the Moquis Indians of New
Mexico; of the awesome majesty and perilousness of the Grand
Canyon; and of the volcanic fury of the Pacific Ocean during a
storm. As Professor Croushore has pointed out in his pioneering
study of De Forest, these descriptions were largely based on
J. R. Bartlett's *Personal Narrative of Explorations and Incidents
in Texas, New Mexico, California, Sonora, and Chihuahua*
(1854) and on J. C. Ives's and A. A. Humphreys' *Report Upon
the Colorado River of the West* (1861). Nevertheless, De Forest
was proud of his landscape painting, and the reviewers also
praised it. *The Nation* found it "admirable. . . . indeed the best
part of the story. All the love tale sinks into insignificance in
comparison."[32]

Using the extravagances of the land as his artistic justification,
De Forest tells an adventurous tale filled with continual crises:
attacks by Apaches, attempts at assassination, perilous journeys
by land and sea, and miraculous escapes from the wiles of
villains. The hero of this romance is Ralph Thurstane. An army
lieutenant, he is a "modest, proud, manly youngster" (38) without the semblance of meanness or treachery. The heroine is Clara
Manoz Garcia Van Diemen. Half American, half Spanish, she is
exceptional in her beauty and purity. Sheerly feminine, she is
a contrast to Mrs. Maria Stanley, the feminist fool and hypocrite
whom De Forest had exploited in *Annie Howard* before her
appearance in *Overland.*

Soon Clara and Ralph are in love, but before these conventional, idealized lovers can be united, there is a pilgrimage to
be made. The overland journey from Santa Fe to California is
made perilous by the machinations of a pair of old-fashioned
villains and their hirelings. The villains are Señor Manuel Garcia,

an aged, dyspeptic "toad," and his potential heir, Carlos Garcia de Coronado, a smoothly polished egoist "as destitute of conscience as it is possible for a member of a civilized society to be" (81). The most notable tool of this pair is the assassin Texas Smith (a character probably inspired by bushwhacker Texas Brown, whom De Forest encountered during his Bureau Major days), and the description of Texas Smith suggests De Forest's indifference to subtlety in *Overland*:

> His intensely black eyes . . . had a stare of absolutely indescribable ferocity. It was more ferocious than the merely brutal glare of a tiger; it was an intentional malignity, super beastly and sub-human. They were eyes which no other man ever looked into and afterward forgot. His sunburnt, sallow, haggard, ghastly face . . . was so marked by hard, and one might almost say fleshless muscles, and so brutalized by long indulgence in savage passions, that it struck you as frightfully ugly. A large dull-red scar on the right jaw and another across the left cheek added the final touches to this countenance of a cougar (20).

Through the watchfulness and bravery of Lt. Thurstane, the villains are foiled, virtue is rewarded, and true love triumphs. The tale is a silly one, ineffective in plot, setting and character, and totally lacking in meaningful theme. The amateurishness is apparent in the way in which the lovers are continually being separated and then—by the miracle of coincidence and the author—stumble over each other again at exactly the right time. The grandiose flourishes with which De Forest describes the glorious West drag on interminably, at times pedantically; and the technicolor setting is obviously more a sop to De Forest's research than it is a justification for the melodramatic plot. Except for Carlos Coronado, who is full of unresolved contradictions, the major characters are either heroes and villains or fools; and the minor characters—the Irishman Sweeney, the German Weber, and the Yankee Cap'n Phineas Glover—are more inspired by stock dialogue and humor than by realistic depth or perception. The sheer melodrama may make the story a "rattling good yarn"[33] to critics like Brander Matthews, but De Forest himself could not have felt the work had much appeal for adults. In his corrected copy, which he hoped to use in some collected edition of his works, he wrote in pencil under the title: "A Story for Boys."[34]

## III   *The Social Historian: Short Fiction*

In his own time De Forest was occasionally called the American Charles Reade. If the remark has any validity, it is most true of De Forest's mid-period as a magazinist, for during that time he especially resembled Reade as a cultural historian with a social purpose. As such, De Forest tends not only to expose social evils but also to preach a particular method of reform. That golden way is moderation, conciliation, and common sense, whether it be in man's religious belief, in reform of the South, in modification of the spoils system in politics, or in extension of the suffrage to the masses.

In a persuasive chapter entitled "De Forest as a Social Historian," Philip Hastings Ford, in an unpublished doctoral dissertation, concludes:

> Almost by definition, a social historian must be at least something of a realist. If he is to present a fictionalized picture of his time, his characters must move in a recognizable setting and they must reflect the attitudes and feelings current in that time and place. Judging De Forest by these criteria, it seems clear that he is a social historian. His writings are accurate reproductions of typical American locales; his characters personify a wide range of American types and classes; and his plots and characters reflect the events and issues of his time.[35]

Though Ford's remark applies only partially to the work of De Forest before 1870, it has considerable validity for many of the short stories and for all of the novels that De Forest published between 1871-78.

Some of the short stories of this period, however, continue to be miscellaneous trivia. To this category undoubtedly belong "The Man With a Nose like an Owl," an unfortunate tale in which De Forest satirized vulgarity and materialism and implied that these traits seemed especially peculiar to the Jewish race; "A Case of Vitrification," in which De Forest revives for the last time his domesticated couple Mr. and Mrs. Pullet and tells a lengthy anecdote about an eccentric who believes his limbs are turning to glass; "The Brigade Commander," in which De Forest shows the ambiguity in character of a great general who is also a great sinner; and "Jenny Gridley's Concession," in which De Forest tells an agreeable tale (or daydream) about a middle-aged, penurious author who wins a youthful heiress and may thereby do what a friend claims is his destiny: to "write masterpieces, instead of being kept down ... to mere ephemeralities because they sell."³⁶

Another group of De Forest's tales of this period treats the South and the Southerner. In one story, "The Colored Member," De Forest treats his material allegorically by telling of a "dusky Faust" corrupted by a Mephistophelian carpetbagger. Indicting the folly of much of American policy in the South after the Civil War, De Forest in this story especially condemns the absurdity of encouraging Negroes, hardly removed from savagery, not only to vote but also to aspire to high elective office. De Forest's objection is not to the Negroes, though he does depict them in "The Colored Member" as resembling monkeys, but to their ignorance. This failing, in De Forest's eyes, inevitably made them easy and pathetic tools for venal carpetbaggers. In the story, De Forest's attitude is apparent through the irony with which he allows a "sagacious bird," the American eagle, to explain government policy to the Negro:

> "You never struck a blow for your liberty, and nevertheless you shall have it. You are as ignorant . . . and as morally degraded as the vulgarest peasant of the oldest despotism of Europe; nevertheless, you shall be a citizen of a great and proud republic, which depends for its strength and honor upon the virtue and intelligence of its citizens. You never governed even yourself, and have not the slightest knowledge . . . of right or wrong in politics; nevertheless I constitute you an elector, with the possibility of being a juror, a dignitary in the commonwealth, an executor of justice, and a lawgiver."
> Having declared thus much, this most ingenious and far sighted of all fowls . . . sailed cheerfully away from the man and brother, leaving him to his own devices.³⁷

In other Southern tales De Forest deals more realistically with his materials. "Was it a Ghost?" satirizes supernatural charlatanry, but is especially memorable for its depiction of a tavern keeper straight out of the Southwestern humorists. His name is Solomon Bodge, and his dialogue is pure cracker, as, for instance, his comments, "We're all right agin, as the temprance man said when he broke his pledge"; or, "Jest remind him of what the lamb said to the wolf. Keep your mouth shet, ef you please"; or, "Never mind my feelins, 's the alligator said to the pickaninny —walk into me with yer boots on."³⁸ A similar character is John Raddle in "Old John Raddle," a tale which contrasts the manners of the high-toned Southron to those of the coarse, illiterate, and drunken low-downer; in making the contrast, De Forest implies that the egoism of the high-toned untouchables can be carried to the excesses of total inhumanity.

Without doubt, however, the best of these realistic Southern tales is "An Independent Ku Klux." If, as some critics suggest, the rise of the middle class in the nineteenth century is reflected in literature by the willingness of writers to depict realistically the lower and middle classes, "An Independent Ku Klux" reveals De Forest's awareness of the importance of this new, democratic material. With real vividness and originality (though undoubtedly influenced by the Southwestern humorists whom he had often read), De Forest captures the dialect, vulgarity, and amorality of his rustic Southern rascal—as, for instance, in the opening of his tale:

> "Say," observed Selnarten Bowen to his wife, Nan Bowen, "these niggers is gone in for stealin' worse'n ever. Hev we lost anythin'?"
>
> Nan Bowen drew herself up to the full height of her five feet nine inches, grappled her mighty hips with her large sinewy hands as if she were about to throw herself at somebody's head, ground her quid of tobacco with a cowlike opening of the mouth and twisting of the lower jaw, and hit a sapling ten feet away with nicotine enough to poison a rattlesnake. . . .
>
> "What hev we got to lose?" said Nan Bowen in a slow, hard, scornful monotone, and with long pauses between her sentence. "What did we ever own? What did you ever own? What is there in our house? Anythin' that niggers would steal? Not as I knows on."[39]

The remainder of De Forest's tale dramatizes an incident in the life of Selnarten, an ignorant rascal who gains much of his food by killing wild hogs. To enlarge his area of operations to nearby Negro pig pens (and to avoid punishment), Selnarten decides to join the Klan. In a mock initiation, typical of the pranks of the Southwestern humorists, Selnarten is abused and ridiculed (though he is unaware of it) by some high-toned lawyers of a nearby village. Told to live "in peace and amity with all men" and to bear "enmity and hate toward wild hogs,"[40] Selnarten leaves his induction convinced that he is now a bona fide Klansman. So persuaded, and certain that his vows do not include Negroes, Selnarten sets out to kill a Negro's pig. In killing the pig, Selnarten also unscrupulously murders its owner and inadvertently sets off a brutal reign of terror that is not ended until martial law is declared in the district.

The ending of the story, so different in tone from the relatively harmless pranks of the Southwestern humorists, bears the imprint of De Forest's experience during his Bureau Major days, and it also asserts De Forest's awareness of the atrocities inherent in such illiterate barbarians as Selnarten. At the same time De Forest makes an implied judgment upon the high-toned squires who deluded Selnarten by the mock initiation. Neither bad nor ignorant people, these men, De Forest suggests, are the hope for the reformation of the South; for most of them, like Squire Jack, do believe it "equally dreadful that the carpet-bag adventurers should plunder the State treasury, and that the reactionist desperadoes who opposed them should bushwhack and maltreat the poor 'niggers.' "[41] At the same time the lack of mature reflection of these Southrons can lead them to ignite such fiery timber as Selnarten, and the lack of leadership from among the squires is at least partially responsible for the hold the carpetbaggers and the desperadoes have upon the state.

A final group of stories of this period is allegorical in tone. Three of these are politically motivated. "Cap'n Phil Glover as President" revives that old Yankee yarn spinner to tell a whopper that implies that President Grant, because of his experience in office, is more qualified for the presidency than is his opponent Greeley. Despite De Forest's loyalty to the Grand Old Party, the story must have been difficult for him to write for he was aware of, and appalled by, the corruption of the men surrounding the President, and he fully knew that he was echoing the cliché by which the Grant forces were trying to frighten the business leaders of America. "The Other Fellow" tells of a senator who sells his soul to the devil (or, perhaps, only to the railroad lobby, for De Forest is purposefully ambiguous) and then is tormented by his vision (caused by either real perceptions or the delusions occasioned by a guilty conscience) that the devil (whom the senator thinks of as "the other fellow") and his agents surround the senator everywhere. "An Inspired Lobbyist," the best of the political allegories, depicts the satanically brilliant scheme of Ananias Pullwool, a lobbyist with the devil in him, to fleece two rival towns, Fastburgh and Slowburgh, which greedily aspire to be the sole state capital.

In addition to these political tales, De Forest published two religious allegories during his career as a professional magazinist. "Father Higgins' Preferment," the last tale in which the satanic Mr. Heller appears, again shows De Forest's ability to mimic Irish speech and again reflects his antipathy to the Roman Catholic Church. More generally, the story asserts, through a dream of Father Higgins, De Forest's conviction that power swiftly corrupts ignorant and indolent men, and they may destroy Christianity while claiming to preserve it. The story attacks the concept that a salvational end justifies an evil means, and the narrative implies that such a belief is a weak rationalization that leads directly to paganism. In indicting the doctrine, which he especially attributed to the Catholic Church, De Forest undoubtedly felt he was exposing the lustful desire for power of the Church.

In one of the last tales De Forest ever wrote, the allegorical "Yesebel," he revealed the tenacious hold that Hawthorne retained upon his art. Set in Puritan Salem, the narrative opens with one of De Forest's typically arresting beginnings (this one, perhaps, inspired by Keats's "Ode on a Grecian Urn"):

> Late in one of the wizard nights of long ago, a flash of lightning revealed a strange picture.
>
> A man in Puritan costume, with a drawn sword in his right hand, was chasing a young girl fantastically attired through a forest.
>
> . . . In this chase there was no advance; the fugitive did not draw away; the pursuer did not overtake. . . . One might have judged the pair phantoms, supernaturally produced and annihilated, rather than human beings.[42]

From this opening, suggestive as it is of the eternal attempt by the grimly religious to capture and to subdue the joyously pagan, the tale turns to the specific illustration. The young girl Yesebel is captured, and this brand plucked from the burning, as her Puritan captor repetitiously calls her, is temporarily tamed. She forgets her pagan songs and her worship of Baal and Ashtaroth. She changes from an elfish nymph, reminiscent of Hester Prynne's Pearl, to a correctly prim and wooden Puritan maiden. One day, however, the young minister Apollos, who has striven hard to bring Yesebel to the true faith, mentions Baal and Ashtaroth, and the names arouse the Jezebel memories in Yesebel. From that time onward, she is again a fairy sprite, luring the young of Salem to midnight revels and seducing Apollos to abandon his crabbed faith. Her victory over Apollos is complete when the two disappear from Salem forever. An old, rationalistic doctor of the town claims to have heard that the two became a fleshly dancer and actor, but in true Hawthornean ambiguity the minister of the town is sure that Yesebel is the devil's creature. Like Hawthorne also, De Forest opposes the dark, grim, Puritan way of life to the joyous animalism of paganism; and the torments of the spiritual struggle of the golden-haired Apollos are reminiscent of similar agonies among Hawthorne's tormented ministers.

In presenting the grim spiritual way and the sensuous animal path, De Forest implies that each needs somewhat of the other; but his ending also implies his knowledge, a little regretful as it may be, that the grimmer Puritanism was a dying faith. Even in the early days of Salem, the young were becoming less and less content with the ways of their fathers, and even such religious enthusiasts as Apollos were easily seduced by the earthly preachments of Yesebel: " 'There is no sin but grief. . . . The nobleness of the soul is measured by its capacity of joy. . . . Look at the beautiful, happy world around us. . . . In such a world why should I not rejoice and smile and dance?' "[43] With his Puritan background, De Forest could no more approve the paganism of such a philosophy than he could applaud the hyterical fanaticism of the Salem with trials. Some middle road must be preferable.

## IV  Kate Beaumont

One of De Forest's favorite subjects during his career as a magazinist was the South. Not only did he treat the subject in numerous essays and short stories, but he also explored it in *Kate Beaumont,* one of his best novels. Even before *Overland* had finished its run in *The Galaxy, Kate* began to appear in January, 1871, in *The Atlantic Monthly.* The latter work De Forest must have subconsciously had in mind ever since he had noted in his Reconstruction articles the need for a novelist to capture the "Chivalrous Southron" before his type disappeared forever. When De Forest began the actual writing of *Kate,* it came, as he noted years later, easily and swiftly:

> Mr. Howells . . . wrote to me for a novel. . . . I wrote the first chapters of "Kate Beaumont" and sent it to him without the first idea how it was coming out. Then I was taken ill and went to Charleston to recuperate. A few weeks later I sent Howells a plot of the book in the rough and went on with the story. Until the end, however, I had no idea how it was coming out. When I read the first four chapters in *The Atlantic* I could not believe that it was my own work. I had written it so hastily that I had forgotten it. I said to myself: "What is Howells doing here, putting in his ideas on top of mine? And who is this character 'Bill,' and what on earth shall I ever do with him?" . . . The book when finished sold very well, and is, I think, about the best thing I ever did.[44]

*Kate Beaumont* is largely set (after some early shipboard scenes) in the South Carolina town of Hartland and its environs, and De Forest drew much of his material from his Bureau Major experiences. The result is considerable attention to commonplace details of setting; and the cumulative effect of these, lacking any Southern mansions and scented magnolia, is destructive of the romantic mood usually found in Southern novels of the time.[45] The emphasis on the ordinary nature of the setting is indicated by the manner in which De Forest introduces the reader to the town of Hartland. He first describes the Presbyterian steeple: "a little, undignified, rusty-white bob of a belfry, which puts irreverent people in mind of a wart." He then proceeds into the church where a fair is in progress: "The greasy wooden seats have been 'toted off'; the tobacco-stained floor has been scrubbed into cleanliness; there are plenty of gayly decked tables, with pretty girls smiling over them." Finally he describes the kind of entertainment typical of such fairs: an exhibition of a "Howling Gyascutus" (which De Forest had seen in Greenville) in which a "man dresses in animal garb and roars in fearful fashion" (32-33). This Realism is strengthened by De Forest's attention to the actualities of Southern speech, from the blandness of Major Lawson ("like warm olive-oil, poured over your head" [29]); to the slanginess of Bentley Armitage; to the garrulousness of Mrs. Chester; and to the illiteracies of such low-downers as Redhead Saxon and his wife Molly. Probably because he was striving for Realism, De Forest affected a more colloquial style in *Kate* than in his earlier works. Long before Howells' advice that American novelists "try to write Americanly . . . use 'Americanisms' whenever these serve,"[46] De Forest was writing such passages as "this was nuts to Jenny" (35); "His candidature might upset Frank's dish of cream" (76); "this courtship must have the go-by" (145); "her Washington whimwham" (146); and "inspired . . . by a bee in her bonnet" (149).[47]

The action of *Kate* has two strands. The dominant one, which Professor Walter Blair suggests may have influenced Mark Twain in his depiction of the feud in Huck Finn,[48] is the feud between the low-country Beaumonts, with their belief in parish representation, and the up-country McAlisters, with their trust in the more democratic electoral system. In this portion of the narrative, De Forest describes at length the growing love between Kate Beaumont and Frank McAlister, the violence of the family feud that keeps the lovers apart, the ultimate union of the young couple, and the beginning of harmony between the families.

The second strand dramatizes the dissolution of the marriage between Nellie Armitage, the sister of Kate, and her handsome but drunken husband, Randolph Armitage. De Forest's treatment of their marriage seems more appropriate at times to Zola's naturalistic epic of drunkenness, *L'Assomoir* (1878?) than to the genteel reticences usual in American fiction of the 1870's.

Both narrative strands in Kate have their weaknesses (most notably in the drawn-out shipboard opening and the swift, summarizing conclusion), and the clumsiness of the narration is especially annoying in such continual, ineffectual transitions as "Affairs of state . . . recall us to Hartland" (109), and "But we must leave the political background . . . and return to the . . . foreground" (110). De Forest himself could not have been unaware of the ineffective dramatization of the end of the novel, for he protested Howells's advice that the last installments of *Kate* be abbreviated:

> I have an idea . . . that, if a serial is *interesting*, the numbers had better be long than short. In the days when I read serials I used to be irritated at getting only a mouthful of sentiment at a time. The veteran English editors . . . give immense spread of canvas to their stories. It seems to me that the *Atlantic* has generally lacked on this point . . . editing too much for Mr. Emerson and other select Bostonians, forgetting that our "select few" is a very few.
>
> The great question of course is—is the story interesting? I was almost discouraged the other day by a leader in the *Tribune* . . . which said that "De Forest is doing good work almost unnoticed." I see few papers, but I fear the man is right. If you think so, let me know, and I will try to put in more stimulus, or, that failing, to be much briefer.[49]

Apparently this plea did not lessen Howells' insistence on greater brevity, and the relatively undramatized scenes of the last chapters was the result.

*Kate Beaumont* is a novel full of incident, from the early savage, animal struggle for escape from a burning ship and the gallant rescue of the heroine by the hero; to assorted brawls, including an orgiastic "cracker ball"; to an attempt by a drunken husband to murder his wife; to an accidental killing of a patriarchal old man; to the recurring complications of what De Forest insistently calls the story of Romeo and Juliet in the American South.

The real interest of the novel, however, is in its variety of characters. Typically, De Forest draws his least effective portraits in his hero and heroine. Kate Beaumont, whom even the sympathetic Howells found a woman of "prevailing passivity,"[50] is another one of De Forest's young ladies on pedestals. She is most imaginatively drawn (though in too summary a fashion) toward the end of the novel when she sees herself as the victim of a pagan God who demands her self-sacrifice. In her illness and delusion she considers abandoning her true love to become the wife of the Reverend Gilyard. When she regains her health, however, she sees, in a moment reminiscent of Penelope Lapham's insight in a similar situation in Howells' *The Rise of Silas Lapham* (1885), that "her late vows of self-sacrifice were senseless" (163). De Forest adds—in a voice suggestive of Howells' indictment of the "gaudy heroines" he so despised—that Kate, in her religious, self-sacrificial delirium "had not been crazed; but she had been near it" (163).

What is true of De Forest's heroine is no less true of his hero. Frank McAlister, despite his European polish and his intellectual superiority to his homeland's barbaric *code duello,* is completely idealized; and his monumental stature does not disguise his origin in conventional romantic literature. He is most interesting when De Forest mocks his love as an "exaltation which was almost mania" (91). The folly of Frank leads him to glory in his suffering, so that he quotes from Schiller like a love-sick puppy, wants to die to prove his love, and wishes to kiss a rail on which the foot of his beloved has rested. Though De Forest depicts satirically Frank's excessive emotionalism, he sympathetically notes, in the vein of romantic convention: "Let us not jeer at him; let us study him reverently. If any man is clean of the world, it is the lover; if any man is pure in heart, it is the lover" (91).

De Forest depicts with greater verisimilitude the other members of the Beaumont and McAlister families. In Kate's father, Peyton Beaumont, De Forest captures a high-toned Southern type. Hot-headed, tender-hearted, and childishly willful, he is addicted to two cocktails before breakfast and to a number of others as the day progresses. Though afflicted with various diseases that stem from his alcoholism, he accepts his pain stoically. Most important, Peyton lives by a rigid code of honor and accepts the *code duello* in all its patterned ceremonial as fundamental to the Southern mode of life. His three sons, one of whom has been trained as a lawyer and another educated as a doctor, are in their own ways as high-toned as their father. None of them stoops to work for a living, and all are egoistically aware of their superior position in society. Even the cynical and sardonic Poinsett Beaumont, who has no intellectual belief in the *code duello*, accepts it as part of the high-toned way of life, and he further accepts his enslavement to a feud whose real cause is veiled in the mists of the past. Though he mocks the Beaumont-McAlister feud (he calls it "our race palladium ... our coat of arms ... the Beaumont established religion" [42]), he also implies fatalistically that intelligence leaves off where honor and the feud begin: "We are drops in a river. I shall fight too someday, though I don't at all crave it" (39). In their enslavement to their code of feudal honor, the Beaumonts, De Forest implies, are no more than barbarian; they are like the Indians to whom he keeps comparing them by references to their war-paint, their sachems, their calumets, and their wampum belt. Moreover the Beaumonts are typical high-toned Southerners in their aggressiveness and their reverence for the *code duello*; they represent the ten or fifteen per cent of adult male Southerners who had been principals in one or more duels.

In addition to these Beaumonts by birth, Kate Beaumont's aunt, Mrs. Chester, and her maternal grandfather, Colonel Kershaw, are important members of the family circles. Mrs. Chester is, perhaps, the most foolish of De Forest's long line of superannuated flirts. Bridling coquettishly in the company of young men, she is mercurially gay at fancied attentions and indignant at imagined slights. Among her fondest memories is the fact that two duels were once fought over her; and, when she feels that Frank prefers Kate to her, she does her mischievous best to cause trouble. A silly woman, Mrs. Chester is also a pathetic one, as De Forest shows when he depicts her crying among a variety of the ballroom dresses of her youth, but De Forest's disgust for her mindless immaturity is greater than his compassion. Eventually the lack of balance of this "cracked old flirt" (67) becomes obvious to her family, and she is put to bed to die of softening of the brain. Her illness is extreme, but her type, De Forest implies, is common in a society that encourages feminine coquettishness, uselessness, and mindlessness. De Forest believed that such antiquated flirts (and their younger and somewhat less repulsive sisters) were more common in the South than elsewhere; but, as he had shown in *Seacliff*, the types also existed in the North and thrived among the leisure classes. Though Lillian Hellman and Tennessee Williams, among others, would eventually capture, with greater art than De Forest ever attained, the complexity, foolishness, and pathos of the aging

Southern belle, De Forest was certainly among the first to suggest that Southern air might produce something other than purity and beauty in woman.

De Forest, however, had learned by the time of *Kate* that environment is not all. It counts, but blood matters too. A few years after *Kate,* De Forest noted how important he felt blood to be; to *The Nation* he wrote that "the better class of whites" in the South would soon overcome the "sanguinary roisters [*sic*]" who were at the time overrunning the country: "the highly-endowed race, the heroic race, the blood race is sure to win."[51]

In Kate Beaumont's grandfather, Colonel Kershaw, De Forest depicted the man of good blood—the true aristocrat, as De Forest conceived him. Such a man De Forest saw in terms similar to the natural *aristoi* whom Jefferson envisioned as the peak of American civilization. In such an aristocrat, the moral, the emotional, and the rational resided in delicate balance. Colonel Kershaw, whom De Forest compares to an elderly, white-haired Washington and whom Peyton Beaumont sees as "the white rose of South Carolinian chivalry" (128), evinces this harmony physically in a "monumental" stature, in a "moral grandeur of expression," and in a "spiritual impressiveness of appearance" (44). More profoundly the Colonel's natural aristocracy manifests itself in his knowledge that the word *honor* means more than vengeance or pride. Most of all, Colonel Kershaw can rise above provincial customs and love of self. Because of his sophistication he wishes an end to the feud and because of his selflessness he can, even when near death, try to avoid inconveniencing others. On his deathbed, a victim of the feud, he knows as only a soldier can (and military imagery clusters around his dying) that peace is better than war and that love is superior to hate. He forgives those who he thinks have shot him, and he begs his hot-headed son-in-law to do his best to end the feud. The triumph of peace is his epitaph, just as his victory is that of common sense over nonsense, law over anarchy, and love over hate. In a time when the Ku Klux Klan was beginning to preach hatred and to practice lawlessness, there was especial pertinence to Kershaw's indictment of the high-toned Southerner's feeling that he, by right, acted by a law above civil laws.

De Forest devotes less attention to the McAlisters than to the Beaumonts. The McAlister women, passive creatures, desire peace but always obey the orders of their men. The McAlister men prefer a more defensive posture in the feud than the more pugnacious Beaumonts; but, though the McAlisters are less sensitive to affronts to their "honor," they are quite willing, save for the love-stricken Frank, to fire back when challenged. Quite seriously, Wallace McAlister comments, when his brother is challenged, that Frank should not appeal to the police for help: "We gentlemen don't do it. . . . Law is for our inferiors" (152). Frank's answer, "Or for our betters" (152), shows that he is allied to Colonel Kershaw by more fundamental things than the "monumental" height with which De Forest endows both of them.

The one McAlister other than Frank that De Forest treats in any detail is Frank's father, Judge McAlister. In appearance elephantine, matronly, and benevolent, the Judge is actually a grave, deliberate, bland, courageous, and, at times, a hypocritical man. An obvious contrast to Peyton Beaumont, the Judge is most so in his devious politics and his egoistic, rationalizing intellect. When the blunt but sensitive Peyton and the subtle but insensitive Judge meet to end the feud, their natural antipathy—suggested by the ornate military dress of Peyton and by the grave, black costume of the Judge—makes it impossible, without each man temporarily rising above himself, to agree to live in peace. In their great moment, however, each man is purified, and the way is open for South Carolina's Romeo and Juliet, each matured by trouble, to cement the union between the families.

De Forest's treatment of the feud suggests his belief (one that was probably responsible in part for Howells' fondness for *Kate*) that there is more folly than villainy in human kind. In his depiction of the marital life of Randolph and Nellie Armitage, De Forest dramatizes as well his conviction that human weakness is more responsible than an evil heart for villainous actions. To make his point, he depicts the marriage of Nellie Armitage, a woman whom Howells remembered as the real heroine of the novel: "A great little creature . . . pathetically, heroically, whimsically alive."[52] Visiting Nellie and her husband, Kate at first sees her sister's marriage as ideal, but after several weeks Randolph must have a spree.

With his backwoods companion Redhead Saxon, Randolph goes to a cracker-ball thrown by two low-down women. Soon he is heated with liquor and full of insolent savagery. By the time he is brought home he is an "image of utter helplessness and clod-like insensibility. One eye was partly open, but there was a horrible glassiness and lifelessness in it. . . . His face was colorless, except a faint tinting of bluish and yellowish shades, as if it were the countenance of a corpse" (101). In his stupor, he is so revolting that his wife first slaps his senseless face, and then reveals to her sister the horror of her marriage. When Randolph awakens, his need for liquor is so great that he beats his brother Bentley in maniacal fury, and then, armed with a knife, goes to his wife's room. There Kate discovers him brandishing the knife over his wife's prostrate body while he demands that she tell where the liquor is hidden. Kate's entrance brings Randolph back to a semblance of reason, and he leaves the two frightened women. Before he goes, however, he tells his wife that he had wanted only liquor, and then adds a final insult: "Do you suppose I wanted *you*" (105)?

Considering the delicacy with which Howells treated, in *A Modern Instance* (1882), the drinking bouts of Bartley Hubbard and the marital relations of Hubbard and his wife, De Forest's frankness must have shocked numerous readers of *The Atlantic*. Just as challenging is his insistence that Randolph's alcoholism is a disease (the hereditary taint also runs through Bentley Armitage) and that the victim should be pitied as well as censured. As with Mrs. Chester, however, De Forest's disgust is greater than his compassion, and he fully discloses his contempt for Randolph in a scene in which Randolph and Redhead Saxon, in a drunken haze, fight a hilariously ceremonial duel without knowing that the bullets they are using are blanks. Most duels, De Forest implies, are fought with little more sense, though with more bloody results; but they are fought by a different class than that of Randolph or Saxon, who are only monkeys imitating the high-toned Southrons they would like to be.

In addition to his major characters, De Forest peoples his setting with numerous memorable minor characters through whom he lends depth and variety to his picture of the antebellum South. Such Negro slaves as Miriam, with her honesty toward her mistress and her belief that duels are Satan's work; such a firebrand orator as General Johnson, with his love for duels, State's rights, and the sovereign South; such a minister as the Reverend Gilyard, dominated by his desire to do his duty and eventually becoming aware of his guilt in not opposing the *code duello;* such a courteous character as the pacific Major Lawson, with his constant flattery and his dream of seeing the story of Romeo and Juliet unfolded happily in South Carolina; such a young, curious, and mischievous young flirt as Jenny Devine; and such a sardonic but pathetic worshiper of Kate Beaumont as the lame Bentley Armitage—all are sketched with vivid Realism. Encountering such characters, one understands, in part, though possibly as much by accident as by intention, the reasons for the Civil War as they were involved in people rather than politics and economics.

Written in a nervous and, in the beginning, an almost telegraphic style, *Kate Beaumont* is one of De Forest's most realistic novels. Especially it is so in its fusion of good and evil in its characters and in its insistence that folly and weakness are more adequate explanations of human error than is the evil of innate depravity. De Forest's fondness for caricature, however, still persists, most notably in Mrs. Chester. So also does his love for the sentimental scene (shown in *Kate* especially in the death-bed portrayal of Colonel Kershaw) and in his tendency toward fine writing. No modern realist, for instance, would dream of describing a meeting of Kate and Frank in such extravagant terms as De Forest: "Their lips, touched by fire from heaven, ennobled language far beyond its wont, and made it like the speech of some better world. Words became emotions, pouring heart into heart, and mingling them forever" (165).

Despite such occasional rhapsodies, *Kate Beaumont* is a worthy novel that blazed a path for more consistently realistic attempts to capture the way people actually are. Howells recognized its merit. Reviewing the novel for *The Atlantic*, he noted that *Kate* was "the first full and perfect picture of Southern society of the times before the war,"[53] and he concluded by asserting that *Kate* proved that America was "not so much lacking in an American novelist as in a public to recognize him."[54]

## V   The Wetherel Affair

De Forest's next novel was the mystery and social satire *The Wetherel Affair*. In 1872 it began to appear serially in *The Galaxy*, and a year later it was published between hard covers. In reviewing the work, *The Nation* proclaimed it an "undeniably American" blend of "Emersonian philosophy, Long Island Sound steamboats, New England religion, and Newport fashion,"[55] while Howells proclaimed that De Forest was "really the only American novelist."[56] In writing to thank Howells for this "stupendous compliment," De Forest implied that he was less than satisfied with the novel; advised Howells not to be discouraged, as he seemed to be, by the difficulties of American authorship, for "We are all incomplete novelists together, much perplexed by the difficulty of making a democratic society picturesque, and doomed perhaps to spend lives in laying foundations for posterity to build upon"; and finally De Forest concluded by once again asserting, through oblique comments upon Howells' idol Turgenev, that De Forest was less sympathetic to Realism than he had formerly been:

> His [Turgenev's] carefully logical characters, who do one thing and keep doing it and do nothing else, are not richly human enough, and to me are not touching. . . . To prefer his tasteful meagreness to the abundance of the great English novelists is much like preferring . . . Racine to Shakespeare. . . . I do not say that Turgeneff [sic] is not able;—merely that he is not prodigious—neither a Thackery [sic], nor a Balzac.[57]

De Forest's dissatisfaction with parts of *The Wetherel Affair* was justified, for the novel is hardly an improvement over his earlier attempt in a similar vein, *Seacliff*. Though there are certainly faults in the earlier work (its dramatic repetitiveness and general prolixity, its dependence on coincidence, and its tendency toward melodrama and caricature), there is also enough acuteness of perception and of graceful expression to make one feel the impact of a unique personality. That impression is largely lacking in *The Wetherel Affair*, while the faults of *Seacliff* are intensified. The result is shallow fiction, full of the triteness of "a friendless waif on the great, pitiless ocean of life" (193); replete with the sentimentality of a hopeless love which ends with the sufferer, in a "dolorous and sublime hour of resignation" (210), thanking the Lord for tears; and overflowing with such religious admonitions as, "We must stoop to figures weighed down by crosses, and look under the acute shadows of crowns of thorns, if we would behold the brows which wear the brightest halos" (124).

Faced with such writing, the reader of today can only marvel that in the novel De Forest should satirize sentimentality in fiction and should lament: "To a person of refined taste the lack of literary culture among the great mass . . . of the so-called reading public is all but incredible. . . . The true secret of gaining the favor of this immensely numerous class of readers is to furnish them with matter just a little better than they could write themselves" (116).

Yet the ironic truth is that De Forest did have cause to complain. *The Wetherel Affair* was incomparably superior to the endless reams of popular moralistic trash that Sylvanus Cobb was publishing in the New York *Ledger*, and it was considerably above the dolorosities and sublimities of those best-selling female

novelists whom Twain satirized in *Huck Finn* and against whom
Hawthorne exploded in 1855: "America is now wholly given
over to a d----d mob of scribbling women, and I should have
no chance of success while the public is occupied with their
trash."[58] Exactly because *The Wetherel Affair* did not have the
thorough melodrama and emotionalism found in the works of
such unrestrained sentimentalists as Augusta Jane Evans, Maria
Cummins, and Mrs. E. D. E. N. Southworth, De Forest's novel
gained no vast shopgirl audience, and its lack of real merit
prevented it from gaining a more sophisticated one. Because it
is so typical in this respect of much of De Forest's work and
because it is a novel which is interesting in conception, if not in
fulfillment, it may be worth while to look in some detail at *The
Wetherel Affair*.

The dual plot puts De Forest's characters, in accord with his
magazinist theory, through a series of extraordinary events which
are largely glued together by the ready cement of coincidence.
One strand of the plot has young Edward Wetherel as its central
character. Edward is a good-hearted bohemian, but even before
the novel begins, his irresponsible and irreligious actions have
offended Judge Jabez Wetherel, his rich and childless uncle.
Soon the two Wetherels have quarreled anew, and Jabez an-
nounces his intention of striking his nephew out of his will. This
Jabez does, but shortly thereafter he is murdered, and no will is
to be found. As the only living heir, Edward Wetherel inherits
the fortune. Though Edward is able to provide evidence that
clears him of the murder, suspicion clouds his name, and he
vows to find the murderer. By the time he has done so, he has
proved himself a chip off the old Puritanic Wetherel tree, and
good thoughts and good works will assuredly follow him all the
days of his life.

The second strand of the plot adds the complications of love.
The heroine of this segment is Nestoria, or Nettie, Bernard. The
daughter of a famous Persian missionary, she has met Edward
Wetherel on her trip to America, where she has come to study
and to do good works. Before she begins these tasks, she lives
for a while in the seaside home of Judge Wetherel. There,
Nestoria resumes her friendship with Edward. Though Judge
Wetherel disapproves, the two lovers soon become engaged.
Shortly after this, Nestoria accidentally sees the murder of Judge
Wetherel. The murderer resembles her fiancé, and she flees in
panic. By the mercy of God, a point De Forest insists upon,
Nestoria survives a perilous sea voyage and arrives in New

York City. There she wanders around the Fulton Market area, which De Forest captures in all the reality of its sights and smells, and after a while she finds a modest room in which to hide from the police. Soon, like so many other sentimental heroines inspired by Richardson, she is torn between her conscience (which tells her to reveal her knowledge of the crime) and her heart (which insists she protect the man she still loves). In following her heart instead of her conscience, Nestoria violates her duty to society, and De Forest condemns her, and those like her, for a romantic soft-headedness that allows crime to flourish. His indictment of Nestoria, however, is gentle; for her sin was almost, not quite, justified by its motivation: love.

After Nestoria has undergone a torment which tests her love and the reader's "sensibility," and after Edward has proved his Puritan rebirth is no fleeting transformation, De Forest draws the two strands of plot together again. Nestoria coincidentally sees the actual murderer, recognizes him, and realizes that she has wronged Edward by her distrust. Edward meanwhile has lured the murderer, an old acquaintance of his bohemian days, into a trap. With the uncovering of the true murderer, love triumphs, and soon Nestoria is in the arms of the man she loves.

The moral of the story is twofold. One is stated by a good, though voluble, Christian: "Appolyon was beaten ... at every point; and those who combated him have been brought through victorious, in spite of their errors" (216). The other is stated by the author, who notes: "There has appeared in this story no grand triumph of conscience or of wisdom, recommendable for wide imitation" (219). The latter moral is obviously De Forest's thrust at the soft heads, both in life and in literature, who preach the wisdom of following, like Nestoria, the natural instincts and the heart's dictates. To such romantic disciples of Rousseau and Emerson, De Forest affirmed the claims of common sense and social responsibility. Nestoria's path was wrong, as she realized, even though her error had no harmful consequences. A saintly hunchback, who also foolishly follows his heart instead of his head, makes the point when he asserts at the conclusion of the novel: "It has turned out well, but not through our merits— only through the compassion of God" (216).

This narrative De Forest tells with a host of ornamental literary allusions, and into it he introduces a swarm of minor characters whom he tends to characterize by Dickensian grotesqueness. Where the genius of Dickens, however, manages to convey humanity within caricature, De Forest creates only puppets.

Where Dickens dramatizes with infinite variety the peculiar traits and the language eccentricities which dominate his memorable creations, De Forest is usually content to repeat endlessly the oddities with which he has endowed his characters. Where Dickens' characters have an inward life that makes them act consistently with the reality they assert, the lack of inward motivation in De Forest's puppets makes them often seem to dance inconsistently and implausibly to satisfy the needs of a plot which De Forest seems to make up as he goes along. At times the sheer goodness of some of De Forest's creations stretches credulity to the breaking point; a good example occurs when four separate characters insist that Edward Wetherel—despite his shady past, despite the suspicion of murder that hangs over him, and despite the fact that his uncle wished to disinherit him—inherit the money that Jabez Wetherel had apparently intended to will to them.

The most prominent of the caricatures in *The Wetherel Affair* are those of Judge Wetherel, Mrs. Dinneford and her daughter Alice, John Bowlder, Count Poloski, and Imogen Eleonore Jones. In Judge Wetherel, De Forest manages to hint at a human beneath the distortion. Old, withered, and skeletal, the Judge is an unbending Puritan, reminiscent of that admirable Calvinist, Dr. Samuel Hopkins of Mrs. Stowe's *The Minister's Wooing*. Like Dr. Hopkins, Judge Wetherel's duty is the dominating force of his life, but at the same time his life is filled with acts of disinterested benevolence, and he "is gentleness itself to the gentle" (19). The silver hair and grave countenance of the Judge make him resemble the patriarchs of old, and the similarity is heightened by the scriptural style in which he talks. An especial admirer of missionaries, he leaves the pamphlets of the American Tract Society on the table of every guest room in his home. Slugabed visitors are awakened, according to the Judge's instructions, by a maid who intones monotonously through the keyhole: "Go to the ant, thou sluggard; consider her ways and be wise" (20). To some of the warmth of Bunyan and a good deal more of the rigidity of Jonathan Edwards (the two men whom he most admires), Judge Wetherel adds a dictatorial strain. He cannot condone the frivolous life of his nephew; when Edward promises that he will transform his life but cannot, without hypocrisy, say he repents his past sins, Judge Wetherel proclaims he cannot enrich a man who has sinned and cannot repent. Soon afterward the old patriarch is dead, and the spirit with which De Forest views him is implicit in the comment: "The severe and somewhat sunless, but conscientious, benevolent, and on the whole beautiful life had ended; and the sincere spirit of the old man, purified through worthy work and worthier aspirations, had risen by mortal violence to divine mercy" (72).

With his other minor characters, De Forest has less success. Mrs. Dinneford, a cousin of Judge Wetherel, is a good Christian but an incurable scatterbrain. She talks ceaselessly and constantly quotes the platitudes of the poet Tupper. (The Edgar Guest of his day, Tupper's volume of blank verses, *Proverbial Philosophy*, had sold over a million copies by 1881.) Her daughter Alice is less of a Christian but more of a scatterbrain. One of De Forest's useless young ladies, a group he never tires of satirizing, she is something of a feminist as well in her defense of her divine right to live without work but with freedom. Her giddiness at one point leads her into an engagement which ends badly and breaks her heart—for an hour or two. At their best, which is seldom, the Dinnefords speak naturally and even memorably. Mrs. Dinneford says on one occasion: " 'We human creatures are a little like cats; we get along best in our own garrets. And it is even so in matters of religion; many people can't worship God except in their own church; indeed it's wonderful how many cat Christians there are' " (20). And her daughter: " 'Young ladies must be proper, and propriety always gives the doldrums, just as measles bring weak eyes. Such hen-coops of old patched-up decorums as we women live in! And if you stick your head out for a grain of corn, somebody is ready to grab you and pull off your feathers and eat you up and pick your bones' " (132).

Another minor character is John Bowlder. A friend of Judge Wetherel, he is a fat, pink, and energetic man who "worshipped Emerson, admired Thoreau, and read much in Walt Whitman" (81). These writers he quotes as often as Mrs. Dinneford quotes Tupper. At times he even attempts his own Whitmanesque "yawp" in poetry; at others, he emulates the precepts of Thoreau. De Forest's good-natured scorn for Bowlder, and the Transcendental folly he preaches but cannot live by, is suggested on one occasion when Bowlder attempts his own Walden experiment "until a party of surveyors found him bedridden with rheumatism and starving, and sent him back to the degrading comforts of civilization" (81). On another day Bowlder is arrested (a policeman suspects him to be a criminal because he is attempting to enjoy exaltation from the dignity of common labor but is in-

appropriately garbed for his work), and he is forced to strip
layer on layer of clothes away so that he can be searched.
Eventually he is seen in his essential hollowness; without his
clothes he is but a "white taper of a figure. . . . Even his conversation, stripped and divested as it was of transcendentalism,
was lean and shrunken" (197).

Just as much a caricature is Count Poloski, who turns out to
be the murderer. He is a dandy pretending to be a count in
hopes of marrying an American heiress, and De Forest's depiction
of him undoubtedly reflects American resentment at the swarm
of foreign nobility who came to American shores, after the
European revolutions of 1848, in order to hunt wealthy wives.
Addicted to bowing, scraping, and hand-kissing, Count Poloski
also insists he is an authority on practically every intellectual
subject. De Forest mocks his artificiality and hypocrisy, but at
the same time De Forest implies that the rudeness of American
manners and the lack of American intellectual sophistication
might be improved a little by more European polish.

The most extreme of De Forest's caricatures, however, is Miss
Imogen Eleonore Jones. A romantic, sentimental schoolteacher,
she reads the *Spasmodic* magazine as closely as Judge Wetherel
pores over his Bible, and her conversation exemplifies the absurd
length to which De Forest could carry his exaggerations. She
befriends Nestoria when she arrives in New York, and guessing
at Nettie's trouble proclaims: " 'Thou art indeed heavy laden.
But fear not and fail not. I will guard thy secret and companion
*thee*. None shall find thee out, nor harm thee. We will walk the
ways of life together' " (101). Or she welcomes a visitor to her
home in such babble as: " 'In the inane wilderness of brick and
mortar which billows and throbs around us there are many, many
abodes far more palatial than this, but none, surely none, in
which you would be received with a simpler, more earnest,
more heartfelt cordiality' " (112). Such satire of the nonsense
that did appear in the New York *Ledger* reminds one of the
speech of some of the characters created by Sinclair Lewis; but,
in comparison to De Forest, Lewis is a master of subtlety.

The major characters of the novel are Edward Wetherel, Nestoria Bernard, and Walter Lehming. The two young lovers are
the superficial, conventional hero and heroine which the
magazine reader of the day expected. Edward is at first a gay
young animal whose egoism is as large as his responsibleness
is small. Because of the twin influences of love and death,
Edward Wetherel changes, or, rather, is resurrected, into the old

Puritan Wetherel mold. In either stage he lacks verisimilitude, for there is no real suggestion of his sinfulness before he is reborn, and there is no internal struggle (or at least no effective dramatization of it) after he sees the evil of his former ways.

Nestoria Bernard, who seems in some ways to be modeled on De Forest's missionary sister-in-law, is at times a clinging vine and at others a sturdy oak—an inconsistency that is not unique in De Forest's portraiture. Petite, blonde, and blue-eyed, she is innocent and religious, the product of a clerical background which reminded her daily that "We are dust and ashes; we are worthless worms of the earth; our sole honor is humility, our sole hope is mercy" (12). After the murder of Judge Wetherel, Nestoria's travail begins. Her first solution of the struggle between her duty and her love is flight; her second, time and prayer. The discovery of the actual criminal implies that, though she has violated her social responsibility, she has sinned for the best of all possible reasons, excessive love; and she can, therefore, depend on the infinite mercy of God, who arranges all things for the cosmic good. Such a thought was common not only to the popular fiction of the day but also to Transcendental philosophy, and De Forest does not mock that one aspect of Transcendentalism. Without a sneer, he allows John Bowlder to quote from Emerson: "A breath of will blows eternally through the universe in the direction of the right and necessary" (82). Unlike Bowlder and some Transcendentalists, however, De Forest insisted upon the reality of evil. The Emersonian conviction that evil was merely the absence of good and all evil was merely potential good in the evolutionary process of becoming actual good—that theory seemed as fanciful to De Forest as it had to Hawthorne and Melville. Evil did exist, and citizens who were morally and politically aware had the social obligation of combating it in their own time and their own country.

The most intriguing character in the novel, though in conception rather than in dramatic realization, is the saintly Walter Lehming. Sickly, dwarfish, hunchbacked, and ugly, he is a dedicated teacher who loves his young charges, and an ill-paid magazine writer who deplores the lack of an international copyright law. As a saint, he looks often at the mirror which shows his misshapen face and then mumbles submissively, "Thus it has pleased God to make me" (149). When he falls in love with Nestoria, he finds it especially difficult to face the mirror, but he does and learns anew: "I must live for others. . . . No one but a dog would live for me" (149). His saintliness leads him to reject that portion of the Wetherel inheritance which the old Judge had intended for him and which Edward begs him to accept. It also compels him to help Edward prove his innocence despite the fact that, by doing so, Lehming loses all hope of winning Nestoria. As a saint, he reconciles, as best he can, the conflicting claims of heart and head, love and duty; but he shows considerable modernity in his sainthood by emphasizing human tolerance and divine forgiveness rather than Puritan dogma. He mediates the rigidity of Judge Wetherel and the folly of the youthful Edward, and in doing so he preaches the golden mean to Edward: "'All extremes of conduct verge on irrationality.... Calvin purified the church, but his preachings were too violent, and there has been a harmful reaction against them. Your well-meaning and pure-hearted uncle was in his way a Calvin. He did you little good while he lived'" (157).

When Edward seems to be in danger of becoming too thoroughly the ascetic, Lehming warns him "to avoid such excesses of austerity. The Divine Reason is perfectly reasonable" (138). In his rational Christianity, Lehming can even oppose the Puritan church's condemnation of the stage, and out of the perfection of his faith, he can accept the utility of all things. From his experience as a teacher watching the growth of children, he can readily embrace Darwinistic theory and even understand "The pleasure which Deity takes in surveying the evolution and glorious unfolding of his creation" (128). Such ideas make Lehming memorable as a conception; but, like so many of De Forest's characters, he is too lacking in shading, too bathetically painted as a man of sorrows, and too much what a sentimental audience wished, to be more than an especially interesting puppet.

In *The Wetherel Affair,* De Forest writes from a lofty, omniscient height. Occasionally in true Victorian fashion he reprimands his characters for their looseness of speech or folly of action, and sometimes he intrudes his own more or less relevant opinions and epigrammatic wisdom into the narrative. Alice Dinneford's infatuation with Count Poloski allows De Forest to lament the American female's infatuation with titles. The weaknesses in the character of Count Poloski give De Forest opportunity to inveigh against foreign dandies and to indict, despite their republican principles, the American people's enchantment with caste and pretension. The impotence of the police to solve the murder of Judge Wetherel (and generally to prevent the rise of the criminal class) inspires De Forest to an outburst against the ineffectuality of American forces of law, and this indictment he then broadens to one on excessive democracy: "A people which suffers itself to be ruled politically by its non-taxpayers, and which degrades its judiciary by making it look for power and honor to ward meeting and other similar sources of popular favor—such a people must necessarily have inferior magistrates and officers of justice, from the highest to the lowest" (205). On the other hand, Edward Wetherel is undoubt-edly speaking for De Forest when Edward proclaims the need of the masses for education. Edward then goes on to indict a system of taxation which is " 'a plundering of the poor' " and a system of tariffs which penalizes the masses and " 'works almost exclusively for the benefit of a few hundred capitalists and monopolists, who are rich enough to overawe and perhaps to bribe our politicians' " (141).

Time and again in such intrusions De Forest showed himself for what he was: a rational, moderate democrat who was deter-mined to oppose both the aristocratic ideals of Europe and the irresponsible chaos of mob rule. Seen in this light, the political commentary supplements the rational religion preached by Lehming. De Forest asserts the golden mean, and, in so doing, he preaches, like his mentor Thackeray, a useful lesson to the fanatics of politics and religion. But possibly *The Wetherel Affair* shows more clearly than any other work of De Forest the fallacy of attempting to find that golden mean in art. In it, compromise breeds only failure: the golden mean between pure art and popular soap opera is a mere illusion.

## VI  Honest John Vane

In *The Wetherel Affair*, despite his pallid love story and his melodramatic mystery, De Forest showed his concern for such real social problems as poverty, crime, venal police and judges, an illiterate citizenry, and burdensome taxation of the poor for the benefit of the rich. Despite the truth of what he had to say, the indictments were in large part responses to the recent exposure of New York's notorious Tweed Ring and were awkward intru-sions upon the narrative. In his next three novels—*Honest John Vane, Playing the Mischief*, and *Justine's Lovers*—he wove his accusations into the texture of three narratives totally different in tone. Undoubtedly influenced by Trollope's parliamentary novels, which he was reading at about this time, De Forest chose his materials from the amalgam of coarseness, social pretentiousness, and wholesale corruption that made up the Vanity Fair of Washington in the 1870's. With the evidence of the gold conspiracy of Jay Gould and James Fisk, the scandalous use of New York's Custom House as a Republican Party machine, the sale by congressmen of West Point cadetships, the exposé of the Crédit Mobilier, and the costly gifts accepted by President Grant himself—with such evidence, De Forest could hardly help agreeing, no matter how much he venerated Grant, with the staunchly Republican *Leslie's Weekly,* which commented on January 13, 1872: "Since the formation of this government there has never been such a series of frauds, defalcations, and peculations, either in number or in magnitude as have characterized the last three years. Should the stealing continue ... it is to be feared we shall have little to save except the national character. ... Down with the Washington Ring."

In his short novel *Honest John Vane,* published in the same year as Twain and Warner's *The Gilded Age,* De Forest expressed for the readers of *The Atlantic* his disgust at the political jobbery that was perverting the name of democracy. For his inspiration he was equally indebted to John Bunyan and the Crédit Mobilier of America. From the first, he took his allegorical tone. In the second, he found the personae and the central action of his story.

De Forest's pilgrim is called Honest John Vane, perhaps as a tribute to Honest John Kelly, the hypocritical boss of New York's Tammany Hall in the 1870's; to Honest John Patterson, the carpetbag senator from South Carolina; and to James G. Blaine, the weathervane speaker of the House of Representatives whose ties to the railroad lobby and to the Crédit Mobilier were common knowledge. In America's Vanity Fair, Vane attempts at first to deserve his Catonian soubriquet. When he learns, however, that Washington's Mr. Christian, Mr. Faithful, and Mr. Greatheart have succumbed to the lobby, he sells his soul cheaply. The purchaser is Darius Dorman, a smoky, claw-like, dusky-eyed lobbyist whom De Forest insistently describes in Mephistophelian terms. After the sale Honest John becomes Weathercock John, and in the raid upon the treasury that signalizes the end of the session he is as greedy as any of the pigs in the House. At the end of the novel, only slightly shaken by a Congressional investigation into corruption, he is still at his work "of enacting the national revenue into the safes of huge corporations ... for the sake of a small percentage thereof to himself" (231).

In *Honest John Vane,* De Forest proclaimed that his work

might be read as a "perversely reversed and altogether bedeviled rendering of the *Pilgrim's Progress*" (224), but the readers of *The Atlantic* in 1873 were undoubtedly less interested in the modern day "Celestial Railroad" than they were in De Forest's indictment of the Crédit Mobilier. It could hardly have been otherwise, for the Crédit Mobilier was the climactic revelation of Congressional corruption in the nineteenth century.

Born in 1864, the Crédit Mobilier was the creation of a number of the major stockholders of the Union Pacific Railroad. A corporation inside a corporation, the Crédit Mobilier took its officers from among men who controlled the Union Pacific, and it had as its ostensible purpose the construction of railroad track for the Union Pacific. In actual practice the aim of the Crédit Mobilier was to divert congressional subsidies, given to the Union Pacific for the creation of a transcontinental railroad, to the pockets of the stockholders of the Crédit Mobilier. Such commercial practices were not unique with the Union Pacific, but the scale was certainly vast. According to the report of the Wilson Committee investigating the Crédit Mobilier, the profit of the corporation, on contracts of around ninety-three million dollars, came almost to forty-four million dollars.

In all likelihood there would have been no more public outcry against the practices of the Union Pacific than there were against the quite similar manipulations of the Central Pacific if there had not been a quarrel among the swindlers over the loot. Echoes of this feud began to be heard as early as 1868, but the quarrel did not become national knowledge until September 4, 1872, when the New York *Sun* published a series of letters from Oakes Ames to Colonel H. S. McComb. Ames—an important stockholder in the Union Pacific, as well as a congressman from Massachusetts—asserted in his letters that he had disposed of a number of shares of stock to influential congressmen whose votes would protect the Union Pacific. Ames's letters named names, and primarily because of this, two investigating committees of Congress began to hear testimony upon the scandal. At first the hearings were behind doors, and then public outcry forced open sessions to be held. Implicated were numerous congressmen, among them such men as Vice-President Colfax; Speaker of the House Blaine; and a future President of the United States, Senator James A. Garfield. The only action of the House investigative committee, however, was the recommendation that Oakes Ames and James Brooks be expelled from their seats, while the investigative committee of the Senate could find only one scapegoat, James W.

Patterson, to recommend for expulsion. Even these penalties, according to the House Committee on the Judiciary, were outside the power of the House; and so Ames and Brooks were reprimanded instead by a vote of "absolute condemnation." It seemed a light punishment to many Americans, and among them were Mark Twain and De Forest, who shouted indignantly of the need for congressional reform.

In the bludgeoning satire of *Honest John Vane,* the Union Pacific becomes the Great Subfluvial Tunnel, the purpose of which is to unite Lake Superior and the Gulf of Mexico, and the Crédit Mobilier becomes a sub-tunnel, the real purpose of which is to defraud the public. Oakes Ames becomes in the novel Mr. Simon Sharp, and though the readers of De Forest's work may not have recognized the servility of Sharp as a characteristic of Ames, they would have had no difficulty in recognizing Ames in De Forest's description of Sharp as "a man of exact arithmetical instincts ... he revolted from ... an unfair allotment of the dividends of dishonor, and insisted that every one should take his own share and no more" (224). Christian and Greatheart, the scapegoats in the novel, resemble Congressman Brooks and Senator Patterson, and De Forest forecast correctly the outcome of even their ordeal when he allowed lobbyist Dorman to assert that eventually all the old congressional war horses would gallop up and down among precedents and counterprecedents until such a dust was raised that everyone would be let off. Finally John Vane is an amalgam of such culprits as John A. Bingham, B. M. Boyer, and James F. Wilson, all of whom managed to tell a story just plausible enough for the investigating committee to allow them to escape. In Vane's willingness to admit that he has "invested" in the Great Subfluvial because he expected to make a profit, Honest John most resembles Representative Boyer, who publicly regretted that he had not profited even more than he had. In the theatricality with which he rejects a seat on the congressional investigative committee, Vane most of all resembles James G. Blaine, who, with similar showmanship, asserted his ownership of Crédit Mobilier stock in the same speech in which he demanded a congressional investigation.

*Honest John Vane* voices De Forest's indignation at the Crédit Mobilier, but even more important the novel probes the sources of that scandal. For De Forest, the most prominent cause is Jacksonian democracy. Such a system encourages the election and corruption of ignorant men, and De Forest's novel is a drama of the inevitable results in such a political system. The first step is election. Because Vane is a likable, ordinary, pliable animal, and De Forest insists on his fleshliness, he is attractive not only to the common man but to the perceptive lobbyist. When the nominating convention of Vane's state cannot choose between Bummer, who is denounced for taking bribes, and Saltonstall, who is attacked for being a gentleman, the delegates are easily manipulated by lobbyist Dorman into nominating Vane. Without any political qualifications, Vane is nevertheless considered able by his constituents to represent them well. Only the few conceive "that he [their representative] ought to be acquainted either with finance, or political economy, or constitutional limitations, or international law, and that furthermore he should be a .person of tried character and honor" (97). These eccentrics, like similar ones in Brackenridge's *Modern Chivalry* (1792-1815), have no influence. They must watch helplessly while De Forest's Vane, or Brackenridge's McTeague, is elevated to heights beyond his mental or moral capacities.

After the election of Vane comes the corruption. De Forest notes, a little snobbishly perhaps, that "there is a rabble in morals as well as in manners, and to this spiritual mobocracy Vane belonged by birth" (170); but the novelist adds a more practical reason for Vane's downfall: his own poverty and his wife's dreams. With a socially ambitious, ostentatiously extravagant, and financially childish wife (and Vane's encumbrance is similar to those of Blaine and Secretary Belknap), Vane is first forced into debt and then into the sale of his vote. De Forest implies that a higher salary than the five thousand a year paid a congressman might have kept Honest John moral longer. Because of this belief, De Forest in *Honest John Vane* has no outburst comparable to that of *The Gilded Age* against the salary grab of 1873 (by which the Forty-Second Congress raised the pay of congressmen by twenty-five hundred dollars and made the raise retroactive for the preceding biennium).

Finally, once he has fallen, there is no hope that Weathercock John will reform. De Forest asserts he is of a "low genus" (180), without proper breeding or education or "sound self-respect and lofty sense of honor" (180). While he had been in Slowburgh where morality was valued, Honest John was moral; but in Washington, where another wind blows, he leans with the prevailing gusts. The scandal by which he is almost exposed does not make him more penitent, only more cautious. He is now of less merit than ever. The solution is to replace him and his

fellows with legislators of education, breeding, and morality—
Brackenridge in *Modern Chivalry* and G. W. Curtis in *Trumps*
(1861) had come to the same conclusion—but De Forest has
no real hope that such an event will occur. Where Twain and
Warner in *The Gilded Age* are buoyantly optimistic about the
future of democracy and apportion just punishment to such
sinners as the adventurous lobbyist Laura Hawkins and the
Bible-spouting spoilsman Senator Dilworthy, and where Henry
Adams in *Democracy* (1881) could, with his back to the wall,
affirm that he believed in democracy, despite all its faults,
because he believed in the evolution of the masses, De Forest
had no such optimistic faith. He wondered, therefore, whether
a "monarchical Prussia ruled by economy and honesty" were
not preferable to "a free America fallen into squandering and
bribery" (223). He feared that the public that had elected Vane
would gullibly keep him in office. De Forest could not forgive
the real villain of *Honest John Vane*:

> the public,—the great soft-hearted American public,—that public
> which has compassion on every species of scoundrel,—which tries
> murderers under jury restrictions warranted to save four fifths of
> them,—which cannot see one condemned to death without
> pleading with tears for his noxious life,—that forgiving, milk-and-
> water public was as mild in its judgment as the Committee [that
> investigated the Subfluvial Tunnel]. It magnified our dishonor-
> able member for not lying, and exalted his name for not commit-
> ting perjury (228).

The indictment of *Honest John Vane* is made with a unity that
is far superior to the shotgun blasts of *The Gilded Age,* and
there is little doubt that De Forest is attacking more serious
problems than the tiny grabs that Twain and Warner were
satirizing in their assaults on the Knobs University bill and the
Columbus River Navigation scheme. In addition, De Forest's
novel lacks the melodrama, full of virtue rewarded and vice
punished, that so vitiates the end of *The Gilded Age*. Despite
these facts *The Gilded Age* may well be the better novel
because there is a vitality in such characters as Beriah Sellers
and Senator Dilworthy that is largely lacking in the allegorical
embodiments of De Forest. The readers of the day at any rate
preferred the farce of *The Gilded Age* to the allegory of *Honest
John*. Perhaps Henry James suggested a reason when, after condemning De Forest's "loose" and "turbid" writing, his "coarse
imagery," and his lack of drama, James noted in dismay that

" 'Honest John Vane' exhales a penetrating odor of what in plain English one must call vulgarity."[59] Howells dissented in *The Atlantic* by claiming that no American yet had produced "so good a political satire as this,"[60] and more recent critics have also revealed less sensitive noses than that of James. Quinn, for instance, calls *Honest John* "one of the best political novels in our fiction,"[61] and Haight proclaims that, as an indictment of lobbying, the novel merits higher praise than *The Gilded Age.*[62]

## VII  Playing the Mischief

De Forest's disillusionment with the workings of democracy, as he had expressed it in *Honest John Vane,* was so great that at times his characters resembled the human vultures that dominated the work of the contemporary political cartoonist Thomas Nast. In *Playing the Mischief,* De Forest continued to expose political corruption, but his inspiration derived more from Thackeray than from the allegories of Bunyan or from the caricatures of Nast. Witty, chatty, and sophisticated, the novel, despite its Victorian length, is written in concise and lucid sentences; and the novelist seems as much amused by the frailties and foibles of the people of Vanity Fair as indignant at them. Gentle irony permeates the narrative, as, for instance, in De Forest's observation that "men of poetic imagination . . . usually are moved by feminine grief, especially when the affected one is fair to look upon" (249); or the heroine's initial emotion upon hearing a rich, elderly man's marital proposal: "she decided, with a spasm of the heart (or, perhaps, it might have been only the diaphragm), that she could not possibly accept him; at least not that afternoon" (256); or, finally, the heroine's attraction toward morality after she hears she may inherit some money if she avoids evil: "Such is the goodness which we inherit from Father Adam's undivided estate of original sin. We are able to love the virtue which pays" (283). In addition to these traits of style, De Forest clings to his fondness for decorative literary allusions, and he continues, though with more artistic control, his love of burlesque. Finally, he seems to be insisting upon the American-ness of his language by his use, without quotation marks, of such colloquialisms as "to get shut of" (47); "she . . . wanted to screw a lot of money out of the treasury" (63); "this would sound spoony" (100); and "his love-cracked noddle" (425).

De Forest's tale, which first appeared serially in 1874 and '75 in the popular liberal-Republican weekly, Leslie's *Chimney*

*Corner,* is realistically simple and commonplace. To Washington he brings the young widow Mrs. Josephine Murray. Then he shows her using her feminine charms to press a claim—one already settled for a modest sum many years before—for a barn destroyed in the War of 1812. Eventually, through sheer duplicity, Mrs. Murray wins an award of $100,000 but not before she has sacrificed all vestiges of sensitivity and morality. After her victory over the honest men of Congress and the nation, Mrs. Murray successfully refuses to pay, either by money or by marriage, the agents whom she has used in forwarding her claim. A triumphant cheat at the end of the novel, she is last seen surrounded by "a gang of affiliated blacklegs" (440) who obviously plan to shear her as she has shorn others.

Fulfilling his desire to be, like Balzac, a "secretary of society," De Forest emphasized setting and character in *Playing The Mischief.* For his materials he had in Washington not only a host of absurd claims and conscienceless claimants but also a city filled with female suffragists and sordid lobbyists. In Congress itself he had a body in which the pre-war leaven of Southern grace and courtliness had been replaced by the grossness of carpetbaggers and scalawags. For his feminine characters he could draw in fact upon such diverse queens of society as the beautiful Kate Chase Sprague, the wife of the wealthy senator, or the extravagant Mrs. "Puss" Belknap, the wife and burden of the Secretary of War. For greater feminine variety, he could turn to such women as Josie Mansfield, the mistress and murderer of the financial buccaneer Jim Fisk; or Vinnie Ream, the sculptress who kept a studio in the basement of the Capitol and lobbied her commissions through Congress so successfully that *The Nation* exclaimed: "legislators . . . made asses of themselves under the influence of what are called 'female charms' but which we shall call . . . the sexual passion"[63]; or Dr. Mary Walker, a suffragette, spiritualist, novelist, and surgeon, who appeared often in Washington society wearing a man's frock coat and trousers; or Christabel Pankhurst, who could advise her weaker sisters in the feminist cause: "You must pray to God and *She* will help you." For his male characters, De Forest could draw upon any number of anonymous journalists whose pens dripped venom and scandal in a period unparalleled for journalistic irresponsibility; or upon such congressional representatives as the Honorable Ben Butler, the former warrior whose energy was almost as great as his conscience was small; or upon the Honorable Zachariah Chandler, the bluff and gruff leader whose swaggering

masculinity and donkeyish laughter were well known throughout
Washington; or upon the Adonis of Washington, Senator Roscoe
Conkling; or finally upon the massive Henry Cooke, the unscrupulous banker whose numerous chins were familiar in the
halls of the Capitol.

Because he drew upon his strength, the materials of reality,
De Forest painted a memorable gallery of portraits in *Playing
The Mischief.* One of his minor triumphs is General Bangs, an
energetic, egoistic politician whose chief aim is power, not in
order to initiate major governmental reforms but merely for the
pleasure in the display of giving orders and receiving submission.
Like Butler, Bangs is a great orator and criminal lawyer—very
criminal, his opponents claim—and he is constantly smiling, lying,
laying pipe, and pulling wires. General Bangs is also fond of
refurbishing his military career, though he does not remember,
as De Forest does, that he was constantly "surrounded by a
staff of newspaper correspondents. . . . They put him at the head
of columns on columns of print. No other general in history
has won so many battles that were never fought" (226). Un-
forgettable also are the sculptress, Miss Appropriation Cohen,
and the feminist Nancy Appleyard. Especially with "Squire"
Appleyard, De Forest has his fun; for, in contrasting the inward
Romanticism and femininity of her nature to the mannishness
of her outer garb, he exposes the shallowness of her beliefs:

> A change of clothes, she thought, was all that was necessary to
> renovate society; and surely nothing would come more naturally
> to the feminine nature. A change of clothes, and, lo! Tyrant Man
> would be dethroned. Woman would mount beside him or above
> him, and Squire Appleyard would be the greatest of her sex. . . .
>
> But meanwhile, with the reformation only just budding, she
> had fallen desperately in love; and here she was crying at a man
> because he would not marry her, and delighted to scoff at her
> Messianic costume (201).

Still another memorable character is old Yankee Jeremiah Drink-
water, who swears to the heroine's fraudulent "affidavy." Solid
as an oak and masculine as a lion, the nonagenarian has the
morals of a pirate and the lungs of a bassoon player, so that,
born later, he "could not have been more naturally a lobbyist, nor
shown himself better suited for a career inside politics" (301).
A comic masterpiece is the lobbyist and former congressman
from Kansas, Jacob Pike. With a language and manner "as vague
as the illimitable West" (372), this member of the "Third House"
loves intrigue more for its own sake than for the money it

brings. Finally, De Forest brings from the South Senator Pickens Rigdon, who, despite his rude mountaineering background, imitates the high-toned Southerner with his courtly manners, his whiskey-perfumed breath, and his lofty air of command. In these and a number of other minor characters, De Forest tried to achieve the national scope which he had recommended that American writers strive for if they would write the great American novel. Possibly in hopes of gaining the kind of breadth he found in Trollope, Thackeray, and Balzac, De Forest imitated their habit of carrying over characters such as Honest John Vane from his previous works.

In his comedy of manners De Forest gives secondary roles to five characters. He is least successful with his two idealized lovers, Belle Warden and Aristides Cato Bradford. The daughter of a veteran female claimant, Belle herself is a chill, moral, and dull young Juno. Bradford is more complicated, perhaps because his physical urges draw him compulsively toward Josephine Murray; but he always manages to control his sexual desires before they endanger his political morality. An honorable war veteran who is repulsed by dishonesty and theft, Bradford is justly the hero of a novel indicting political corruption, but De Forest is aware that Bradford is a limited man with "a soul of a single virtue" (415). To the political honor he so cherishes, he must add "the honey of sympathy" (415) before he is a full man. Marriage to Belle will not only enrich his heart but strengthen his integrity, and possibly, with her to urge him on, his campaign against special legislation may some day meet with success. In *Playing the Mischief,* however, he speaks to empty seats, for the House belongs to Honest John Vane, General Bangs, and their ilk.

More interesting than Belle and Bradford are Josephine Murray's relatives, the Reverend Murray and his wife, and Colonel Julian Murray. Rigidly orthodox in his religious convictions, the Reverend Murray has married a woman twenty years older than he and has devoted his life to her happiness. Such self-abnegation has made him a nervous gossip whose life is an example both of moral spotlessness and perfect waste. De Forest, though charitable toward the Reverend's selflessness, pronounces his own acceptance of the divine wisdom of man's general egotism when, as the author, he asserts: "If we were all divested of self-preserving egotism, and robed for life in the innocent swaddlings of unmixed love, we should probably lose our civilization, dress in fig-leaves, and become extinct" (391). Which is to say that the tension between man's selfishness and selflessness should be resolved in only one way: in balance, the divine balance. The Reverend Murray's self-abnegation is just as much a flaw, though not so destructive a defect, as the selfishness of Josephine Murray, who is "uncommonly clever" but "still ... had the thoughtless whims of a child, who kills birds or kittens without knowing that it hurts them" (426).

The Reverend Murray's wife is a tremulous old gossip who is still fond of society; she is characterized especially by her Dickensian habit of echoing the end phrases of everything her husband says. Like her husband, Mrs. Murray is titillated by the scandal purveyed by the *Newsmonger,* and though the two old people condemn what they read, their disapproval resembles "the grimace and the wiping of the mouth with which an ancient drunkard apologizes for his dram" (219). De Forest's indictment of the publishers and writers of such trash is more hearty. The writers, he asserts, have an "abominably copious sewer of an imagination" (218), and one such writer's conduct during the Civil War De Forest fumingly recalls through the words of the veteran Bradford: " 'He would lurk ten miles from a battle-field, under protection of the brave men who were bleeding and dying in the front, and write letters of solid slanders against them.... At the Red River, where we fought side by side with the Sixteenth Corps, he represented that we were broken through by the enemy, and that the Sixteenth Corps had to march over us.... For mean and wicked malice I never heard the like of these stories' " (233).

The most interesting of the Murrays, however, is Colonel Murray. With his soldier's lingo and wisdom, his impeccable military honor, and his rational religion, he resembles in his lofty moral beauty the white rose of Southern chivalry, Colonel Kershaw. In his wisdom Colonel Murray can discuss religion with Reverend Murray and can attempt, unsuccessfully, to show the good minister that a rational religion does not demand the existence of a devil, and that Darwinism does not invalidate essential Christian doctrines: " 'The Church actually did not know what a great and beneficent Deity it worshiped until the vastness of His creation was revealed to it by the anathematized star-gazers. Well, it accepted astronomy, and it has grown mightier on it. Some day it will accept evolution, and grow mightier on that' " (101). (Perhaps because of fear of offending the orthodox and perhaps because his own religious convictions had become more supernatural, De Forest cut the long dialogue on evolution from the manuscript which he wished eventually printed in an edition of his *Collected Works.*)

In his military fatalism and in his Christian charity, Colonel Murray can even exonerate Josie of blame in the deaths of the Reverend Murray and his wife, for from Colonel Murray's point of view "Life is a battle" (390), and the participants in the struggle kill one another not out of malice but to save oneself: "You get your ball, and it does for you. But the man who fired it did not aim at you. . . . Josie's faults are selfishness, dishonesty, and lying. She is not malignant" (390). Like De Forest himself, this "entirely sane Don Quixote" (97) is a patrician veteran ever ready with such apothegms as "Go through life by easy marches" (97); and, like De Forest also, Colonel Murray's reading has become increasingly scientific with age: "What with Max Muller and Whitney, and Galton and Lecky, and Spencer and Darwin, and forty more amazing chaps, I am up to my eyes in new ideas all the while" (104). Even the abundant white hair and the benevolent yet resolute look of Colonel Murray forecast precisely the appearance of De Forest in his later years.

The dominating characters of *Playing the Mischief*, however, are Josephine Murray and her two most persevering suitors, Sykes Drummond and G. W. Hollowbread. Drummond is a vulgar and pugnacious congressman with diabolical energy and a donkeyish laugh. In him is naked power, "the iron hand without any glove at all" (128); and his contempt for the weakness of others makes him quick to expose frailty and to gloat over it. His black eyes glow with unconcealed glints of passion, and his masculinity makes Squire Nancy, with whom he toys sexually, unable to look at him "without palpitating from beaver to boots" (129). Intelligent, he is partially able to control his gloating and his laughter when Josie points out to him that these personality traits only make enemies, but De Forest asserts the superficiality of the change (and reveals his own belief in biological determinism) when he comments: ". . . we are our ancestors over again. . . . Circumstances and education vary the transmitted type more or less in exteriors, but not at all in its inner nature. . . . This Sykes Drummond . . . , no matter how he might strive to polish his manners, would always be, in emergencies, and in forgetful moments, coarse, insolent, and masterful" (386).

To use such a creature and successfully to cast him off unpaid, as Josie does, is implausible; however, De Forest's increasing plot skill is apparent in the stroke by which he makes the action believable. What De Forest does is to have Drummond pretend to gentlemanliness so that he may completely win Josie's heart. After Josie's claim has been granted, therefore, Drummond writes a letter in which he releases her, because of her changed financial circumstances, from her engagement to him. At first femininely touched by Drummond's action, Josie quickly sees through it and accepts Drummond's offer. Drummond is left cursing over her letter to him and complaining: "She does not even thank me for my services. . . . In any body else I should call that ingratitude" (442).

The comic masterpiece of De Forest's novels may well be Congressman G. W. Hollowbread. In his works, and especially in *Playing the Mischief*, De Forest, like Hawthorne, constantly implies that human wisdom lies in the golden mean (in the delicate balancing of the heart and the head) and that human folly and villainy stem from a disproportion between heart and head. In Josie's elderly courtier Hollowbread, De Forest dramatizes a normally intelligent and conscientious man who loses both morality and common sense because he cannot control his heart. A masculine counterpart to the superannuated female flirts of whom De Forest is so fond, Hollowbread is a sartorial marvel from his dyed hair to his polished boots to his remarkable apparel "furnished with pads, straps, and springs. . . . It [seemed as if the clothing] might have buzzed and scrabbled away, of its own motion and internal force, like a clockwork locomotive" (183).

After Josie has "embezzled" the attention of Hollowbread in the first few paragraphs of the novel, he is the fool of love; even he realizes his absurdity as he wheezily searches for Josie's residence in a "maniacal rain" (66) that douses his hair and soaks him with humiliation and wrath. Josie's laughter, as she steps warm and dry from Hollowbread's carriage, forecasts Hollowbread's fate, and that prophecy is abundantly clear to Hollowbread himself after the Presidential reception where Josie uses him and his prestige and then leaves him wet and alone in the wintry wind. Walking home and thinking of her, Hollowbread realizes that Josie "will be the death of me" (146); and, by the time Josie is through with him, he is a broken man "ghastly in countenance and woe-begone in expression" (434), but worshiping until the end before the shrine of love. After Josie breaks her engagement to him, he becomes mentally ill, like Mrs. Chester of *Kate Beaumont;* but, where De Forest is totally contemptuous of Mrs. Chester, he is more sympathetic to Hollowbread. The result is a combination of absurdity and pathos that makes this elderly Mark Antony more human than any of the other elderly flirts of De Forest.

Ultimately, however, the achievement of *Playing the Mischief* rests on the bare and attractive shoulders of Josephine Murray. In the rogue tradition in literature, Josie may owe something to Twain and Warner's lobbying adventuress Laura Hopkins, who also has the devil in her; but Josie resembles even more Thackeray's Becky Sharp and De Forest's own Mrs. Larue. Reviewing the novel in *The Nation,* Henry James, appalled, denied the "slightest interest" in Josie because she is "a lying, thievish, totally heartless little jade without the faintest vestige of a moral nature."[64] De Forest's constant allusions in Indian terms to Josephine show that he is just as aware as James that he is dealing with a moral savage, but she is superficially an agreeable one, as De Forest noted in the ironic sentence with which he opened the novel: "Josephine Murray was one of those young women whom every body likes very much on a first acquaintance" (43).

In exploring Josie's audacious egotism, her instinctive lying and coquetting, her fondness for the unusual for its own sake and her love of love *pour le sport,* her chameleon agreeableness because of her lack of moral convictions, her artistic appreciation of moral beauty while completely lacking morality herself, her intelligence and wit and ready rationalizations, and her obsession with money and display—in dramatizing these facets of "the fine lady of the century" (161), De Forest illuminated a complexly real human. Through the moral blindness of Josie, he also made his essential point. To Josie he gives the defense of her plundering of the public treasury. She feels there is only justice in the payment of her claim, for, as she maintains, her tax upon the public is "only a quarter of a cent a head. The Crédit Mobilier took a dollar a head" (338). To her at least, there is unassailable logic in her contention that claims are an accepted part of American life: "There is something of the sort in almost every trade and profession. Bankers sell doubtful stocks to their customers, and don't hold their heads any lower for it.... Ever so many men are drawing irregular allowances.... Are women to have no such chances?" (337).

Such a defense of swindling does not persuade Colonel Murray, but it is hardly unique to Josie or the nineteenth century. If, as De Forest implies, Josie is sick and her perfidies are uncontrollable by herself alone, if she is as "possessed" by her heredity as Murray by his and Drummond by his, then it is

the obvious duty of society to curb her predatory nature. Society
has that power if it will but use it. If, however, honorable men
will neither vote nor enter Congress, then the governing body
of America will become the den of thieves that De Forest had
forecast that it might in the end pages of *Honest John Vane.*

Confronted with such characters and ideas as these, the
reviewers of *Playing the Mischief* shuddered in disgust. Henry
James complained that "De Forest has a great deal of cleverness,
but he overdoes his realism."[65] The reviewer of *Harper's* asserted
that De Forest should have devoted more time to "the brighter
and better side of American politics," and then he questioned the
taste of the "scalping" of well-known Washingtonians.[66] George
P. Lathrop in *The Atlantic* praised De Forest's humor and
then genteely commented that "The vulgar phases of society . . .
cover such a wide area . . . that they must be treated cautiously,—in glimpses only." Because De Forest had been excessively
attracted to the "vulgar phases of life . . . so plainly everywhere
around," he had succumbed to the "serious danger" (apparently
Realism) that was harming the work of American novelists.[67]

Such reviews did make *Playing the Mischief* something of a
*succès de scandale,* so that its sale of over six thousand copies
in book form made it the best-selling novel De Forest published
in his lifetime; but even today the novel has not received the
critical praise that is its due. No twentieth-century critic,
however, has been quite so unjust as Edmund Wilson.[68] One
can understand, if not agree with, Wilson's complaint that the
novel is "insupportably tedious," for De Forest is, perhaps, somewhat repetitious in his situations; and it is undeniably true that
his characters, like those in *Vanity Fair,* are much the same at
the end of the novel as at the beginning. However, Wilson's
statement that *Playing the Mischief* reveals De Forest's inability
to dramatize a scene is peculiar, for the novel is composed in
scenes which fully and dramatically explore individual and
national morals and manners. (The Presidential reception scene,
which runs some forty-five pages, has dialogue and visual effects
that seem almost cinematic.) Wilson's reference to the last scene
of *Playing the Mischief* as an illustration of De Forest's dramatic
weakness is especially unjust, for De Forest had no intention of
dramatizing that scene with the same kind of fullness that he had
used in the masterfully comic opening scene between Josephine
and Hollowbread. To have fully explored the last scene would
have necessitated another novel, that of the defeat of Josephine
and the revels of the animals over her carcass, and De Forest

was wise to imply and not to dramatize the despoliation of Josephine. He would have been even wiser to have ignored the moral convictions of his Victorian audience entirely and to have allowed Josephine, without the shadow of poetic justice hanging over her, to exult over her spoils.

## VIII  Justine's Lovers

In the last of his Washington novels, which he published anonymously in 1878, De Forest again illuminated his preoccupation with the golden mean, the divine balance, and because of this, *Justine's Lovers* may deserve some critical attention. The novel purports to be the autobiographical "confession" of Justine Vane, and the action is largely schoolgirl moonglow. When the novel begins, Justine and her recently widowed mother are living in well-to-do splendor in their palatial Boston mansion. Then Henry Starkenburgh, a rich young giant with the voice of an organ, enters the life of Justine. With this "Titan," the young heiress falls in love, and soon afterward the engagement of the couple is announced. Starkenburgh's physical stature, however, is larger than his moral one; and, when Justine's mother loses her fortune, Henry asks to be released from his engagement. The remainder of the novel depicts the attempts of the two women, totally unprepared for either work or struggle, to cope with life and poverty in the boardinghouse worlds of Boston and Washington.

Such a dilemma, De Forest could have depicted grimly and naturalistically, coolly and objectively, or warmly and sentimentally. Out of his desire to gain a popular audience, De Forest chose, as he admitted, "to imitate the ordinary 'woman's novel,'" and he was pleased at the fact that "Not a critic in the U. S. questioned the sex of the writer...."[69] In typical soap-opera vein, De Forest agonizes, with some realistic touches, over the difficulties of indigence and the harshness of humanity, but his prevailing tone asserts the brevity of poverty and the general goodness of mankind. By the end of the novel, De Forest has made another point dear to the heart of the sentimentalist: virtue and goodness in woman bring not only love but financial rewards. To dramatize this latter conviction, De Forest provides Justine with two gallants: a kind, rich, and sickly courtier, and a handsome, youthful, and selfless physician. From the courtier, who dies while Justine is engaged to him, Justine receives a new inheritance; and from Dr. Caswallon,

Justine will, no doubt, gain love and marriage. A sentimental reader could hardly ask for more.

To such romanticism, De Forest did add some realistic touches. Justine and her mother, for instance, discover the sheer indignity of destitution, and De Forest uses Justine's quest for a government post in Washington to show the humiliations that beset the poor. To beg for work and be rejected, to be told to be quiet and to have to obey meekly, to be insulted and to be able only to blush—these things are the facts that Justine thinks of when she notes "An experience of the reality makes one utterly impatient of the people who babble sentimentally" (9). Even more truthful to the facts of life was De Forest's disclosure that his heroine could act according to the dictates of her stomach rather than of her heart. One such instance occurs when Justine accepts the proposal of her elderly admirer, not because of the impulse of romantic love but because of the message of common sense which preaches (as does Justine's mother) that security is preferable to starvation. More fully, Justine's romantic image of herself is shattered when her elderly admirer dies and she does not as yet know that she is his heiress. At that point Henry Starkenburgh, who has already heard of her inheritance, writes to her and offers his hand in marriage anew. Though Justine knows how contemptible Henry is, and knows further that she does not love him, she is driven by "the irresistibleness of that tyrant, poverty!" to "feel that I *must* take him; that I did not want to, but simply must" (122). Though luck saves Justine from accepting Henry in fact, she has done so in thought and has implicitly accepted her mother's discovery that "there is one purpose in life worth notice, and that is ... not to starve" (121). Such violations of romantic credo make Justine fall below her ideal conception of herself, but she rises to a greater reality than those marvels of Mrs. Southworth who forever manage to preserve their honor both of body and of mind.

In Justine and her mother, De Forest showed two women learning to temper romantic emotionalism with hard common sense. In his polished villain Henry Starkenburgh he creates a monster whose excessive rationalism cuts him off from the nobler emotions of human kind. Starkenburgh's common sense makes him propose to Justine when she has money, and his prudence makes him draw back when Justine has lost her fortune. To him no other course is possible, and he cannot see the possibility of a more altruistic view. When Justine complains, after his second proposal, of his hot and cold conduct, he tries to make her see that she is "too sensitive, and too ... romantic." He explains that "Between persons of like fortune marriage is suitable, and is a subject of rational discussion and agreement" (129). Where excessive emotionalism has made Justine blind to Henry's real nature, excessive practicality makes Henry as grotesque as his proud, egoistic caricature of a mother.

Without doubt, *Justine's Lovers* preaches the beauty and the wisdom of the golden mean in matters of the affections, but De Forest also insists that the path between extremes is the road of wisdom in other realms. The foolishness of those radicals who agitated for complete Negro suffrage, De Forest disposed of through a wise old Negro mammy who tells of the uselessness of a round hole at the top of the entrance to her home: " 'Why, y see, my old man ... he built this shanty; an we had a cat, an' I kinder insisted that cat should have a hole to come in by, an' he cut one. But when he come to set up the do', that was the hole in the top on't. An' the cat he lived an' died, an' never got no good out on't, no more'n cullud folks doos out o' votin' '" (104).

De Forest also advises that radical reforms be avoided in the Civil Service. To dramatize this dominant political point of the novel, De Forest has Justine humbly apply for a Washington appointment. Then De Forest paints with a bitterness undoubtedly based on his own experiences as an office seeker, the portrait of a cold and ambitious politician, glad to be of use to those who can repay his favors but cool and even sadistic to those who need help the most. This callousness toward human need, De Forest complains, is a concomitant of the severity of the civil-service reforms inaugurated by President Hayes. Heartless administrators like the secretary of the civil service might dream of nobler ideals than the spoils system, but they might also tend toward inhumane rigidity of administration. The reformers would be wise, asserts De Forest, to temper their intellectual systems with some warmth of heart, to remember that people have intangible virtues as well as tangible abilities. Justine's lovers, all those good, kind people who helped her in her need, might not have the culture and the intellect of the secretary of the civil service; but from De Forest's point of view they have better qualifications for the post than its unnamed holder.

Such an argument for moderation in civil-service reform was, of course, consistent with De Forest's fondness for the golden

mean, but it is also undoubtedly true that the reasoning itself
stems from De Forest's bitterness at his treatment by Washington.
Creative rationalization may, of course, inspire both convincing
arguments and great art—but *Justine's Lovers* is neither of these.
The reviewer for the New York *Post* was charitable when he
proclaimed that the work was obviously by a "bright, clever,
witty and wise woman."[70] In our own time Arthur Hobson
Quinn is more accurate in his proclamation that *Justine's Lovers*
has "a few good moments, but they are very few."[71]

## IX  *Weakening Artistic Powers and Declining Productivity*

De Forest was always sensitive to criticisms of his work, and
at times when his work was condemned, he even burned
manuscripts over which he had labored;[72] without doubt the
harsh reception given *Playing the Mischief* and *Justine's Lovers*
must have affected him deeply. By 1879, also, the youthful deification he had once felt for literary men was waning, and he
announced publicly that he now believed "that the man who
best manages his fellow men—the great general or the great
statesman—is the leading man in the world in regard to ability."[73]
These feelings De Forest reflected in his final period, 1879-81,
as a magazinist. In a review of *The Life of David Glasgow
Farragut*, he emphasized his admiration for the disciplined life
of that religious and tender naval leader. Reviewing Froude's
*Caesar: A Sketch,* De Forest noted the literary fame of Froude
but, nevertheless, criticized the diffuse and rhetorical style of
the study and found especially regrettable the fact that a great
general should be analyzed by an author who knew nothing
about things military and was a little contemptuous of them.
As if to remedy the injustice done by Froude's volume, De
Forest published his own essay on "Caesar's Art of War and of
Writing." Showing his thorough familiarity with military strategy,
he praised the soldier-statesman Caesar for the promptness of
decision, rapidity of execution, and variety of methods that made
his genius unparalleled even by Napoleon. In addition De
Forest implied the things he valued in literary style when he
commented: "the constant composition of orders and instructions
teaches a general to be lucid and short, and leads him to look
upon the contrary qualities with distaste. . . . Caesar . . . produced
the best military narrative that ever was written."[74]

De Forest's feeling for the pre-eminence of military leaders
and statesmen is also apparent in his long essay on "Our Military

Past and Present" in which he ventures to advise America's leaders about the conduct of military affairs. Basing his advice on the nation's military past, De Forest concluded from the evidence that five steps were vital to future American security. Specifically, he first argued that the various state militia should be abolished, for, with few exceptions, the history of such militia was a "monotonous record of disaster and disgrace."[75] Second, he counseled that the state militia be replaced with a force of national volunteers. Third, he advised the creation of a sufficient permanent army. Fourth, he advocated the establishment, even in peace, of a national guard. Fifth, he suggested the wisdom of giving military instructions, based on the realities of war and not on the romanticizations of popular fiction, in high schools and universities. This advice is practical throughout, and Caesar might have praised the concise, lucid style.

De Forest, however, was no Caesar, and he had no worlds to conquer except literary ones. Though his interests by now were really elsewhere, he made two more attempts in this period to capture the popular audience that had so long eluded him. In 1879 he anonymously published *Irene the Missionary* in *The Atlantic*. Set in Syria during the Maronite and Druse warfare of 1859 and 1860 and drawing for its climax on the actual massacre of the Christians in Damascus on July 6, 1860, *Irene the Missionary* is as much travelogue as novel. The work drew upon the recollections of the Syrian landscape, folk, and customs which De Forest had treated earlier in *Oriental Acquaintance*. Especially, *Irene* was indebted to De Forest's memories of the Reverend Pomroy, who served as the novel's saintly Reverend Payson, and to his recollections of the Presbyterian mission where Dr. Henry De Forest and his wife had worked so arduously.

De Forest had no illusions about the merit of *Irene*. Occasionally he thought that some of his readers might conceive the author to be a young lady missionary. The fancy tickled De Forest, and the possibility was not at all remote. Save for De Forest's insistence on attempting his own version of Howells' realism of the commonplace, the narrative might easily have been duplicated by one of America's moral, sentimental females. Irene Grant, the heroine, is full of virtue, piety, and dullness; and, as De Forest conceded, "would have been a more entertaining personage had she been something of a flirt" (212). The death of her clergyman father has left her a penniless orphan, a staple of sentimental fiction; and her journey toward a strange land where she might serve as a benefactress to humanity was one of the more common daydreams of the Victorian era. Surrounding Irene constantly "is an atmosphere tinged with sober philanthropy and devoutness.... But this solemn pressure was no hardship, because it was no novelty and because it coincided with her conscience" (162).

The story of Irene takes place near ancient and exotic Mt. Lebanon, but her drama remains essentially the one that feminine hearts eternally love to ponder: the choice among suitors. Though Irene also feels she has the choice between love and duty, De Forest minimizes that conflict, and as a matter of fact, the choice among suitors lacks dramatic tension. The least attractive of Irene's courtiers is Porter Brassey, the American consul. A crass vulgarian with dreams of a political career, he has a taste for wine, cards, and American companionship; and he brings into the novel its only bite and life. In his nationalistic pride he is so contented with the American language that he belittles all others, and he is so fond of the varied splendors of America that he is sure that anything that can be found elsewhere can be found bigger and better in good old West Wolverine, U. S. A. Though Mr. Brassey plays the game of love craftily, his "shagbark rusticity and unpolished gnarliness" (185) leave Irene unmoved, and neither his amorous pertinaciousness nor his endowment of a Damascan mission softens her contempt for him.

A more attractive suitor is Doctor Macklin. In a land where doctors are more welcome than doctrines, Dr. Macklin's ministrations are necessary to the spiritual work of the mission. Though the doctor complains occasionally that he wishes he had less work and the minister had more, the doctor's dedication is apparent in the scorn with which he brushes aside the importance of the ague that often drives him, as it had Dr. Henry De Forest, shivering to his bed. Occasionally brusque and hotheaded, the doctor is always devoted to Irene; but, though he may deserve to be loved, his suit causes Irene more pleasure than pain. The reason is that her heart belongs to Hubertsen De Vries, a rich, suave, young American archaeologist. A comment that De Forest makes upon general female character is more reminiscent of the De Forest of *Playing the Mischief* than of the female author De Forest was pretending to be:

No matter for native dignity, for conscious worth of character, for noble or even sacred purposes in life. They all seem to fail . . . in presence of a fact which appeals to natural desires and strong needs of feminine nature. Money is power, and therefore aristocracy; moreover, it means decoration, beautifulness, and the gratification of vanity; finally, it shields one from bitter labor and the world's roughness and scorns. . . . the drift is toward the glitter (165).

Money moves Irene's heart toward De Vries, but he is a worthy young man as well. Something of a scholar, De Vries has considerable biblical and ethnological knowledge. He plans to write an exhaustive "History of the Rise and Decline of the Philistines," and some of his theories, such as his surmise that the biblical estimates of the size of the Philistine army are probably vast exaggerations, are reminiscent of De Forest's speculations on the Indians of Connecticut. Though not averse to an occasional innocent flirtation and not unaware of the pleasures of cards and wine, De Vries is happier in the moral atmosphere around Irene than he is elsewhere. When De Vries risks his life, in typical Fenimore Cooper vein, to rescue Irene from the terrors of Damascus during the massacre of 1860, her heart is completely won. She wishes to shout her love for him when he proposes, but one problem remains: the fact that her religion differs from his. (Precisely how their religions differ, De Forest does not tell, but De Vries' belief in a creator does not keep his Protestantism from seeming more liberal and rational than the orthodoxy of Irene.)

Irene looks for council to the Reverend Payson, a rather conventional figure of a tolerant, modest, and holy man, living in the world but a little above it and a trifle absent-minded in it. The Reverend Payson shows true Christianity in his espousal of religious tolerance—an attitude that De Forest contrasts satirically to the fanaticism of fundamentalist and millenarian religionists—and soon afterward the marriage follows. After that— that's another story, as De Forest says. Typical of many popular novels of the time, however, he does provide a few glimpses of the future: De Vries is to command wisely and fight valiantly during the Civil War; Porter Brassey is to go to Congress; and Dr. Macklin is to return to America, find and marry a young lady surprisingly resembling Irene, and then return happily married to his mission post in Syria.

In its own time *Irene* aroused some interest because of its exploration of a land where the sublime past seemed forever brooding upon the beautiful present, but unfortunately De Forest never fully realized either the contrast between Syrian life and American manners or the subtleties of his American and Syrian characters. While the novel was appearing in *The Atlantic,* the New York *Times* complained that "Irene and her confederates"

make "one long for the good old cannibal days."[76] Most critics
have agreed. Among the few exceptions was *The Atlantic,* which
loyally praised *Irene* for depicting missionaries as ordinary people
living real, though commonplace, lives.[77] And Edmund Wilson has
recently added to his eccentric judgments on De Forest by praising *Irene* as "one of the most readable of De Forest's novels."[78]

The last novel that De Forest published during his career as
a magazinist was *The Bloody Chasm,* which was first published
in 1881 and then reprinted a year later under the title *The
Oddest of Courtships.* Quite possibly inspired by the popular
success of *A Fool's Errand,* Albion Tourgée's dramatization of
the failure of American Reconstruction policy, *The Bloody Chasm*
dramatized De Forest's feeling that the hatred and bitterness
occasioned by the war would die down in time. Like a passionate
but foolish woman, the South, De Forest affirmed, could be won
back to belief in the Union by kind and sympathetic courtship.
Though the idea was neither original nor profound, De Forest
might have used the actualities of his experiences in South Carolina to write a moving and truthful allegorization of the agonies
of Reconstruction. *The Bloody Chasm* is not such a book.

The novel opens shortly after the end of the Civil War, and
the contrivance which dominates the narrative is the fancy of
Silas Mather, an elderly Bostonian, that his Northern nephew,
Colonel Harry Underhill, marry Mr. Mather's Southern niece,
Miss Virginia Beaufort. When the old Puritan dies, he leaves a
fortune to Miss Beaufort, but it is to come to her only if she
marries Underhill. Despite her pride in her Southern lineage and
her hatred for the Yankees who killed her brothers in the war,
Miss Beaufort is forced by poverty to agree to such a marriage.
Underhill, out of kindness and a "poetic" temperament, accepts
the union also. Miss Beaufort comes to the ceremony gowned in
black, suggestive of the South's feeling that forced union with
the North is a funereal occasion, and soon afterward the couple
part. Miss Beaufort has never seen the face of her husband and
never intends to, and from that fact comes the odd courtship
in which a husband changes his name in order to woo his own
wife. Underhill vows he will win that beautiful stronghold "as
surely as the North won the South" (145). Eventually Miss
Beaufort, like Miss Ravenel before her, is converted by love
into a recognition of Northern virtue. She loses her Southern
bitterness so completely that she speaks fondly of her husband's
irregular courtship as a "regular Yankee trick. Oh, you darling
humbug" (299).

The plot of *The Bloody Chasm* is obviously absurd, even in a summary which omits the coincidences and digressions, and the characters are impaled upon the implausibilities of the allegory. The novel's only interest is in its renewed expression of the figure in the carpet in De Forest's work: his conviction of the superiority of moderation over extremes. Most fully in *The Bloody Chasm,* De Forest dramatizes the folly of fanaticism through Virginia Beaufort. A gentlewoman, she is "the product of years of grandeeism and civil war" (92). The subjection of the South has humiliated her, but this "flower of the low country" (26) has learned little through defeat. Her pride in her aristocratic Beaufort blood, her love for the South, her hatred for the North—these have only been intensified by the war. What she must learn is the narrowness of her view, and this she discovers when she uses the Yankee dollars of Silas Mather to move to Paris. With time and study comes a new knowledge, and she changes from a creature who was "a little like a noble savage" to one "fit to be a queen of civilized men" (218). With a new environment comes a greater cosmopolitanism, and she discerns that Charleston is but a hamlet and that the greatness of America lies largely in its unity. Most important, she finds that her hatred is dying with the passage of time. Though she clings to her bitterness as best she can and though she feels guilty at betraying her dead, she will no longer dispute with those who tell her that "true policy, as well as true magnanimity, consists in forgetting our enmities as faithfully as we remember our friendships" (206). Even her pride in her hatred is attacked when she hears that the soldiers of the war have lost their rancor, and only the women and the politicians keep the animosity burning. Slowly she becomes willing, as her view enlarges, to forgive, and in time she is fully conquered by the devotion she gives her husband. By her love, which is only possible because she has lost her insularism, Virginia bridges the chasm between North and South, and De Forest implies that only through a similar loss of sectionalism and rejection of hatred can a stable union between North and South be created.

De Forest makes much the same point through the old Boston Puritan, Silas Mather. Walking around the ruins of the city of Charleston, the stern old Puritan views the decimation as an act of Providence visited upon a modern Babylon, and with satisfaction he muses that this is the just result of rebellion and undeniable proof of "the overruling watchfulness of a holy Creator and Governor" (21). This vengefulness, however, is mastered by a greater passion—the love Silas has for his wife. Because of her deathbed request that Silas aid her Southern kinsmen, he conquers his rancor, humbles his pride, and does his best to aid his niece despite her bitterness toward Yankees. His victory over hatred makes Silas a larger and more Christian man than the rigid abolitionist he once had been. Out of his love for his wife, his compassion for his niece, and his forgiveness of the South, he makes his strange bequest, and by his desire for union between North and South, he personally spans the bloody chasm before his death.

Where Silas and Virginia conquer the narrowness that causes hatred and fomented the Civil War, Harry Underhill has a moral breadth, despite some sexual weaknesses, that saves him from fanaticism. His tolerance, like that of an old Southern general named Hilton, stems from the experiences of war. These have taught him objectivity, for "A soldier learns. . . . to worship valor no matter where found" (239). This ability to see both sides makes Colonel Underhill able to write a moving poem about Southern valor, and in another way it makes him able to see the lesson of such pictures as the "Decline of the Romans" and "Calling of the Condemned": " 'The one is a protest against unbridled Caesarism, and the other a protest against unbridled democracy. I presume that they were placed opposite each other by design. It is as much as to say, 'That leads to this and this leads to that' " (244). From this ability to see the horror of extremes come compassion, moderation, and common sense. Though the United States might have underrated these values during the Civil War, they were desperately needed, as the carpetbaggers and Klu Klux Klan had shown and still were showing during the Reconstruction. *The Bloody Chasm* is a reminder of that need.

The best writing of *The Bloody Chasm* comes in the early pages, where De Forest realistically depicts the destruction, poverty, and humiliation that the war brought Charleston. In these early pages, too, De Forest depicts at some length the only two people in *The Bloody Chasm* that have the feel of reality. These are the old Negro servants, Phil and Mauma Chlo. Obviously inspired by the cliché of the devoted slave, forever loyal to the kind old master, Phil and Mauma, at least before they come to Paris, go somewhat beyond the stereotype. They are proud to be free and are willing to say so even in Charleston: "Niggers is dreffull poo' folks dese yere days. All de same, we'd ruther be our own poo' folks, an' not somebody else's" (31).

They are memorable for their simple morality, their common sense, and their lack of hatred—all of which contrast strikingly to the artificiality and folly of the Southern aristocracy.

Perhaps the most annoying of the many flaws of *The Bloody Chasm* is the thematic confusion De Forest engenders by a subplot in which Colonel Underhill dallies with a young Catholic songstress named Norah Macmorran. His interest in her is largely inspired by his love for music, and his renunciation of her comes from his feeling that she belongs to a different religion and a lower social caste from him. From the situation De Forest manages to wring a good deal of sentiment, but the inspiration of Colonel Underhill's affection seems frivolous (and becomes unintentionally comic with such statements as "I really ... want a musical wife, so far as I want one at all" [106]), while the renunciation of Miss Macmorran because her family is "not of our sort" (108) shows ideas of caste that conflict with the democratic theme implied in the dominant narrative. The musical motivation suggests the shallowness of character and the implausibility of action which exist throughout *The Bloody Chasm,* while the disorder in theme reflects the confusion that De Forest personally had about the extent to which democracy should extend. Though he could respect the humble laboring class, embodied in such characters as Miss Macmorran's washerwoman mother, and though he was certain that the Negroes deserved to be free, he was still sure that the Macmorrans and the Negroes were different from the Underhills, the Beauforts, and the De Forests. Common sense, for De Forest, implied that a marriage between an aristocrat and a member of the lower classes had little chance of success. Blood was blood and environment was environment. Puritans should marry Puritans; Catholics, Catholics; Negroes, Negroes. In time perhaps the social chasm might be bridged, but for De Forest it was probably deeper than the bloody chasm.

By the time of the publication of *The Bloody Chasm,* De Forest was close to being an unknown American writer, and the novel was virtually ignored by reviewers. Even *The Atlantic* could find no space for a notice. The only review of any significance appeared in *The Nation.* The reviewer, Arthur G. Sedgwick, lectured De Forest for writing a romance, and then noted that De Forest did have some talent as a humorist and should work that vein more fully in the future.[79] To the grey-haired author of *Miss Ravenel* and *Playing the Mischief,* this advice must have seemed hilarious.

### CHAPTER 5

# 'To Leave a Small Monument'

## I  *Last Years: 1881-1906*

IN 1880, after he had received his B.A. degree and then spent a year at the Yale Medical School, Louis Shepard De Forest set out to study medicine in Germany. With his son gone, John W. De Forest became increasingly restless in New Haven. In June of 1881 he left for New York City. Almost a year later he wrote Professor Eaton of Yale that possibly some day he might return to New Haven. Because of that he wished his membership renewed in St. Hubert's, a shooting club where he and Eaton were friendly rivals. Referring to the dyspepsia that plagued him in his later years, De Forest recommended the Swedish Movement Cure that he had been undergoing in New York, but he confessed that the cure was "not, alas, a panacea; it will not save a man from catching cold."[1]

By 1883, De Forest had returned to New Haven, where, for the most part, his life was uneventful and secluded. De Forest may well have been moodily thinking of his own situation as an American democrat aware of the weaknesses of American democracy when he wrote the scholar Thomas Lounsbury to congratulate him upon his biography of James Fenimore Cooper. Praising Lounsbury for doing justice to the "noble, hearty, fervid nature" of Cooper, De Forest added that he was especially pleased that Lounsbury had "done justice to some of the curs that nagged him [Cooper]. What an insight you have into the mingled donkeyhood and malignity and indolence of contemporary criticism."[2] When Lounsbury responded to this praise, De Forest wrote again to repeat it; but, as if fearful that his health and his work might be threatened, De Forest concluded: "I write all this because I don't make calls. I have positively given up going out evenings. My mornings are spent in writing and my afternoons in hard walking, both necessary."[3]

During these months the urge to travel must have gnawed at

De Forest. This desire he satisfied momentarily by a visit to Nova Scotia in August, 1883. From Halifax, at any rate, he responded to Thomas Bailey Aldrich's request for a novel for *The Atlantic* by writing that he was doing another kind of work and that he would certainly "not write a novel for a year or two, if indeed I ever do. Meantime I am glad to hear that American novels sell, though it sounds like a fairy story."[4]

What De Forest was working upon was undoubtedly a genealogical study of the De Forest line. Upon this study De Forest, in his later years, spent considerable money and vast amounts of time. In 1884, despite his modest finances and uncertain health, he set out for Europe to continue his exploration of his family crest and ancestry. From Nice he wrote his son a bit of fatherly advice upon the study of languages (French and German, he felt, were far superior to Spanish, both in practical and literary merit). Then, after some humorous comment upon the madness of carnival time in Nice, he compared the petty losses of the British in the Sudan to the destructiveness of the battles of the Civil War. The end of the Sudanese revolt, in which spears were fighting against guns, seemed inevitable to him: "good shooting rules the world now; and if one side can shoot and the other can't, it's no fair fight."[5] A month later, when he learned that his son had signed up for more academic courses, De Forest wrote a lecturing epistle. Noting how "very extraordinary" it was that Louis had not yet received his degree, De Forest asserted that Louis should finish his doctorate studies immediately. Insistently De Forest repeated that he had little money to spare and "We should be in a very bad box if we should find ourselves . . . obliged to work our way home in the steerage."[6] Because of his perilous financial situation, De Forest wrote from Paris to James Russell Lowell, the American Ambassador in London, to ask if there was any chance that the English might be interested in De Forest's work. Not without pathos is De Forest's comment: "You remember that Miller succeeded with the English when he had failed with his own countrymen."[7]

Though Lowell had neither financial nor artistic encouragement to offer his countryman, the De Forests, father and son, did manage to return to America without working in the steerage. A year or so after his return to New Haven, De Forest wrote the editor of *The Century* to inquire if the magazine might be interested in a manuscript that De Forest had recently completed. *The Century* answered briefly that the magazine had manuscripts for several years in advance. To this chilly response De Forest answered by sending a brief description of his novel:

It is called *A Daughter of Toil:*—One of the romances of working life.

It is the story of a poor and good girl, who by dint of worth and favoring chances, struggles up to—the best she can get. The heroine and her fortunes are drawn from life, though the incidents are greatly disguised through a sense of decorum. The scene is mainly in New York City, with episodes in the country and in Europe.

The characters, both high and low, are largely portraits. The plot partakes of the nature of romance; that is, when we see such things we call them romantic. The treatment is straightforward narration, with a great deal of dialog and very little analysis.[8]

The outline did not entice *The Century,* and other magazines were no more encouraging. When De Forest began to read the magazine version of Howells' *The Apprenticeship of Lemuel Barker* (published in book form as *The Minister's Charge*), he noted the similarity between his own novel and that of Howells. To his friend he wrote to avow that *A Daughter of Toil* was not an attempt to grasp "at your thunder."[9] The completion of Howells' novel left De Forest full of "wonder and praise," and in admiration of Howells' "realistic philosophy and . . . martyr like valor in standing to a true confession of it," De Forest asked:

How dare you speak out your beliefs as you do? You spare neither manhood nor womanhood, and especially not the latter, though it furnishes four-fifths of *our* novel-reading public. . . .

Indeed I wonder in my admiration of your heroism, if you quite know what you are about. You are exposing to view the base metal and coarse clay of which nearly the whole American people is fabricated; and meantime this slag and half-baked mud is so conceited of itself, and so shop-girlishly touchy in its conceit!

Finally, in this long letter, De Forest noted that in *A Daughter of Toil* he had an old gentleman, not to be mistaken for himself, speak out against the Howellsian Realistic credo. That old codger, with his coat of arms and his preference for high-born heroes to low-born clods, had to be given his say, proclaimed De Forest; for "What less can a sincere minded novelist do? Though I regret to confess that I am not always sincerely spoken in my stories." Curiously, however, De Forest then avowed that he was not totally unsympathetic to the old gentleman's view, and he lectured Howells upon Realistic and Romantic fiction:

> I do believe, unlike yourself apparently, that the two kinds of fiction are equally allowable and in a certain sense equally true. Each is the result of a selection; for we cannot tell the whole life, even of a country village; we must choose some characters for our painting, and shut our eyes to others. Now we may select the Othello and Desdemona of the place, who go together to flashing ruin; or we may select the Lem Baker [sic] and Stira [sic] Dudley who fizzle out like the mass of vulgar-born people. Let each one select what he can best paint.[10]

In a diplomatic response to De Forest, Howells claimed that he would be interested to see what De Forest's aristocrat had to say upon Realism; noted that possibly De Forest had less sympathy than he himself for "poor, silly American girls"; and then acknowledged: "it was your bold grappling with the fact of the robust lives ... of our nation that gave me courage to deal with it in Lemuel and 'Modern Instance.' It's odd that no one touched it before you."[11]

De Forest needed such praise, and Howells' letter—as well as his acclaim of De Forest in the February, 1887, *Harper's*—led De Forest, after thanking Howells, to comment sardonically: "Can it be ... that I was a great man once for a little while, and missed knowing it? If so, I hope the thing will yet come to light publicly,—say after we get an international copyright law passed,—a century or so hence."[12] One reason that De Forest so needed Howells' praise was that for the first time in his career he was finding it difficult to publish his work. No one would accept *A Daughter of Toil,* and De Forest probably destroyed it in despair—or at least De Forest's son remembers that his father in despondency burned about this time a long manuscript.[13] That mood could only have been intensified when De Forest finished an early version of what was probably *A Lover's Revolt*—at least he described the work he sent *The Century* in 1887 as "a historical novel of the Revolutionary period"[14]—and no one was willing to publish it either as a magazine serial or as a book.

The chill of publishers, the unprofitability of novel writing, the decline of De Forest's artistic powers, and the fact that in 1888 De Forest was willed around $20,000 on the death of his first cousin Erasmus L. De Forest—all these undoubtedly account for the relative literary silence of De Forest after 1885.

He was never, however, able to give up entirely his dream of literary fame, and so in the last twenty years of his life he did a good bit of literary dabbling. One result of this avocational interest was the publication in 1898 of *A Lover's Revolt*, a work which De Forest claimed to have rewritten three times in the five years before its publication. This novel brought De Forest briefly out of the obscurity into which he had fallen, and a visitor from the New York *Times* interviewed De Forest at New Haven's Hotel Garde. In this large, shabby railroad hotel, where he lived intermittently from 1890 until the onset of his fatal illness in 1903, De Forest had a third floor room which was furnished with a bed, traveling trunk, two easy chairs, a table, and a "library" in the clothes closet. Here De Forest read the few novelists he was still interested in—Howells, Zola, and Tolstoi—and immersed himself in the scientific and ethnological interests that so absorbed him in his declining years.

In this setting, De Forest struck the interviewer as a "hale and hearty ... well preserved gentleman" with a cheerful, breezy manner and a fondness for a nomadic hotel existence. Noting De Forest's "straight carriage" and "kindly eye," the interviewer then let De Forest lapse into reminiscence about his military and artistic career, his new novel, modern writing generally and Stephen Crane particularly, and De Forest's interest in genealogy. For his new novel, the white-bearded author, so strongly resembling the stereotyped vision of a Southern colonel, made no great claims; he only asserted that he had attempted to show how sentiment and pride had much to do with causing the Revolutionary War. For *The Red Badge of Courage*, as an example of the new fiction—"so entirely different from the way they used to write in my day"—De Forest had considerable praise. At the same time the old realist could not help noting that, though Crane's depiction of battle was excellent, "I never saw a battery that could charge at full speed across a meadow."[15]

In addition to his work upon *A Lover's Revolt* in these years, De Forest searched painstakingly and lovingly for the De Forest crest, castle, and coat of arms, and his work eventually bore fruit in 1900 as the genealogical study *The De Forests of Avesnes*. Of more literary significance, De Forest collected and organized his Civil War and Reconstruction essays into two complete manuscripts; collected his fugitive verse; and occasionally fretted over the four verse-tales that he published as *The Downing Legends*. An anonymous, condescending review in the Baltimore *Sun* (August 29, 1901) implies the state of De Forest's reputation at the time by the critic's mocking confession that "J. W. De Forest is, as we learn from the title page of the work before us, author of fourteen previous works, and alas! we have never heard of him before this day."

Closer to his heart than his poetic efforts, which De Forest himself compared to the preoccupation of "the bedridden granny who whiled away the hours in getting the cracker crumbs out of the bed,"[16] was De Forest's desire to see a collected edition of his works published before his death. He first began to think of the edition around 1884, and early in that year he wrote to Harper's about the possibility of acquiring the copyright for *Miss Ravenel, Playing the Mischief*, and *Justine's Lovers*. The terms which Harper's suggested were beyond de Forest's purse, and for the next three years he attempted, unsuccessfully, to interest a publisher in the collected works. On May 2, 1887, he again wrote to Harper's. Noting the uselessness of the Harper plates for a uniform edition, he offered seventy-five dollars for the three novels, said he could afford no more, asserted that the sale of the collected edition would probably not cover his own expenses, and concluded: "My only object is to leave a small monument for myself. And I must hurry."[17] Soon afterward, Harper's accepted De Forest's offer and returned him the copyright of his novels. De Forest set about making minor revisions, and Howells encouraged him, perhaps without even being aware of De Forest's dream, by writing that possibly a uniform edition of De Forest's works would now sell: "I do believe the public has been growing toward your kind of work. . . . Good Lord! When one thinks of Stevenson and Haggard selling their tens of thousands and you lacking a publisher, it is hard to be patient."[18] No publisher, however, shared Howells' optimism, and the passage of time made De Forest himself more and more unable to bear the costs of publication. Though Howells, as late as 1895, was still pressing the idea of a uniform edition,[19] De Forest by then had long abandoned the project.

In his later years, despite the bequest of his cousin in 1888, simple survival became something of a problem for De Forest. As early as 1890 he applied for a Civil War pension, and in 1902 he renewed his application. Of the latter petition, De Forest's son has noted: " . . . he was always hard pressed—in some years desperately so—for money. Some four years before his death his health was failing and his expenses mounting and he applied for a service pension—$12 a month. I was on the Pension Board at the time but was not present for the examination. The pension was given on account of the heart disease which finally caused his sudden death."[20]

In 1903, a year before his pension began, De Forest was admitted to the New Haven Hospital. Largely bedridden for the rest of his life, he spent his last months at his son's home in New Haven. His granddaughter still recalls the groans that came from De Forest's room during those last painful months, but she remembers also that De Forest never faltered in his religious faith.[21] In his son's home De Forest died on July 17, 1906. He was buried in the Grove Street Cemetery of New Haven. The simple tombstone that marks his grave is figured by a crossed saber and a pen. At the entrance to this cemetery there is a list of the distinguished people buried there. De Forest's name is not among them.

## II  *Last Publications*

Though the fiction and the poetry that De Forest published in his later years are not great art, nor even significant literature, they are worthy of brief examination if only because they are so illuminative of the central weakness in De Forest's body of work. That weakness is an inconsistency of tone, and it shows up dramatically in *A Lover's Revolt* and in the two volumes of poetry *Medley and Palestina* and *The Downing Legends*.

De Forest's last novel resembles in some ways his first, *Witching Times*. Set during the beginnings of the American Revolution, *A Lover's Revolt* combines historical narrative with a love tale. The former, into which De Forest introduces in minor roles such historical personages as the American patriot Dr. Joseph Warren and the British soldier General Gage, dramatizes such historic events as the battles of Lexington, Concord, and Bunker Hill; it ends with the British abandonment of the city of Boston and the entrance of the victorious American troops, an event which De Forest makes simultaneous with the death of an old Tory sycophant who "dies like an empire in convulsions" (413). Among the conquering forces is the hero of the novel, Asahel Farnlee, who enters Boston with "his black eyes sparkling and his dark aquiline face flushed with triumph, an incarnation of the coming republic" (416).

The subordinate narrative works, though in tragic vein, the one subject that De Forest felt continually appealed to an American audience: the sexual triangle. The figures in the triangle are the British soldier, Captain Moorcastle; the American patriot, Asahel Farnlee; and the foolish heroine, Huldah Oakbridge. Huldah's tragedy begins when she rejects the true love of "Ash" Farnlee in order to strive to capture the epaulettes of Captain Moorcastle. By rejecting a man who looks upon her as an equal in order to fawn upon a Briton who sees her as a mere colonial, Huldah invites her own humiliation. In the agony she goes through upon being spurned by Moorcastle, Huldah goes mad, and her insanity brings about her accidental death while she is wandering in search of her British captain.

In both his war narrative and his love tale, De Forest insists upon one point: dignity, respect, and love can only exist among equals. The master-subject relationship between England and America breeds contempt on one side and toadyism on the other, and only when these castes of mentality have disappeared can better relationships begin. The novel dramatizes the American victory on the field of battle, but in a last-page poetic "Sequel" De Forest complains that the "brave continentals" died fruitlessly. Americans still remain colonials, he asserts; and he especially laments the fate of "Yankeedom's artists" who "abide in shadows till Britons have praised." In the last stanza of the "Sequel," De Forest, like Emerson, Melville, and Whitman before him, demands that the American Eagle shout a "Clamor of challenge, a yawp claiming your soul as your own," and he invites the American people to "Rise and declare what you like, nor care if you like it alone" (417).

Such is the action of the novel and its hortatory "Sequel." Of these materials De Forest might have made a memorable tale, and A Lover's Revolt does have some segments that are admirably done: the initial description of Boston accumulates the details of commonplace sights and sounds that make for reality; De Forest's probings into the mind of "Ash" Farnlee before, during, and after battle have passages that are not greatly inferior to the psychological penetration of The Red Badge of Courage; passages in the warfaring adventures of the Yankee Bumpkin Abner Sly capture the dialect, shrewdness, hypocrisy, practicality—the tang, in short, of a native type; and, finally, De Forest's depiction of Huldah Oakbridge's mad wanderings has effective moments, as, for instance, when De Forest, undoubtedly remembering the climactic scene of Hawthorne's "My Kinsman, Major Molineux," has Huldah pause in her ramblings to observe the horror of her Tory uncle being daubed with tar and feathers: "And when the shining stickiness descended upon the hair and flinching features and decent raiment of the victim ... the poor, light-headed girl poured forth scream on scream of laughter, so shrilly wild that the noisiest louts there present faced about with open mouths to stare at her" (388).

These elements of *A Lover's Revolt* are, without doubt, effective. Nevertheless, and contrary to Edmund Wilson's opinion that *A Lover's Revolt* is De Forest's "most genuinely searching novel,"[22] the work rivals *Overland* as a tale for adolescents. The plot, in its continual shifts from love story to war narrative, seems disconnected, and probably the best part in the entire novel is the six-chapter digression upon the humorous adventures and misadventures of Abner Sly. Numbers of De Forest's people are caricatures whose actions are as implausible as their mentality is unreal; and, in its lack of restraint, the portraiture of such Tory bootlickers as Uncle Fenn and Sister Ann becomes unintentionally comic. The infatuation of Huldah for Captain Moorcastle is based upon one family dinner, one short kiss, and no more than three hours of conversation; and, though her lovesick foolishness can be believed, her madness lacks sufficient motivation. The writing of the novel is pedestrian, and it overflows with a chauvinism that made even the loyal Howells complain that it was "too thumpingly patriotic for my pleasure."[23]

One climactic scene may suggest some of the defects of *A Lover's Revolt*. Near the end of the novel Captain Moorcastle discovers Ash Farnlee working in Boston as an American spy. When the two men confront each other in Ash's place of concealment after he has spared Captain Moorcastle's life, the captain does not wish to be the cause of Farnlee's capture and execution. Moorcastle, therefore, offers Farnlee the excuse that he may well have come to Boston to see Huldah, not to spy. Despite the peril that an admission of his spying implies, Ash Farnlee, because of his honor, cannot accept the invitation to lie and thus save his own skin as well as aid the American cause. Such simplified morality is implausible, but the improbabilities of the scene increase as the two men turn to meditations upon their relationship to Huldah. When Ash tells of his agony at the loss of his beloved, Moorcastle, who has been painted previously as the epitome of snobbishness and egoism, gasps sympathetically and seems to be suffering physically. Then, because he feels that he is responsible for making Ash suffer over the loss of Huldah, Captain Moorcastle decides that he cannot possibly turn in his prisoner to the British authorities. After this remarkable *non-sequitur*, the two men begin to meditate upon the causes of the war. Ash notes that he had had no interest in politics until Huldah's preference in lovers made him resent the assumption that Englishmen were superior to Americans, and Captain Moorcastle philosophizes that Ash's feeling "points to a war for independence. It's a deeper question than the question of taxation" (364). Ash agrees that the fundamental causes of the war go deeper than economic ones, and he asserts that only "blood, and much blood" (365) will settle the quarrel.

After this friendly personal and philosophic discussion, Moorcastle aids Farnlee to escape, and then the Briton resigns his commission because he feels that he "has dishonored his military oath by freeing Ash" (367). For a while he is bitter against women because he feels that it is they who get him into such moral dilemmas, but De Forest notes that his bitterness is only momentary, for he is one of those men "whose lives are ruled by the impulses of temperament as a St. Vitus patient is jerked hither and thither by his malady" (367).

This scene and its aftermath are interesting because they so obviously reveal De Forest's artistic incongruities. On the one hand the scene is an endeavor to make Captain Moorcastle something more than the conventional hard-hearted, swaggering, egoistic villain he has hitherto been—an attempt to endow him with the kind of realistic complexity that De Forest had achieved with Colonel Carter in *Miss Ravenel*. At the same time the scene is a perfect example of the necessities of a romantic plot situation triumphing over the truth of character, for until this point Moorcastle and Farnlee have been instinctively hostile toward each other—Moorcastle's contempt for Americans has previously made Farnlee writhe with humiliation and hatred—and it is impossible to believe in the sudden cordiality and consideration the two men show each other.

This scene illustrates in yet another way De Forest's confused mixture of Realism and Romance. In his urge toward Realism De Forest is attempting to give the true, ordinary, commonplace cause of the war when he has his characters suggest that hurt pride, not economic causation or philosophic abstractions, made the war inevitable. On the other hand, the cause De Forest advances is a glaring oversimplification, in its way comparable to the deep-dyed villains and the snow-white heroines that inhabit the worst of romantic fiction. Because of this mixture of Romanticism and Realism, *A Lover's Revolt* is one of De Forest's more disoriented novels, and its failure, as in so much of De Forest's fiction, stems from the fact that De Forest was unable to achieve the artistic discipline or perception or integrity to

decide what he wanted to do and to do only that. Edmund
Wilson is wrong when he claims that De Forest's mind "never
attained to anything like a real point of view, to any sort of
general philosophy of society, politics, morals,"[24] for De Forest
did, in his continual espousal of political and religious moderation, have a general philosophic point of view. What De Forest
didn't have was an adequate philosophy and a consistent
practice of realistic art. In his art he too often attempted a
kind of artistic moderation, a little bit of Realism and a little
bit of Romance, and this inconsistency of tone is the greatest
cause of the weakness of so much of De Forest's fiction. Born
earlier or later, De Forest would undoubtedly have been a less
confused writer, and perhaps a less interesting one. His fate,
however, was to be an artist who points both backward and forward, and his art was most meritorious when it looked forward.

De Forest's role as a transitional writer whose talent is
realistic and satiric, not romantic, is shown in no place more
clearly than in his verse. De Forest was no poet. In his wiser
moments he realized it, as when he wrote his brother George
to confess that his verses lacked "much poetic vigor or originality.... The odor of Parnassus is not very strong in them."[25]
Despite this knowledge, De Forest could never quite forget the
dream of poetic fame, and in the last years of his life, he
published at his own expense two volumes of verse, much of it
written many years earlier. The worst of his poetry is the
mystically religious work that makes up the "Palestina" section
of the volume *Medley and Palestina*. Its "grim ... versification
and phraseology," as one critic put it,[26] may be suggested by
the two opening stanzas of "Hosea's Curse":

> Ephraim forgetteth Sinai's El,
> And buildeth fanes to calves of gold;
> His Baalim-stones are manifold,
> His altars burden hill and dell.

> Yet shall he tremble with affright
> Because of the shame of Beth Aven,
> Where batten the vulture and raven,
> And smoke of offering dims the sight (156).

Not quite so grim, and certainly not so full of the eternal
allusions to Baal, Ashtaroth, Agag, Amulek, Edom, Yahveh, and
the like, is the "Medley" section of *Medley and Palestina*. The
war poems of this section, however, are filled with clichés and
chauvinism, and most of the other lyrical poems of the section

owe as much to Poe and Longfellow as to De Forest. A typical passage from one of the battle poems, this one celebrating the arrival of Sheridan at Winchester, implies their merit:

> He came! the Roland of our cause!
> He came! we needed but his glance
> To halt, to rally, and advance,
> To strike as 'twere a dying blow,
> And see the day all laureled go (17).

The opening of "The Owl" indicates one essential source of De Forest's poetic indebtedness:

> All day he sits in his virtuous dome
> On the mantel stand of the hotel hall,
> And stares at naught like a scornful gnome,
> Regardless of me, and thee, and all . . . (31).

Of the entire volume, the only verses that have anything approaching merit are those of "The Lottery Valentine," discussed earlier, and the two satirical forays "Lochinvar in the South" and "Judge Boodle." In "Lochinvar" De Forest mocks the romantic vein he has been striving so desperately to mine in other poems, and though the stanzas are certainly not high poetry, they are, as suggested by the opening lines, at least mildly humorous:

> Oh, young Lochinvar is around in the South!
> He has plenty of muscle and plenty of mouth;
> Through all the Tar Country his gun is the best,
> And his knife is plumb ready inside of his vest (89).

Mark Twain, with his contempt for the caste of mind that glorified Sir Walter Scott in the American South, would have liked "Lochinvar," and he would also have appreciated De Forest's other poetic satire "Judge Boodle." Reminiscent of *Playing the Mischief,* the poem has moments of good fun as Judge Boodle helps his lady fair, a humorous portrait of *la belle dame sans merci* luring the judge on to hell, to gain a claim for recompense for a horse long dead. In his efforts

> . . . Boodle every wire did pull,
> Rolled logs with all creation,
> And piped our glorious Capitol
> To push his legislation (93).

Such verses as these indicate that De Forest's rhyming talents, such as they were, lay more in the direction of satire, so closely aligned to Realism, than to lyricism, so intimately connected with Romanticism. In his second volume of poetry, a collection of four stories in rhyme that he called *The Downing Legends,* De Forest shows even more vividly the unresolved tensions between Romance and Realism that so often vitiated his art. In these legends, as Edmund Wilson has noted in *Patriotic Gore,* De Forest attempted to combine high "literary" poetry with colloquial rustic verse, and his best achievement came when he was imitating Lowell's Yankee *Bigelow Papers,* not when he was striving to climb the peaks of Parnassus. One example may suffice. In "The Witch of Shiloh," a poetic version of De Forest's story "Yesebel," De Forest is imitating Keats and Poe, but the word-magic of these great Romantics is obviously missing from the opening stanza of "The Witch":

> The night was marvelous to hear;
> It had a strangely mingled mell.
> It bellowed like a raging mere;
> It hissed with flights of spirits fell.
> The night was like a demon's dream,
> (A demon dreaming deep in hell),
> A dream of blast and roar and gleam
> And formless horror throned supreme (3).

Though their source is even more apparent, the rustic portions of the poem are somewhat better. Voiced through the mouth of De Forest's clownish hero Adam Downing, whom De Forest, out of his aristocratic predilections, views pessimistically as "The germ of Yankee might and merit,/A demiurge, a type, a fate,/Precursor of a coming nation" (4)—voiced so, the Yankee portions of the poem have at least the virtues of straightforwardness and wit. Downing's initial vision of the witches of Shiloh may serve as a case in point:

> "I watched 'em through my kitchen winders,
> A-whirlin' down the blowy weather,
> Now scalin' round like paper cinders,
> Now flockin clost as bees together.
> The wings were flimsy, torn an' scurvy,
> Consid'able like paper money;
> An' when they tumbled topsy-turvy,
> 'Twas partly horrid, partly funny;
> While as for music, any boodle
> Of summer frogs in Shiloh ditches,
> Will yowp a sweeter Yankee-Doodle
> Than all your singin'-schools of witches" (26-27).

In all four of the Downing legends, De Forest continued to use, side by side, both the high and the low poetic styles, but consistently he failed to fuse them into a single artistic entity. That failure represents the failure of much of his art, and it stems from the fact that De Forest desired to explore new realistic, democratic ground but could never quite forget the romantic, aristocratic territory he wished to leave behind. Undoubtedly he would have been a more consistent realist if there had been a greater audience for the kind of truths he told in *Miss Ravenel* and *Kate Beaumont*—truths concerning war, marriage, and morality that went far beyond the genteel Realism of the commonplace preached by Howells. Undoubtedly De Forest would have been a greater artist if he had possessed the single-minded devotion for Realism and democracy and the passionate hatred of Romanticism and aristocracy that characterizes the work of Howells and of Twain. Undoubtedly De Forest would have written less commercial trash if he had never betrayed his art, as he admitted he had to Howells, and had instead attained the high-minded dedication that illumes the life of Henry James.

Nevertheless it still remains true that De Forest deserves to be remembered as something more than a historical curiosity whom it is polite to proclaim "the first American realist." He is that—his accomplishment in *Miss Ravenel* alone merits that recognition—but he is more than that. He is the author of a significant body of work exploring the social history of America through specific national traumatic experiences from the time of the Salem witch trials to the period of corruption in Washington during the period of Grant's administration. He is the creator of a gallery of characters, national in scope, that range from Southern ladies to low-down Carolina crackers, from Northern financiers to Washington politicians, from self-serving Puritan theologians to self-sacrificing men of war, and from giddy, aging Southern belles to shrewd, amoral flirts of both the American North and South. At his best, De Forest is a novelist of manners, most critical of American vulgarity, materialism, and narrowness; and his contrast of people and classes and geographical section illuminates with wit and wisdom the strengths and weaknesses of American democracy as well as the frailties and foibles of humanity. For his best work, De Forest still deserves an audience. William Dean Howells exaggerated, but in the right direction, when he proclaimed of De Forest: "I have thought it more discreditable to our taste than to his talent that he has not been recognized as one of our foremost novelists."[27]

# Notes and References

## Chapter One

1. In J. W. De Forest's *The De Forests of Avesnes* (New Haven, Connecticut, 1900) and in his "The Founder of New York" (*American Historical Register*, II, May, July, 1895, 881-90, 1172-80), De Forest claims Jesse De Forest deserves credit as the original founder of New York. Charles M. Dozy, archivist of Leyden, Holland, makes similar claims in a letter to Mr. George W. Van Sailen, New York *Tribune* (March 18, 1895), p. 8. Mrs. R. W. De Forest, however, in *A Walloon Family in America* (New York, 1914) I, 28-148, effectively shatters this theory.

2. Instructions in manuscript in the David Curtis DeForest collection, Historical Manuscripts Room, Yale University Library.

3. Reverend Hollis A. Campbell, William C. Sharpe, and Frank C. Bassett, *Seymour, Past and Present* (Seymour, Connecticut, 1902), p. 235.

4. John Hancock De Forest to "Dear Boys," De Forest collection, Yale University Collection of American Literature. Much of the biographical information in Chapter I is based on information in this collection. Unless otherwise noted, references throughout this study to De Forest letters are from it. Letters from the David Curtis DeForest collection in the Historical Manuscripts Room of Yale University will be noted as from that collection.

5. To Dr. Henry De Forest, February 24, 1834, in David Curtis DeForest collection.

6. *The Nation*, VI (February 6, 1868), 107.

7. To George De Forest, February 24, 1834, in David Curtis DeForest collection.

8. February 16, 1837, in David Curtis DeForest collection.

9. John W. De Forest, *History of the Indians of Connecticut* (Hartford, 1853), p. 357.

10. Facts noted in William Sharpe, *Seymour and Vicinity* (Seymour, 1878), p. 70.

11. To Dr. Henry De Forest, February 27, 1827, in David Curtis DeForest collection.

12. February 27, 1837, in David Curtis DeForest collection.

13. John W. De Forest, *Oriental Acquaintance* (New York, 1856), p. 1. Future references to *Oriental Acquaintance* in this section of the chapter will be noted in parentheses in the text. I shall in future similarly indicate page references to the other volumes of De Forest when the particular work seems plainly indicated by the text. In most instances I shall use the original edition of a work as listed in the "Selected Bibliography" of this book. Because they are more readily available, I have chosen to use the later editions of *Miss Ravenel's Conversion from Secession to Loyalty* (New York and Toronto, 1955), *Honest John Vane* (State College, Pennsylvania, 1960), and *Playing the Mischief* (State College, Pennsylvania, 1961). Any reference to other editions will be indicated by footnotes.

14. To George Sergeant, February 11, 1847, in David Curtis DeForest collection.

15. *Miss Ravenel's Conversion from Secession to Loyalty*, Rinehart editions (New York and Toronto, 1955), p. 71.

16. In *History of the Indians of Connecticut*, front pages.

### Chapter Two

1. "Olimpia Morata," *The New Englander*, XIII (May, 1855), 217.
2. Letters to Messrs. Dix and Edwards, October 9, 1856, in the Library of the Historical Society of Pennsylvania.
3. This paragraph is based upon the material in Harriet's commonplace book in the De Forest collection of the Yale University Library.
4. *The Atlantic Monthly*, IV (July, 1859), 131.
5. *Putnam's Monthly Magazine*, VIII (November, 1856), 544.
6. In the De Forest papers at Yale there is a letter by Louis Effingham De Forest to Mrs. Anne Jenovese (June 18, 1935), in which Mr. De Forest notes that in J. W. De Forest's personal library there were a number of volumes of De Quincy, including *Confessions of an English Opium Eater* and *Suspiria de Profundis.*
7. *Harper's New Monthly Magazine*, XIV (March, 1857), 517.
8. *Putnam's Monthly Magazine*, X (July, 1857), 50.
9. *The Atlantic Monthly*, VI (September, 1860), 312.
10. G. Harrison Orians, "New England Witchcraft in Fiction," *American Literature*, II (1930), 67.
11. J. W. De Forest, "Witching Times. A Novel in Thirty Chapters," *Putnam's Monthly Magazine*, VIII-X (December, 1856, to September, 1857), X, 403. Future clear references to *Witching Times* will be noted by volume and page number in parentheses in the text.
12. Edwin Oviatt, "J. W. De Forest in New Haven," New York *Times* Saturday Supplement (December 17, 1898), p. 856.
13. *Patriotic Gore: Studies in the Literature of the Civil War* (New York, 1962), p. 680.
14. *Literary History of the United States*, ed. Robert E. Spiller, *et al.*, rev. ed. (New York, 1953), p. 881.
15. New York *Times* (June 25, 1859), p. 2.
16. *Ibid.*

### Chapter Three

1. "Charleston Under Arms," *The Atlantic Monthly*, VII (April, 1861), 494.
2. *Ibid.*, p. 505.
3. *Ibid.*, p. 497.
4. See Gordon's S. Haight's introduction to the Harper edition of *Miss Ravenel's Conversion* (New York, 1939), p. xi.
5. Chronology in De Forest family papers, De Forest collection, Yale University Library.
6. J. W. De Forest, *Poems: Medley and Palestina* (New Haven, 1902), p. ix.
7. Letter dated April 6, 1862, in *A Volunteer's Adventures*, (New Haven, 1946), p. 9. Further quotations from *A Volunteer's Adventures* in this section of Chapter III will be indicated in parentheses in the text.
8. *Miss Ravenel's Conversion*, p. 174.
9. Letter to Andrew De Forest, August 7, 1864.
10. *A Volunteer's Adventures*, p. xvii.
11. *Ibid.*
12. "De Forest, Van Petten, and Stephen Crane," *American Literature*, XXVII (January, 1956), 578-80.

13. William Dean Howells, *Criticism and Fiction* (New York, 1891), p. 73.

14. In *Literary History of the United States,* p. 881.

15. *Criticism and Fiction,* p. 73.

16. Certificate signed by Surgeon E. A. Parks in De Forest collection.

17. Jay B. Hubbell, *The South in American Literature* (Duke University Press, 1954), p. 394.

18. *A Union Officer in The Reconstruction,* ed. James H. Croushore and David Morris Potter (Yale, 1948), p. 61. Future references in this section to *A Union Officer* will be indicated by parentheses in the text.

19. The phrase was inspired by Josiah Wedgewood's famed medallion (1787) of an enchained slave kneeling with his arms stretched toward heaven. The inscription asked, "Am I not a man and brother?" and the question was popularized by the antislavery society of London.

20. Southron was used by Sir Walter Scott to differentiate an Englishman from a Scotchman. Southern speech patterns often made Southron out of Southern, and American Southerners after Scott often made of the mispronunciation a sign of aristocracy. Northerners often derided the mispronunciation and the false pride, the provincialism, they felt it showed.

21. Anonymous, "Chivalrous Southrons," VI, 96-128.

22. *The Nation* (March 12, 1868), p. 208.

23. Shields McIlwaine, *The Southern Poor White from Lubberland to Tobacco Road* (Norman, Oklahoma, 1939), p. 91.

24. *Harper's New Monthly Magazine,* XXXV (August, 1867), 365.

25. *Harper's New Monthly Magazine,* XXXI (October, 1865), 570.

26. *Ibid.*

27. To "Dear sirs," Feb. 1, 1867, *Galaxy* Correspondence in New York Public Library.

28. To "Messrs. Church," Feb. 17, 1867, *Galaxy* Correspondence.

29. "My dear sir" [of the firm of Harper's], December 28, 1865. Ms. at Harper and Brothers. Photostat at Yale.

30. Messrs. Harper & Brothers, May 2, 1887.

31. *The House of Harper* (New York, 1901), p. 244.

32. See Cowie, *The Rise of the American Novel* (New York, 1948), p. 513; and Wagenknecht, *Cavalcade of the American Novel* (New York, 1952), p. 106.

33. Oviatt, "J. W. De Forest in New Haven," p. 856.

34. *Ibid.*

35. In an excellent article in which he defends De Forest's Bunyanesque title in *Miss Ravenel,* Professor Cecil Moffitt discusses in detail the resemblance of De Forest's novel to another lengthily titled novel: *The Pilgrim's Progress From this World to That Which is to Come.*

36. William Dean Howells, *Heroines of Fiction* (New York and London, 1901), II, 157.

37. William Dean Howells, *My Literary Passions* (New York, 1895), p. 223.

## Chapter Four

1. The ultimate cause of this schism, if such did indeed exist, is hardly discoverable at this late date. A Freudian critic, however, could hardly fail to detect in *Miss Ravenel* an excessive attachment between Dr. Ravenel and his daughter, and such a reader might easily find evidences

of a similar relationship between Dr. Shepard and his daughter. Certainly Mrs. De Forest was not averse to spending long periods with her father and away from her husband.

2. *Medley and Palestina* (New Haven, 1902), p. 43. First printed as "A Sigh" in *The Galaxy*, X (July, 1870), 96.

3. *Medley and Palestina*, pp. 46-47.

4. September 21, 1868. In Houghton Library of Harvard University.

5. (New York, 1873), p. 124.

6. To "Dear Sirs" [editors of *The Galaxy*], February 8, 1870. In *Galaxy* Correspondence, New York Public Library.

7. To the "Editors" [of *The Galaxy*], September 28, 1869. In *Galaxy* Correspondence, New York Public Library.

8. To Nathaniel Hawthorne, [June 1 (?) 1851], quoted in *The Portable Melville*, ed. and with an introduction by Jay Leyda (New York, 1952), p. 430.

9. "The Novels of Mr. De Forest," *The Atlantic Monthly*, XXXII (November, 1873), 621.

10. The articles appeared in *The Galaxy*, Vols. XIV, XV, for the months of October, November, and December, 1872, and January, 1873.

11. The articles appeared in *Harper's New Monthly Magazine*, Vol. LVI, January and February, 1878; and *The Atlantic Monthly*, Vol. XLI, April, 1878.

12. *The Atlantic Monthly*, XLI (February, 1878), 156.

13. "Crumbs of Travel," *The Atlantic Monthly*, XXXVIII (December, 1876), 701.

14. *Ibid.*, p. 705.

15. "An Independent's Glance at the South," *The Nation*, XXIII (September 28, 1876), 196-97.

16. March 1, 1877. In Yale University Library.

17. March 1, 1877. In Houghton Library of Harvard University.

18. *Justine's Lovers* (New York, 1878), p. 53.

19. March 11, 1879, in Houghton Library, Harvard University.

20. *Ibid.*

21. *Lippincott's Magazine*, VI (August, 1870), 196.

22. *Ibid.*, p. 198.

23. *The Atlantic Monthly*, XXIV (October, 1869), 397.

24. *Ibid.*

25. *Ibid.*, p. 390.

26. *Hearth and Home*, II (February 12, 1870), 122.

27. *Hearth and Home*, II (February 19, 1870), 138.

28. *Hearth and Home*, II (February 5, 1870), 106.

29. *Hearth and Home*, II (February 26, 1870), 154.

30. *Hearth and Home*, II (March 19, 1870), 347.

31. "The Great American Novel," *The Nation*, VI (January 9, 1868), 28.

32. XIII (December 28, 1871), 423.

33. "Best Sellers Long Ago," New York *Times* (September 5, 1920), Section 3.

34. See Mrs. Anne D. Jenovese's uncompleted doctoral dissertation, done at the University of Pennsylvania and with the cooperation of Dr. Louis Effingham De Forest, in the De Forest collection of Yale University, Chapter VI, p. 5.

35. "The Techniques of J. W. De Forest, Transitional Novelist" (Ohio State University), 1953, p. 97.

36. *Harper's New Monthly Magazine,* LVII (August, 1878), 450.

37. *The Galaxy,* XIII (March, 1872), 294.

38. Sunday New York *Times,* January 17, 1875, p. 3.

39. *The Galaxy,* XIII (April, 1872), 480.

40. *Ibid.,* p. 484.

41. *Ibid.,* p. 483.

42. *The Galaxy,* XXI (March, 1876), 343.

43. *Ibid.,* p. 355.

44. Edwin Oviatt, "J. W. De Forest in New Haven," New York *Times,* Saturday Supplement (December 17, 1898), p. 856.

45. This point is made effectively in "The Techniques of J. W. De Forest," pp. 43ff.

46. *Criticism and Fiction* (New York, 1891), p. 137.

47. Ford's "The Techniques of J. W. De Forest" discusses De Forest's diction at considerable length and notes that De Forest's use of vernacular and colloquial words was most common from 1871-75 and probably reached its peak in 1875 in *Playing the Mischief.*

48. *Mark Twain and "Huck Finn"* (Berkeley, 1960), pp. 218-19, 225, 234-35.

49. Letter to Howells, May 27, 1871. In Houghton Library of Harvard University.

50. *Heroines of Fiction* (New York and London, 1901), II, 154.

51. "An Independent's Glance at the South," *The Nation* (September 28, 1876), p. 196.

52. *Heroines, loc. cit.*

53. "Recent Literature," *The Atlantic Monthly,* XXIX (March, 1872), 364.

54. *Ibid.,* p. 365.

55. "Recent Novels," *The Nation,* XVIII (May 21, 1874), 336.

56. "Recent Literature," *The Atlantic Monthly,* XXXIV (August, 1874), 229-30.

57. De Forest to Howells, July 21, 1874. In the Rutherford B. Hayes Library.

58. To William D. Ticknor, January 19, 1855, quoted in *The Portable Hawthorne,* ed. and with an intro. by Malcolm Cowley (New York, 1948), p. 624.

59. *The Nation,* XXIX (December 31, 1874), 442.

60. XXV (February, 1875), 238.

61. Arthur Hobson Quinn, *American Fiction* (New York, 1936), p. 170.

62. See *Literary History of the U. S.,* p. 883.

63. "Sex in Politics," XII (April 20, 1871), 271.

64. "New Novels," *The Nation,* XXI (August 12, 1875), 106.

65. *Ibid.*

66. "Editor's Literary Record," *Harper's New Monthly Magazine,* LI (September, 1875), 602.

67. "Recent Literature," *The Atlantic Monthly,* XXXVII (February, 1876), 238-39.

68. See *Patriotic Gore,* p. 713.

69. Note by De Forest to W. M. Griswold in *Descriptive Lists of Novels,* ed. William M. Griswold (Cambridge, Massachusetts, 1893), pp. 82-83.

70. (May 31, 1878), p. 1.

71. *American Fiction*, p. 173.

72. See Anne D. Jenovese, "John William De Forest," Chapter VII, p. 1.

73. New York *Tribune* (February 20, 1879), p. 4.

74. *The Atlantic Monthly*, XLIV (September, 1879), 288.

75. *The Atlantic Monthly*, XLIV (November, 1879), 566.

76. (May 19, 1879), p. 3.

77. "Recent Novels," *The Atlantic Monthly*, XLV (May, 1880), 680.

78. *Patriotic Gore*, p. 714.

79. "A Novel of the Rebellion," *The Nation*, XXXIII (November 10, 1881), 376-77.

### Chapter Five

1. April 23, 1882.

2. January 25, 1883, Lounsbury papers, Rare Book Room, Yale University Library.

3. January 28, 1883, Lounsbury papers.

4. August 6, 1883, Houghton Library, Harvard University.

5. February 16, 1885. In the possession of Mrs. William Durrie Waldron of New York City.

6. March 4, 1885. In the possession of Mrs. William Durrie Waldron.

7. May 8, 1885, Houghton Library, Harvard University.

8. April 24, 1886, *"The Century* Collection," New York Public Library.

9. June 24, 1886, Houghton Library, Harvard University.

10. Save for the initial one, the quotations of this paragraph are from De Forest's Letter to Howells, December 6, 1886, in Houghton Library of Harvard University.

11. December 9, 1886.

12. January 24, 1887, Houghton Library, Harvard University.

13. See Anne Jenovese's uncompleted dissertation, Chapter VII, p. 3.

14. De Forest to "Dear sir," April 19, 1887, in *"The Century* Collection," New York Public Library.

15. The quotations of the paragraph are from "J. W. De Forest in New Haven," New York *Times* book section (December 17, 1898), p. 856.

16. De Forest to Brander Matthews, January 29, 1902, in the Brander Matthews' Collection of Columbia University Library.

17. May 2, 1887.

18. September 2, 1887.

19. See Howells to De Forest, January 14, 1895.

20. Louis Shepard De Forest to Louis Effingham De Forest, February 2, 1936.

21. Interview by James F. Light of Mrs. William Durrie Waldron, 925 Park Avenue, New York City, December 23, 1961.

22. *Patriotic Gore*, p. 736.

23. "The New Historical Romances," *The North American Review*, CLXXI (December, 1890), 948.

24. *Patriotic Gore*, p. 739.

25. November 11, 1852.

26. [T. Wentworth Higginson], "Recent American Poetry," *The Nation*, LXXIV (May 29, 1902), 430.

27. *My Literary Passions* (New York, 1895), p. 223.

# Selected Bibliography

## PRIMARY SOURCES

A. *Bibliography*

HAGEMANN, E. R., "A Check List of the Writings of John William De Forest (1826-1906)." *Studies in Bibliography*, VIII (Charlottesville, Virginia, 1956), 185-94.

B. *Manuscript Materials*

De Forest collection in the Yale Collection of American Literature. The central repository of De Forest materials, including numerous letters of the family of John Hancock De Forest to each other and ten letters of W. D. Howells to J. W. De Forest; financial and legal documents pertaining to the De Forest family; and publication facts and correspondence relevant to J. W. De Forest's writing. In addition there are seventeen De Forest manuscripts, including revised versions of *Miss Ravenel's Conversion from Secession to Loyalty, Kate Beaumont,* and *Playing the Mischief;* a chronology of the life of J. W. De Forest prepared by his grandson Louis Effingham De Forest and corrected by his son Louis Shepard De Forest; Harriet De Forest's commonplace book of poetry; and an uncompleted doctoral dissertation done by Anne D. Jenovese with the cooperation of Louis Effingham De Forest.

David Curtis DeForest collection, Historical Manuscripts Room, Yale University Library. Materials concerning this distinguished brother of John Hancock De Forest but with a few papers relevant to J. W. De Forest.

The Houghton Library at Harvard University holds thirteen letters of De Forest to Howells, written between 1868-90, and a few minor letters to T. B. Aldrich, J. R. Lowell, and Messrs. Dix and Edwards.

The W. C. Church Manuscript Collection of the New York Public Library contains seventeen letters by De Forest, written between 1867-77 and all relevant to his writings for *The Galaxy;* the Century Collection of the New York Public Library holds three minor letters of De Forest concerning his writing.

Columbia University Library holds six letters of De Forest, all except one to Brander Matthews, written in De Forest's later years.

Mrs. William Durrie Waldron of New York City, the granddaughter of J. W. De Forest, has in her possession a number of De Forest's letters of his later years to his son Louis Shepard De Forest, as well as a few minor items relevant to J. W. De Forest's interest in genealogy.

A number of minor items are held by the following: the Rutherford B. Hayes Library (one letter by De Forest to Howells); the Johns Hopkins University Library (a brief life in De Forest's hand); the Shea Collection of the Riggs Memorial Library of Georgetown University (a brief life in De Forest's hand); the Chicago Historical Society (two items of trivia); and the Historical Society of Pennsylvania (four unimportant letters and a manuscript page in his own hand of De Forest's *A Lover's Revolt*).

## C. Published Works

*The History of the Indians of Connecticut from the Earliest Known Period to 1850*, Hartford, Connecticut: W. J. Hammersley [*sic*], 1851. Subsequent editions were published by Hamersley in 1852 and 1853; by Joel Munsell, Albany, New York, 1871; and by Archon Books, with an intro. by Wilcomb E. Washburn, Hamden, Connecticut, 1964.

*Oriental Acquaintance: or, Letters from Syria*, New York: Dix, Edwards and Company, 1856.

"Witching Times. A Novel in Thirty Chapters," *Putnam's Monthly Magazine*, VIII-X (*December*, 1856–September, 1857). This novel did not receive book publication.

*European Acquaintance; Being Sketches of People in Europe*, New York: Harper and Brothers, 1858.

*Seacliff; or The Mystery of the Westervelts*, Boston: Phillips, Sampson and Company, 1859.

*Miss Ravenel's Conversion from Secession to Loyalty*, New York: Harper and Brothers, 1867. Subsequent editions have been published by Harper and Brothers, intro. by Gordon S. Haight, New York, 1939; and by Rinehart and Company, ed. and with an intro. by Gordon S. Haight, New York, 1955. The 1939 edition follows De Forest's revision of the 1867 manuscript as based on the revised text held by the Yale University Library; the 1955 edition follows, with minor typographical corrections, the original edition of 1867.

"Della; or The Wild Girl," *Hearth and Home*, II (February 5–March 19, 1870). This novel did not receive book publication.

"Annie Howard," *Hearth and Home*, II (March 19–May 21, 1870). This novel did not receive book publication.

*Overland*, New York: Sheldon and Company, 1871.

*Kate Beaumont*, Boston: J. R. Osgood and Company, 1872. A subsequent edition, based on the revised text held by the Yale University Library, was published in the "Monument Edition" of the Bald Eagle Press, State College, Pennsylvania, ed. and with an intro. by Joseph Jay Rubin, 1963.

*The Wetherel Affair*, New York: Sheldon and Company, 1873.

*Honest John Vane*, New Haven, Connecticut: Richmond and Patten, 1875. A subsequent edition was published in the "Monument Edition" of the Bald Eagle Press, State College, Pennsylvania, ed. with an intro. by Joseph Jay Rubin, 1960.

*Playing the Mischief*, New York: Harper and Brothers, 1875. A subsequent edition, based on the revised text held by the Yale University Library, was published in the "Monument Edition" of the Bald Eagle Press, State College, Pennsylvania, ed. with an intro. by Joseph Jay Rubin, 1961.

*Justine's Lovers*, New York: Harper and Brothers, 1878. [Published anonymously.]

*Irene the Missionary*, Boston: Roberts Brothers, 1879. [Published anonymously.]

*The Bloody Chasm*, New York: D. Appleton and Company, 1881. A subsequent edition was published under the title *The Oddest of Courtships; or The Bloody Chasm*, by D. Appleton and Company, New York, 1882.

*A Lover's Revolt*, New York: Longmans, Green, and Company, 1898.

*The De Forests of Avesnes (and of New Netherland) a Huguenot Thread in American Colonial History, 1494 to the Present Time,* New Haven, Connecticut: The Tuttle, Morehouse and Taylor Company, 1900.

*The Downing Legends: Stories in Rhyme,* New Haven, Connecticut: The Tuttle, Morehouse and Taylor Company, 1901.

*Poems: Medley and Palestina,* New Haven, Connecticut: The Tuttle, Morehouse and Taylor Company, 1902.

*A Volunteer's Adventures,* ed. James H. Croushore, with intro. by Stanley T. Williams, New Haven, Connecticut: Yale University Press, 1946.

*A Union Officer in the Reconstruction,* eds. James H. Croushore and David M. Potter, New Haven, Connecticut: Yale University Press, 1948.

## SECONDARY SOURCES

A. *Doctoral Dissertations*

CROUSHORE, JAMES H. "John William De Forest: A Biographical and Critical Study to the Year 1868." Yale University, 1944. A pioneering study, most valuable for its biographical thoroughness.

DAVIDSON, JAMES. "John William De Forest and his Contemporaries: The Birth of American Realism." New York University, 1957. Discusses De Forest's relationship to Hawthorne, Transcendentalism, and Realism; and attempts, without much success, to show the influence of De Forest upon Howells and James.

FORD, PHILIP HASTINGS. "The Techniques of J. W. De Forest, Transitional Novelist." Ohio State University, 1953. A valuable study weakened by Ford's attempt to defend De Forest's worst writings by claiming they are really parodies, perhaps unconsciously so, of bad writing.

GARGANO, JAMES W. "John William De Forest: A Critical Study of His Novels." Cornell, 1955. Lucid, perceptive, thorough criticism of the major novels.

HAGEMANN, E. R. "John William De Forest and the American Scene: An Analysis of his Life and Novels." Indiana University, 1954. Introductory essay upon De Forest's life followed by superficial criticism.

JENOVESE, ANNE D. "John William De Forest, Realist and Soldier." Uncompleted doctoral dissertation done around 1935 for the University of Pennsylvania. A copy of the manuscript is in the De Forest collection of Yale University; this work has some value because Mrs. Jenovese had the cooperation of Louis E. De Forest.

NALL, ALLEN KLINE. "A Critical Evaluation of John William De Forest." University of Texas, 1952. An attempt to weave together a critical and biographical study but weakened critically by the tendency to give mere plot summaries.

SCHUSTER, RICHARD. "American Civil War Novels to 1880." Columbia, 1961. Places *Miss Ravenel* among other Civil War novels, praises De Forest's treatment of character and military background, and claims that *Miss Ravenel's* one flaw is its lack of central unity.

B. *Books and Periodical Articles*

BROOKS, VAN WYCK. *New England: Indian Summer.* New York: E. P. Dutton, 1940. Notes De Forest's work had a "breadth of understanding and a truth to actuality that were unique at the moment" and echoes Howells' assertion that De Forest's work was too virile for an audience largely composed of women.

CAMPBELL, HOLLIS A., *et al. Seymour Past and Present.* Seymour, Connecticut: W. C. Sharpe, 1902. Useful for background information upon De Forest's early environment.

CARTER, EVERETT. *Howells and the Age of Realism.* Philadelphia and New York: Lippincott, 1950. Numerous passing references, occasionally distorting the content of De Forest's writing, which praise De Forest's realism and satire.

COWIE, ALEXANDER. *The Rise of the American Novel.* New York: American Book Co., 1948. Perhaps the best published treatment of De Forest's major works (especially *Miss Ravenel* and *Honest John Vane*) with the conclusion that De Forest's work was weakened by his lack of "a steady and all-absorbing aim" but, nevertheless, he deserves "more consideration than he has thus far received. . . . "

CROUSHORE, JAMES H., and POTTER, DAVID M. Introduction to J. W. De Forest's *A Union Officer in the Reconstruction.* New Haven: Yale University Press, 1948. Discussion of historical backgrounds of the Freedmen's Bureau and appraisal of De Forest's role as a Bureau Major and his writings about his experiences.

GORDON, CLARENCE. "De Forest's Novels," *Atlantic Monthly,* XXXII (November, 1873), 611-21. Probably inspired by Howells, this is the most thorough study of De Forest's work to appear in his lifetime.

HAGEMANN, E. R. "John William De Forest and *The Galaxy,* Some Letters (1867-1872)," *Bulletin of the New York Public Library,* LIX (April, 1955), 175-94.

HAIGHT, GORDON S. In Spiller, R. E., *et al. Literary History of the United States,* rev. ed. in one volume. New York: Macmillan, 1953. Brief but perceptive discussion of De Forest's major works with the claim that he was "The first American writer to deserve the name of realist."

————. Intro. to J. W. De Forest's *Miss Ravenel's Conversion from Secession to Loyalty.* New York and London: Harper, 1939. Brief but intelligent appraisal of De Forest's original Realism in character portrayal, in *Miss Ravenel.*

HOWELLS, WILLIAM DEAN. *Heroines of Fiction,* Vol. II. New York and London: 1901. General comments on De Forest's work with especial attention to *Kate Beaumont.*

————. *My Literary Passions.* New York: Harper, 1895. Notes of *Miss Ravenel*: "I had a passion for that book, and for all the books of that author."

HUBBELL, JAY B. *The South in American Literature: 1607-1900.* Durham: Duke University Press, 1954. Notes that De Forest's Reconstruction essays emphasize the Southern traits which especially irritate Northerners but the writings are nevertheless "one of the shrewdest appraisals of the Southern character ever written."

MCILWAINE, SHIELDS. *The Southern Poor White from Lubberland to Tobacco Road.* Norman: Oklahoma University Press, 1939. Claims that De Forest "must be reckoned the most significant in literary anticipations of all the writers who depicted the 'low-down people' from the late sixties to 1900."

MCINTYRE, CLARA F. "J. W. De Forest, Pioneer Realist," *University of Wyoming Publications,* IX, 1 (August 31, 1942), 1-13.

MOFFITT, CECIL. *"Miss Ravenel's Conversion* and *Pilgrim's Progress," College English,* XXIII (February, 1962), 352-57. Shows allegorical similarities.

O'DONNELL, THOMAS. "De Forest, Van Petten, and Stephen Crane," *American Literature,* XXVII (January, 1956), 575-80. Suggests the influence of De Forest upon Crane through De Forest's war comrade and Crane's teacher Van Petten.

ORIANS, G. HARRISON. "New England Witchcraft in Fiction," *American Literature,* II (1930), 54-71. Claims *Witching Times* is "the only fictional treatment which provides a comprehensible and psychological account of scenes, actors, and motives in that mad delusion."

OVIATT, EDWIN. "John De Forest in New Haven," New York *Times,* Saturday Supplement, December 17, 1898. An interview with the aging author in which he comments upon his work.

POTTER, DAVID M. "John William De Forest," *New Haven Colony Historical Society Papers,* X (New Haven, 1951), 188-203. Sensible survey of De Forest's life and works with the conclusion that De Forest, after the failure of *Miss Ravenel* to win an audience, attempted to win a broader response to his art by experimenting with various fictional modes.

QUINN, ARTHUR HOBSON. *American Fiction: An Historical and Critical Survey.* New York: Appleton-Century-Crofts, 1936. Notes De Forest's Realism and claims he "painted pictures of our national life which no nation should willingly permit to remain in obscurity."

RUBIN, JOSEPH JAY. Intro. to J. W. De Forest's *Honest John Vane.* State College, Pennsylvania: Bald Eagle Press, 1960. Valuable discussion of De Forest's life, work, and reading, with especial consideration of *Honest John Vane.*

––––––. Intro. to J. W. De Forest's *Playing the Mischief.* State College, Pennsylvania: Bald Eagle Press, 1961. Valuable, though somewhat disconnected, discussion of some of the major ideas of De Forest's work, with especial attention to the Washington background and the variety of characters in *Playing the Mischief.*

––––––. Intro. to J. W. De Forest's *Kate Beaumont,* State College, Pennsylvania: Bald Eagle Press, 1963. Valuable but rather clumsy and disconnected treatment of De Forest's Southern experiences and writing with especial emphasis on *Kate Beaumont.*

SHARPE, WILLIAM C. *Seymour and Vicinity.* Seymour, Connecticut: Record print, 1878.

STONE, ALBERT E., JR. "Best Novel of the Civil War," *American Heritage,* XIII (June, 1962), 84-88. Claims *Miss Ravenel* is the best novel of the Civil War and attempts to substantiate the claim by brief analysis and comparisons.

WAGENKNECHT, EDWARD. *Cavalcade of the American Novel.* New York: Holt, 1952. Notes De Forest is "perhaps the most unjustly neglected of all American writers."

WILLIAMS, STANLEY T. Intro. to J. W. De Forest's *A Volunteer's Adventures.* New Haven: Yale University Press, 1946. Intelligent analysis of De Forest's realistic treatment of war.

WILSON, EDMUND. *Patriotic Gore: Studies in the Literature of the Civil War.* New York: Oxford University Press, 1962. The longest essay yet published on De Forest. This sympathetic article quotes at length from De Forest's writing but is weakened by occasional errors of fact.

# Index

107; death of Mrs. De Forest and lessening artistic productivity, 108; travel in New York, Nova Scotia, and Europe, 164-65; difficulty in publishing work, 165-67; literary dabbling and attempts to publish a *Collected Works*, 168-69; impoverished last years in New Haven, 168-69; death, 170

WRITINGS OF:

Index